Introduction to English Linguistics

Introduction to English Linguistics

Second revised edition

by

Ingo Plag
Maria Braun
Sabine Lappe
Mareile Schramm

Mouton de Gruyter
Berlin · New York

Mouton de Gruyter (formerly Mouton, The Hague)
is a Division of Walter de Gruyter GmbH & Co. KG, Berlin.

The first edition was published in 2007.

The Library of Congress has cataloged the first edition as follows:

> Plag, Ingo.
>   Introduction to English linguistics / by Ingo Plag ... [et al.].
>   p. cm.
>   Includes bibliographical references and index.
>   ISBN 978-3-11-018969-8 (pbk. : alk. paper)
>   1. English language.   I. Title.
>   PE1075.P493   2007
>   420—dc22
>   2007023193

Bibliographic information published by the Deutsche Nationalbibliothek

The Deutsche Nationalbibliothek lists this publication in the Deutsche Nationalbibliografie;
detailed bibliographic data are available in the Internet at http://dnb.d-nb.de.

ISBN   978-3-11-021408-6

© Copyright 2007, 2009 by Walter de Gruyter GmbH & Co. KG, D-10785 Berlin.
All rights reserved, including those of translation into foreign languages. No part of this
book may be reproduced in any form or by any means, electronic or mechanical, including
photocopy, recording or any information storage and retrieval system, without permission
in writing from the publisher.
Cover design: Martin Zech, Bremen.
Cover photo © by Scott Liddell/morguefile.com.
Printed in Germany.

Preface to first edition

This book is the product of a truly joint effort of its four authors. Each of us contributed substantially to the overall design and content of the book, and to all chapters, while at the same time being chiefly responsible for one or two chapters, respectively. Mareile Schramm was the leading author of the phonetics chapter, Sabine Lappe was in charge of phonology and semantics, and Maria Braun of morphology and pragmatics. Ingo Plag took care of the introduction, the syntax chapter, the chapter on extensions and applications, was responsible for the glossary, and coordinated the project.

This introduction is, however, not only the collaborative work of the four individuals whose names appear on the outside cover. A whole group of people has supported us in the realisation of the book in various ways. We have to thank our student assistants for their help at various stages of the project, as well as for their careful reading of chapters and commenting expertly on content and presentation: Christian Grau, Christina Kellenter, Kristina Kösling, Henner Metz, Taivi Rüüberg, and Linda Zirkel. We are also very grateful to our colleagues Verena Haser, Sabine Jautz, Gero Kunter, and Jaye Padgett, who provided critical comments on some of the chapters. Special thanks go to Phil Mothershaw-Rogalla for providing us with pertinent speech data, and to Lutz Arndt for his invaluable assistance in the usual domains (what would we do without you?). As always, Gisela Schwung was there when organisational problems needed to be solved.

Finally, we want to thank all our students in Marburg, Hannover and Siegen who – over many years – have attended our introductory courses to English linguistics. They have served as guinea-pigs for our didactic experiments and have forced us to explain even complicated matters in an ever more comprehensible way. Special thanks go to the students in the two introduction to linguistics courses we taught in the summer semester of 2006. These students were the ones on which we tried out the first versions of our chapters, and they not only provided valuable feedback but also made it clear to us that writing this book is really worth the effort. Teaching a subject like linguistics to beginners is a true challenge, but also a great source of inspiration and joy.

Preface to second edition

The first edition of this book has been received very favourably by its readers. Many people sent us very encouraging comments and made very useful suggestions to further improve the book. The team of authors has therefore decided to revise and enlarge this introduction to meet the demands of their readership and, of course, to eliminate some of the errors contained in the first edition. The most important change is that we have added material to make the book more easily usable in university settings outside Europe, North America in particular. The new introductory chapter gives more detailed information on this point.

We would like to express our sincere gratitude to all students and colleagues that have provided us with feedback on the first edition, and to our student assistants Miriam Führer, Andreas Ganacki, Jennifer Schluer and Josephine Thomschke for their help with the preparation of the manuscript.

Table of Contents

Preface	v
Abbreviations and notational conventions	x
Introduction	xi

1. The sounds: phonetics ... 1
   - 1.1. Introduction ... 1
   - 1.2. Spelling vs. pronunciation: the representation of speech sounds ... 2
   - 1.3. Producing sounds ... 7
     - 1.3.1. The nature of speech sounds ... 7
     - 1.3.2. The vocal tract ... 8
   - 1.4. How sounds differ from each other: the classification of speech sounds ... 9
     - 1.4.1. The classification of consonants ... 10
     - 1.4.2. The classification of vowels ... 16
   - 1.5. Conclusion ... 24
   - Further reading ... 24
   - Exercises ... 25

2. The sound system: phonology ... 29
   - 2.1. Introduction ... 29
   - 2.2. Introducing order into the chaos: the phoneme ... 29
   - 2.3. The key to finding the order ... 35
     - 2.3.1. Minimal pairs ... 35
     - 2.3.2. Distributional characteristics of allophones ... 37
     - 2.3.3. Observing allophonic alternations in different word forms ... 39
   - 2.4. More about the sound system of English ... 42
     - 2.4.1. Allophones of /l/ ... 42
     - 2.4.2. Stop phonemes ... 45
     - 2.4.3. A slightly more complex case: /ɹ/ ... 50
   - 2.5. The syllable ... 54
     - 2.5.1. The structure of the syllable ... 54
     - 2.5.2. Syllabification ... 59
     - 2.5.3. The syllable and allophonic processes: /l/ revisited ... 63
   - 2.6. Conclusion ... 65
   - Further reading ... 65
   - Exercises ... 66

3. The structure of words: morphology 70
   3.1. Introduction 70
   3.2. Minimal building blocks: morphemes 70
   3.3. Types of morphemes 75
   3.4. Morphological analysis of words 78
   3.5. Realisation of morphemes: allomorphs 82
   3.6. Morphological processes: inflection and derivation 89
   3.7. Word-formation 93
       3.7.1. Introduction 93
       3.7.2. Affixation 94
       3.7.3. Compounding 99
       3.7.4. Conversion 104
       3.7.5. Shortening 106
   3.8. Conclusion 108
   Further reading 108
   Exercises 109

4. The structure of sentences: syntax 111
   4.1. Introduction 111
   4.2. The building blocks: words and phrases 114
       4.2.1. Constituency tests and phrases 114
       4.2.2. The internal structure of phrases 121
   4.3. The functional level: subjects, objects, adverbials, predicates 128
   4.4. The mapping of form and function 135
   4.5. Conclusion 136
   Further reading 137
   Exercises 137

5. The meaning of words and sentences: semantics 140
   5.1. Introduction 140
   5.2. What does 'meaning' mean? Words, concepts, and referents . 140
   5.3. Compositional and non-compositional meaning ... 149
   5.4. The network: organising word meaning 155
       5.4.1. Words and other words 155
       5.4.2. Same or different? 163
   5.5. Conclusion 170
   Further reading 172
   Exercises 172

6. Studying language in use: pragmatics 176
   6.1. Introduction 176
   6.2. Expressing intentions through language 177
      6.2.1. Using language to act: speech acts 177
      6.2.2. Speech acts: a closer look 179
      6.2.3. Classifying speech acts 181
      6.2.4. Realisation of speech acts: direct and indirect speech acts 187
      6.2.5. Performing speech acts successfully: felicity conditions 189
   6.3. Understanding utterance meaning 192
   6.4. Exploring pragmatic principles 195
      6.4.1. The Cooperative Principle 195
      6.4.2. Politeness 202
   6.5. Conclusion 206
   Further reading 207
   Exercises 207

7. Extensions and applications:
   historical linguistics, sociolinguistics and psycholinguistics 210
   7.1. Introduction 210
   7.2. Historical linguistics: how languages develop 210
   7.3. Sociolinguistics: the social significance of language 219
   7.4. Psycholinguistics: how do we store and process language? . . 224
   7.5. Conclusion 227
   Further reading 228
   Exercises 228

Glossary 231
References 246
Subject index 251

Abbreviations and notational conventions

A	adjective
Adv	adverb
ANC	American National Corpus
AP	adjective phrase
BNC	British National Corpus
C	consonant
$C_{[+\text{voice}]}$	voiced consonant
$C_{[-\text{voice}]}$	voiceless consonant
IPA	International Phonetic Alphabet
N	noun
NP	noun phrase
P	preposition
PP	preposition(al) phrase
RP	Received Pronunciation
S	sentence
V	1. verb
	2. vowel
VP	verb phrase
#	word boundary
*	impossible or ungrammatical sound sequence, word or sentence
.	syllable boundary
σ	syllable
'	stress on the following syllable
/ /	phonological (i.e. underlying) representation
[ ]	1. phonetic representation
	2. structural boundary (in morphology and syntax)
—	position of a sound to which a phonological rule applies
{ }	morpheme
|	read: "in the context of"
< >	orthographic representation
CAPITAL LETTERS	concept
SMALL CAPITAL LETTERS	lexeme

Introduction:
what this book is about and how it can be used

Although language is a topic of interest for most people, having and using language is usually taken for granted. This book does the exact opposite, it asks all kinds of questions about language and introduces its readers to its scientific study. The most fundamental question that still amazes most linguists is the following. How can it be that a speaker utters some kind of peculiar noise, and only milliseconds later a listener knows what the speaker has conceived shortly before, or during, the moment that noise was uttered?

This introductory textbook will take you on a tour through the complexities involved in answering this question. In doing so, the present book is mainly concerned with one particular language, English, but often comparisons are made with other languages, German in particular. As a textbook for an undergraduate readership our book presupposes no prior knowledge of linguistics and introduces and explains linguistic terminology and theoretical apparatus as we go along. Important technical terms appear in **bold print** when first mentioned. Crisp definitions of these terms can also be found in the glossary, and more elaborate information can be easily found via the subject index.

The purpose of the book is to enable the students to engage in (and enjoy!) their own analyses of the English language on all levels of description. Taking a problem-oriented approach, we do not present linguistics as a fixed set of knowledge, but as a systematic way of analysing and understanding language phenomena. After having worked with the book, the reader should be familiar with the basic methodological tools to be able to systematically analyse language data and to relate their findings to theoretical problems. The book is not written in the perspective of a particular theoretical framework and draws on insights from various research traditions.

Introduction to English Linguistics can be used as a textbook for an introductory course on linguistics, as a source-book for teachers, or as a book for self-study by beginners and more advanced students (e.g. for their exam preparation). For each chapter there are a number of basic and more advanced exercises, which are suitable for in-class work or as students' homework. The more advanced exercises include research tasks, which also give the students the opportunity to use the different methodological tools introduced in the text. Each chapter is also followed by a list of recommended further readings.

As every reader knows, English is spoken by hundreds of millions of speakers and there exist numerous varieties of English around the world. The variety that has been taken as a reference for this book is Standard British English, with the standard accent Received Pronunciation. We make, however, frequent reference to other varieties of English, especially to North American English, where important differences occur. With regard to most of the phenomena discussed in this book, different varieties of English pattern very much alike. However, especially concerning pronunciation there are significant differences observable between different varieties. Furthermore, the symbols for the representation of speech sounds in writing, i.e. the symbols of the phonetic alphabet, are not used in the same way across continents. In this second edition, we now provide a more detailed discussion of the differences between British and North American pronunciations, and explanations and documentation of the differences in the transcription conventions. Given that the standard American and British English varieties are only two varieties among many, we trust that the book will enable the readers to adapt and relate the findings presented with reference to these two varieties to the variety of English they are most familiar with.

The structure of the book is as follows. Chapters 1 and 2 are devoted to the analysis of the sounds and the sound system of English. Chapters 3 and 4 deal with the internal structure of words and sentences, respectively, while chapter 5 is devoted to the study of meaning. Chapter 6 focuses on the use of language and how interlocutors reach their communicative aims. Finally, chapter 7 takes a look at three subdisciplines of linguistics in which the concepts developed in the first six chapters are employed to answer questions relating to the history of language, the social significance of language, and how language is represented and processed in our minds.

The authors welcome comments and feedback on all aspects of this book, especially from students. Only if students tell their teachers what is good for them (i.e. for the students), teaching can become as effective and enjoyable as it should be for both teachers and teachees (oops, was that a possible word of English?).

Chapter 1
The sounds: phonetics

1.1. Introduction

Speaking is such a normal and everyday process for us that most of the time we do not consciously think about what we are doing. Fortunately, you might say. Imagine you had to think carefully about every sound in every word in every sentence you want to produce. It could take hours to finish a single sentence. Luckily, there is no need for this: we have developed such efficient routines for speaking that most of the necessary actions do not require conscious thought. You could compare it to walking: once you have learned what to do, some sort of automatism takes over.

This works fine as long as we stick to our respective native language. The situation changes, however, when we start learning a new, foreign language. Not only are the words different, but in many cases the foreign language also has some sounds which are unfamiliar. German learners of English, for instance, very often have problems with the "lisping" sound in words such as *bath*, *therapy*, or *mathematics* (we use italics whenever we cite words as examples). There are no German words which include this type of sound. That does not mean, of course, that native speakers of German cannot achieve a correct pronunciation of *bath* or *therapy*, but before they can do so they have to learn how to produce the new sound. English learners of German, on the other hand, encounter the same problem with the vowel that appears in German *Müsli* 'muesli' and *Hüte* 'hats' (we use single inverted commas to indicate the meanings of examples cited). This vowel is not part of the pool of sounds which English speakers use to construct the words of their language, the English **sound inventory** (we use bold print whenever we introduce an important new term).

There are some general conclusions we can draw from this. Firstly, languages may use only a subset of all possible speech sounds. In fact, there is no language which makes use of all of them. Secondly, languages differ in which sounds they include in their inventory: German uses a different selection than English does. Foreign language learners are thus bound to encounter sounds which do not occur in their native language and which they do not have routines for. They have to learn the gestures necessary to produce these unfamiliar sounds. In other words, learners have to find out which muscle movements in which combination and sequence are required for the production of the respective new sound.

There is an entire subdiscipline of linguistics, **phonetics**, which deals with these and other characteristics of speech sounds. It focuses on questions such as the following: What types of speech sounds do we find in the languages of the world and in individual languages? How can we describe these sounds? Which criteria can we use to distinguish different sounds?

Several approaches have been taken to the investigation of speech sounds and different branches of phonetics have developed, each focussing on a different aspect of speech. Articulatory phonetics aims at describing the process of articulation. How do we create speech sounds? In what way does the production of one sound differ from that of another? Which articulation-related criteria can we use to distinguish and classify different speech sounds? Acoustic phonetics, on the other hand, concentrates on the physical properties of the speech sounds themselves. What is the physical reality of a speech sound and how can we measure acoustic differences between speech sounds? Which physical properties are characteristic of particular sounds? Finally, auditory phonetics investigates how speech sounds are perceived and processed by the listener. In the following sections we will deal mostly with articulatory phonetics.

The remainder of this chapter is structured as follows: section 1.2. introduces some notational conventions used in phonetics which are essential for the discussion of speech sounds. In 1.3. we give a general overview of the nature of speech sounds and their production before discussing in more detail how we can describe and classify sounds in section 1.4., focussing on the sounds we find in English. A conclusion in section 1.5. summarises the findings of this chapter.

1.2. Spelling vs. pronunciation: the representation of speech sounds

We said above that the sound that occurs in English *therapy* and *mathematics* does not exist in German. What about the German words ***Therapie*** or ***Mathematik***, you might want to object. The letters are the same, alright. However, if you pronounce the words, you find different sounds in English and in German: only English has the lisping sound that we referred to earlier, whereas the corresponding sound in the two German words is the same as that which occurs initially in words such as *Tee* 'tea'.

What does this tell us? For one thing, the examples show that we have to strictly distinguish between letters and sounds, since we do not always get the same sound for the same letter. Even within a single language, there is no one-to-one correspondence of sound and orthographic symbol. Some more examples of this phenomenon are given in (1):

(1) knight   would   who
     doubt   honest   though

If we assumed that every word in (1) had the same number of letters and sounds, we would expect the word *knight* to consist of six distinct sounds, *would* should have five sounds, and so on. If you listen to someone pronouncing these words, you will notice that, clearly, this is not what we find. Some of the letters do not seem to have a corresponding sound at all: all of the above words have more letters than sounds. The conclusion we can draw from this is that spelling does not necessarily reflect the sound structure of words, or, to put it differently, spelling and pronunciation are two pairs of shoes and ought to be kept apart. To illustrate this point further, let us investigate some more words. What can you find out about the relation of spelling and pronunciation when looking at the words in (2)?

(2) a. rune   b. beat
         who   head
         shoe   great
         moon   heard
         you   heart
         true

If you pronounce the words in (2a), you will realise that they all share the same vowel sound. Yet, they differ in spelling. For one and the same vowel sound, we find an amazing total of six different spellings. Turning to the words in (2b), we observe a related phenomenon, again focussing on the vowels and their representation in writing: This time, the spelling is the same in all five words, <ea>, but the pronunciation is a different one each time.

It is obvious from the examples above that spelling does not help us if we want to talk about and refer to sounds, since the correspondence between letters and sounds is not one-to-one. This, however, is exactly what we would like to have when we talk or write about sounds, so that, whenever we use a certain symbol, people know exactly which sound we are talking about. Therefore phoneticians have established transcription systems which have a separate symbol for each sound. The most well-known and most standardised transcription system is the **International Phonetic Alphabet (IPA)**. You may already be familiar with phonetic transcription from dictionary entries or the vocabulary parts of your foreign language textbooks in school, where the

IPA or a similar system of phonetic symbols is used to indicate the pronunciation of words. Many (though not all) of the symbols in fact look like ordinary letters, but it is important to keep in mind that, unlike letters, phonetic symbols directly represent sounds in a one-to-one fashion. In order to indicate which kind of unit we are talking about, we use two different sets of brackets: angled brackets "< >" for letters, and brackets "[ ]" for sounds. Thus, for instance, the orthographic representation of the word referring to a piece of garment you wear on your feet is <sock>, but the representation of its sounds, its 'phonetic representation', is [sɒk]. In the latter case each symbol represents uniquely one sound.

Of course, if you want to use the IPA symbols, you need to be familiar with the correspondences between symbols and sounds. Which sound does a given symbol refer to? There is no way of telling just from the look of it. You can think about phonetic symbols as labels of some kind, not unlike labels you use for musical notes, for instance. The names we use to distinguish different notes, such as 'a', 'g', or 'd', enable us to talk about these notes without giving complicated examples and explanations. Phonetic symbols function in much the same way.

The list in (3) gives the IPA symbols and sample words for all sounds that occur in the standard accent of British English, which is known under the name of **'Received Pronunciation'** (**RP**). Note that the complete IPA includes many more symbols for sounds which languages other than English have in their inventories, but these need not concern us here. The interested reader may find the complete list of IPA symbols on the inner back cover of the book. IPA fonts for your computer can be downloaded from the internet. (The International Phonetic Association (also IPA for short) provides a useful overview of websites at http://www.arts.gla.ac.uk/IPA/ipafonts.html.)

(3) The sounds of English (RP); IPA transcription; pertinent letters in bold print

	IPA symbol	example		IPA symbol	example
a.	[p]	**p**ie	b.	[iː]	b**ea**t
	[t]	**t**idy		[ɪ]	b**i**t
	[k]	**k**ite		[e]	b**e**d
	[b]	**b**uy		[æ]	b**a**d
	[d]	**d**ie		[ɜː]	b**ir**d
	[g]	**g**uest		[ə]	**a**long
	[m]	**m**ighty		[ʌ]	c**u**t
	[n]	**n**ight		[uː]	b**oo**t
	[ŋ]	ki**ng**		[ʊ]	b**oo**k
	[f]	**f**ight		[ɔː]	b**ough**t
	[v]	**v**an		[ɒ]	wh**a**t
	[θ]	**th**ink		[ɑː]	b**a**th
	[ð]	**th**ey			
	[s]	**s**ee	c.	[eɪ]	d**ay**
	[z]	**z**ero		[aɪ]	b**uy**
	[ʃ]	**sh**ine		[ɔɪ]	b**oy**
	[ʒ]	vi**si**on		[əʊ]	b**oa**t
	[h]	**h**ide		[aʊ]	h**ow**
	[w]	**w**hite		[ɪə]	h**ere**
	[l]	**l**ight		[eə]	h**air**
	[ɹ]	**r**ide		[ʊə]	t**our**
	[j]	**y**oung			
	[tʃ]	**ch**urch			
	[dʒ]	**G**eorge			

We will be using the IPA system for all transcriptions in the remainder of this book. Note, however, that for traditional reasons a slightly different transcription system is often used in the literature on North American varieties of English. In some texts you will thus encounter symbols that don't occur in IPA transcription. While there is some variation, you are most likely to come across a set of symbols such as the one in (4). The examples given are not for RP this time, but for what has been termed **General American**, the standard reference accent of North American English, for which the symbols are typically used.

6   *The sounds: phonetics*

(4) The sounds of General American; American transcription conventions; pertinent letters in **bold** print

	phonetic symbol	example		phonetic symbol	example
a.	[p]	**p**ie	b.	[i]	**bea**t
	[t]	**t**idy		[ɪ]	b**i**t
	[k]	**k**ite		[e]	l**a**te
	[b]	**b**uy		[ɛ]	b**e**d
	[d]	**d**ie		[æ]	b**a**d
	[g]	**g**uest		[ə]	**a**long
	[m]	**m**ighty		[ʌ]	c**u**t
	[n]	**n**ight		[ʊ]	b**oo**k
	[ŋ]	ki**ng**		[u]	b**oo**t
	[f]	**f**ight		[o]	b**oa**t
	[v]	**v**an		[ɔ]	b**ou**ght
	[θ]	**th**ink		[a]	p**o**t
	[ð]	**th**ey			
	[s]	**s**ee	c.	[ay]	b**uy**
	[z]	**z**ero		[oy]	b**oy**
	[š]	**sh**ine		[aw]	h**ow**
	[ž]	vi**s**ion			
	[h]	**h**ide			
	[w]	**w**hite			
	[l]	**l**ight			
	[r]	**r**ide			
	[y]	**y**oung			
	[č]	**ch**urch			
	[ǰ]	**G**eorge			

If you compare the two lists in (3) and (4), you will notice that many symbols are in fact identical. Concerning the consonants, American conventions deviate in only a handful of cases from the IPA, for instance in using [č] and [ǰ] instead of IPA [tʃ] and [dʒ] for the initial and final sounds in *church* and *George*, respectively. More substantial differences can be found in the realm of the vowels. Note, however, that, at least partially, the usage of different vowel symbols results from actual phonetic differences in the vowel sounds. In other words, the vowels of General American are not exactly the same as those of RP, so that even if we used the same transcription system for both accents, the inventories would look different. We will investigate some of these differences in section 1.4.2. below.

The lists in (3) and (4) give you some idea of the variety of speech sounds we are dealing with in phonetics even if we restrict ourselves to the sounds that occur in just one accent of one language. How do we arrive at such an amazing diversity of sounds? In order to answer this question, let us take a closer look at how speech sounds are produced.

1.3. Producing sounds

1.3.1. The nature of speech sounds

If you have ever tried speaking immediately after running hard, you will have found that this is a difficult thing to do while you are panting for air. That is, of course, because we need air not only to breathe, but also to speak. You will notice that it is possible for you to produce sounds breathing in as well as breathing out. The latter method, however, clearly demands less energy and is the most common one in the languages of the world. For instance, all English sounds are usually produced with air being pushed out from the lungs through the mouth or nose. Technically, this mechanism is called 'pulmonic egressive airstream mechanism'. Other mechanisms such as, for instance, pulmonic ingressive (with sounds being made while breathing in) are possible, but they are regularly used only in a minority of languages and will not be considered here in more detail.

Of course, breathing out cannot be all we do when we speak. We are able to produce and distinguish a large variety of speech sounds, but what exactly is it that makes these sounds differ from each other? What makes [s] as in *sand* different from [h] as in *hand*? What distinguishes the initial sound [b] in *bat* from the initial sound [p] in *Patrick*? It "sounds" different for sure. Let us think about what this "sounding different" means for a moment.

Essentially, what we perceive as sound is air vibration. When we speak, air is pushed out of our mouth or nose and the neutral surrounding air pressure is disturbed. When the resulting sound waves, i.e. variations in air pressure, hit our ears, the air vibrations are interpreted as one sound or another. This happens not only for speech, but for all kinds of sounds. Take an organ in church, for instance: with its many tubes it produces a variety of different sounds, some of which sound higher and some of which sound lower. These differences in sound quality we perceive are related to differences in the vibration of the air. In a wider tube the air has much more space for vibration, whereas in a narrow tube, it soon hits the walls and is thrown back. This results in a greater number of vibrations (cycles of variation in air pressure) or a higher **frequency** of the sound, which we then perceive as a relatively higher note.

8   The sounds: phonetics

Although speech sounds are much more complex than the simple notes in this organ example, the mechanism is basically the same: air is pushed through a system of individually shaped tubes, so to say, all of which influence the final sound quality. The detailed properties of sound waves are beyond the scope of this chapter. Instead we will have a closer look at the "tube system" that produces them.

1.3.2. The vocal tract

Figure 1.1. shows a picture of the so-called **vocal tract**, that is the entire passage above the larynx. This is where speech sounds are shaped. Often, you will also find references to the 'vocal organs', a term that refers to all parts of the body involved in speech production, including also the parts up to the larynx such as lungs and trachea (windpipe).

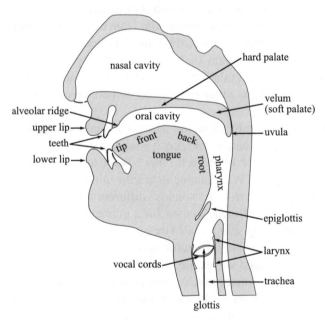

Figure 1.1. The vocal tract

As the picture shows, the vocal tract is divided into two main cavities that provide resonating space, i.e. space for the vibration of the passing air: the nasal cavity and the oral cavity, the latter of which includes the mouth and the pharyngeal areas. When air is pushed from the lungs, it passes through the larynx and the upper cavities of the vocal tract. For each of the various distinct sounds that we can produce, the airstream is modified in a unique way.

At this point, the interesting question to ask is how we can describe the differences in this modification. If the vocal tract were a simple tube, we could state the width and length of that tube, and that would most probably be it. Obviously, the situation is more complicated here. How can we describe differences in the shape of a complex system such as the vocal tract? Measuring distances in units such as centimetres or millimetres as you could do for tubes makes no sense at all in this case. The dimensions of the vocal tract are different for each speaker, yet all of us can pronounce sounds such as [t] or [g]. Thus, where numerical measures do not help us, anatomical ones do: You can see in figure 1.1. above that phoneticians have come up with a number of labels for different parts of the vocal tract. These labels are used to make rather precise statements about where in the vocal tract individual sounds are produced. We refer to all parts of the vocal apparatus which are involved in speech production as **articulators**, making a further distinction between 'active' and 'passive' articulators. The former include all those articulators which can be moved (i.e. the tongue, the lips, and the lower jaw), while the latter term describes those articulators which cannot change their position (e.g. the upper teeth, the hard palate, etc.).

Equipped with this set of reference points in the vocal tract we can now set out to explore what gives different sounds their individual qualities. As we will see, these qualities will refer to the manner (how is a sound produced?) and place of articulation (where is a sound produced?) of the respective speech sound.

1.4. How sounds differ from each other: the classification of speech sounds

If someone asked you whether [p] is more similar to [s] or to [iː], you might be tempted to say that [p] and [s] are more alike, because they are both consonants, whereas [iː] is a vowel. Indeed, the distinction between consonants and vowels plays an important role in phonetics. But what is this difference really? How do we determine whether a sound is a consonant or a vowel? Which properties do [p] and [s], for instance, share that make them consonants and distinguish them from vowels such as [iː]? Which features allow us to tell [p] and [s] apart as different consonantal sounds? The following section will be concerned with these problems. In order to facilitate the discussion, we will take an intuitive approach here to what is a consonant or a vowel.

Later on we will see which criteria we can use to formally distinguish the two classes of sounds. We will start by looking at the production of consonants and establish criteria for their description and classification. With these tools at hand, we can then test whether it makes sense to apply the same kind of categories to vowels, too, and if not, why not.

1.4.1. The classification of consonants

Each of the pairs of sounds in (5) illustrates one of the three criteria used to distinguish consonants. In each case, the two given sounds differ crucially in one aspect.

(5) a. [b] and [d] as in *bark* and *dark*
 b. [b] and [w] as in *bin* and *win*
 c. [z] and [s] as in *zoo* and *Sue;*
   [b] and [p] as in *bin* and *pin*

Let us start by having a look at the sounds in (5a). If you pay attention to what the articulators do when you say [b] and [d], respectively, you can easily detect a difference between the two sounds: for [b] your lips come together, while for [d] your lips are spread. Now concentrate on what your tongue does during the production of [d]: it touches the roof of your mouth just behind your upper front teeth, at the small bump called alveolar ridge (cf. figure 1.1.). For [b] you will find that the tongue is in a completely different, very low, position, not touching the roof of the mouth at all. We can therefore distinguish [b] and [d] by the different positions of the articulators during the production of each sound. At the place where the articulators come together for each sound, the airstream coming from the lungs is obstructed. Since the position of the articulators varies for different sounds, also the point of obstruction varies accordingly. Linguists therefore use the point of closest constriction in the vocal tract as a criterion for the description and classification of consonants. The technical term for this is **place of articulation**. Figure 1.2. illustrates the shape of the vocal tract for [b] and [d], respectively.

Sounds which, like [b], are characterised by a constriction at the lips are called **bilabial** sounds (involving both lips), whereas the place of articulation of [d] is referred to as **alveolar** (with an obstruction at the alveolar ridge). As you can see, place of articulation features correspond to the articulators involved. Moving from the lips further to the back of the mouth, we distinguish the following places of articulation: **Labio-dentals** involve only the lower lip and additionally the upper teeth. An example of a labio-dental sound is [f]. If we talk about **dental** place of articulation, however, the lips do not play a role

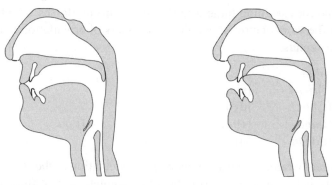

Figure 1.2. Difference in place of articulation: [b] versus [d]

in production. These sounds are produced with the tongue immediately behind the upper front teeth or even protruding between upper and lower front teeth, as in [θ]. The latter place of articulation is sometimes more specifically referred to as **inter-dental**. In **palato-alveolar** sounds, such as [ʃ], the constriction is between the hard palate and the alveolar ridge, slightly further back than for alveolar sounds, such as [s]. For a purely **palatal** sound such as [j], the tongue is raised toward the hard palate. An obstruction at the velum as in [k] gives us a **velar** sound, and finally, if the airstream is obstructed at the glottis, as in [h], we talk about **glottal** place of articulation. Note that sounds with varying places of articulation also differ in terms of which part of the tongue is involved in their production. For instance, in alveolar sounds, such as [s] or [d], it is the tip of the tongue that causes the obstruction, whereas in velar sounds, such as [k] or [g], the relevant part of the tongue is the back.

We have given only one sound as an illustration for each place of articulation here. Turning to the examples in (5b) above, however, you will see immediately that two sounds can share the same place of articulation and still differ in quality. In the production of both [b] and [w] in *bin* and *win*, the air is obstructed at the lips, and [b] and [w] can consequently be classified as bilabial sounds. You will notice, however, that the way in which you produce the two sounds is different. For [b] you briefly close the lips and stop the airflow completely. You momentarily hold your breath, so to say, before you release the air again. You can feel this release as a small burst of air. For [w], by contrast, the lips get close, but leave a passage for the air to pass through. Thus, the airstream is obstructed in different ways for [b] and [w], respectively, and this difference results in different sound qualities. The various production methods of consonants are referred to as their respective **manner of articulation**. We can use this specification as a criterion for classifying consonants and for assigning them to different groups or classes. The bracketed sounds of the words below illustrate the manners of articulation that we find in English sounds.

(6) a. [p]*an* [k]*ing*
    b. [f]*riend* [s]*and*
    c. [tʃ]*urch* [dʒ]*ungle*
    d. [l]*and* [ɹ]*ing* [w]*e* [j]*ou*
    e. [m]*ean* [n]*ever* *ki*[ŋ]

You are already familiar with the manner of articulation of the sounds in (6a). The pattern is the same as for [b] above: a complete stop of the airflow followed by a release. Sounds which are produced in this way are referred to as either **stops** (because the airflow is stopped completely) or **plosives** (because of the burst of air at the moment of release, which sounds like a small explosion). English stops include all of the following: [p, b, t, d, k, g].

Turning to the examples in (6b), we can now use the newly gained criteria to conclude that [f] and [s] cannot be stops, since there is continuous airflow throughout the production of these sounds. However, the airflow is not unobstructed. For [f], for instance, the lower lips and the upper front teeth come very close together, leaving only a narrow passage through which air can escape. When the air passes through this slight opening, the result is audible friction, a characteristic noise after which this class of consonants is named **fricatives**. Among the English sounds, [f, v, θ, ð, s, z, ʃ, ʒ, h] are classified as fricatives.

Having learned about stops and fricatives, you may be surprised that the examples in (6c) are shown as a distinct group. Didn't we say that [t] is a stop and [ʃ] a fricative? Why then does [tʃ] (and likewise [dʒ]) appear here with its own entry? The reason is that the sound sequences [tʃ] and [dʒ] behave differently from any other sequence of fricative plus stop. For instance, they are the only such sequences which can occur initially in English words (cf. examples above). Since no other stop-fricative sequence is allowed in this position, it is assumed that the special behaviour of [tʃ] and [dʒ] results from an equally special status: They are regarded not as two separate units, but as a single one. Nonetheless, phonetically, [tʃ] and [dʒ] combine two different manners of production: a stoppage of the airflow, followed by a prolonged release with only a narrow opening and therefore audible friction. The linguistic term for these complex sounds is **affricates**.

The next group of sounds in (6d) is traditionally subdivided into two subclasses, the so-called **liquids** [l] and [ɹ] on the one hand and the so-called **glides** or **semi-vowels** [w] and [j] on the other hand. However, what is more important than this distinction is what all four sounds have in common. If you compare the manner of articulation of [l, ɹ, w, j] with what we have seen so far for stops or fricatives, one difference you will notice is that the four sounds are created with much less turbulence in the airstream. There is certainly no complete closure, and the articulators leave enough space for the air to pass without audible friction. Phoneticians use the term **approximants** for this type of sound, in which the articulators approach each other, but do not cause a strong constriction in the vocal tract. English has only these four approximants. Among them, [l] is usually referred to as a 'lateral approximant', because the air escapes at the sides of the tongue instead of down the centre of the mouth as in the three other, 'central approximants'. Test this difference for yourself: you will notice that for the production of [l] the tip of your tongue touches the alveolar ridge, so the air cannot escape centrally. However, it can still flow around the sides of the tongue. If you let loose the tip of your tongue and close off the sides of your mouth instead, you end up producing [ɹ]. Thus, [l] and [ɹ] have the same, alveolar, place of articulation, but the shape of the tongue and the path of the airflow distinguish the lateral [l] from the central [ɹ].

So far, we have established four different classes of consonants: stops, fricatives, affricates, and approximants. According to the data in (6e), there is yet another group, consisting of the sounds [m], [n], and [ŋ]. Concerning articulatory gestures, can you find any similarities or differences to any of the other classes? In what way is the airstream obstructed when you say [m], for instance? You will immediately have observed that throughout this sound, your lips are closed, that is, no air can escape through the mouth. The complete closure reminds us of the class of stops, and indeed, you will find [m], [n], and [ŋ] treated as stops in some textbooks. However, they do not share the second characteristic feature of stops such as [p] or [t], i.e. the sudden release of air, and thus [m], [n], and [ŋ] cannot be referred to as plosives. Certainly you have found out by now why there is no such burst of air in these sounds: They do not show a sudden release, because the air continues to flow throughout the sound, only it escapes through the nose instead of the mouth. How does this work and why does it not happen in other cases? In order to answer this question, let us have a look at the positions of the vocal organs for [b] and [m], respectively, illustrated by the two figures below.

The position of the velum is what makes all the difference. During the production of most sounds it is raised, thus stopping air from flowing up into the nasal cavity. This is the position it has for [b] above as well as for all English stops, fricatives, affricates, liquids, and glides. Only for one class of consonants the velum is lowered, leaving an open passage from the oral to the nasal

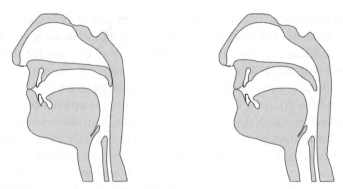

Figure 1.3. The vocal tract during the production of [b] and [m]

cavity, so that the air can escape through the nose. These sounds are called **nasals**.

English has only the three nasal consonants mentioned above: [m], [n], and [ŋ], which differ only in their place of articulation. Of course, even though the air escapes through the nose, the place of articulation criteria still hold for nasal consonants. The different shapes of the vocal tract affect the air vibration and thereby the resulting sound quality for nasals just as they do for oral sounds.

In this section we have so far discussed how we can distinguish consonants by their place and manner of articulation and assign them to different classes according to these criteria. It is now time to deal with the last remaining criterion for the classification of consonants, which we illustrated by the opposition of the two sounds [z] and [s] as well as [b] and [p] in (5c) earlier on.

Regarding place and manner of articulation features, the classification of [z] and [s] is the same: both are alveolar sounds and both are fricatives. You can clearly hear that there is a difference between the two sounds, though. Thus, there must be some additional parameter which we have not taken into account so far and which causes the difference in sound quality between [z] and [s]. You can even feel the difference: Put your finger on your throat in the area of your glottis while saying [z]*oo* and [s]*ue* and you will notice a vibration that is present during the [z] in *zoo*, but not during the [s] in *Sue*. Analogous distinctions can be made between [b] and [p] in *bin* and *pin*.

The vibration you feel during [z] (and the vowel [uː]) is that of the **vocal cords** or 'vocal folds', two small muscular folds which are located at the lower end of the larynx (cf. figure 1.1.). When air is pushed from the lungs, it goes up through the trachea and the larynx, passing through the opening between the vocal cords (the **glottis**). The flexibility of the vocal cords makes it possible to vary the width of this opening. When the vocal cords are apart, the air can pass relatively freely into the vocal tract. In this case, no vibration of the vocal cords is caused. This is the normal situation when we breathe out, but also in many speech sounds such as [p, t, k, tʃ, f, θ, s, ʃ, h]. These sounds are called **voiceless**.

However, the vocal cords may also come together to close the space between them. If the airstream from the lungs now pushes its way through, it forces the vocal cords apart. Since the folds are very elastic, they bounce back to their original position close to each other, and the cycle of opening and closure repeats itself. The result is a vibration of the vocal cords: the vibration you felt in our small experiment above. Sounds which are produced with this vibration are said to be **voiced**. They include all vowels, approximants, and nasals, but also a number of fricatives, stops, and affricates.

Finally, we are in a position to uniquely identify each consonant of English by stating its articulatory properties. The criteria are usually given in the sequence: 1. voicing, 2. place of articulation, 3. manner of articulation. The phonetic symbols can thus be regarded as abbreviations for specific combinations of articulatory features: [p] means a voiceless bilabial stop, [v] a voiced labio-dental fricative, [ŋ] a voiced velar nasal, and so on.

The inventory of RP English consonants is given in table 1.1. in a so-called consonant chart. The sounds are sorted in different columns according to their place of articulation and in different rows according to their manner of articulation. In cells with more than one symbol, the left one describes a voiceless sound and the right one a voiced sound. Note that stops and fricatives often come in pairs: one voiced and one voiceless sound for the same place of articulation. In cells with only one symbol, you will find that this symbol usually occupies the right-hand side of its cell, indicating that the corresponding sound is voiced. The only exception is the symbol for the glottal fricative, which is left-aligned, reflecting the fact that [h] is a voiceless sound.

Table 1.1. The consonants of English (RP); IPA symbols

	bilabial	labio-dental	dental	alveolar	palato-alveolar	palatal	velar	glottal
plosive	p b			t d			k g	
fricative		f v	θ ð	s z	ʃ ʒ			h
affricate					tʃ dʒ			
nasal	m			n			ŋ	
approximant	w			(central) ɹ (lateral) l		j		

16 *The sounds: phonetics*

In this section we have seen that consonants can be described and classified according to their articulatory characteristics. The three main criteria we need to distinguish different consonants from each other are voicing, place of articulation, and manner of articulation. In the following section we will turn our attention to the large group of sounds we have not dealt with yet: the vowels.

1.4.2. The classification of vowels

When we started out with the classification of sounds we said that the most basic distinction that is usually made is between consonants and vowels. Bearing in mind that differences in sound quality result from different modifications of the air stream, it would only seem reasonable to assume that the production of vowels is somewhat different from the production of consonants. However, before we jump to any conclusions, let us see what happens if we try to use our consonantal criteria to describe and classify different vowels. Consider the vowels in the examples below. Can you identify different manners of articulation or pinpoint the respective place of articulation for each vowel? What can you say about voicing?

(7) a. beat — bet — bat
 b. beat — boot
 c. beat — bit

Let us start with the simplest case, voicing: you can feel your vocal cords vibrating in all vowel sounds above. This is the usual case with vowels: unlike consonants, which can be either voiced or voiceless, vowels are almost always voiced. Therefore, we would not gain much by using voicing as a criterion to classify vowels. But what about manner of articulation? Is the airstream obstructed in different ways for the vowels [iː] as in *beat* and [e] as in *bet*, for instance? Clearly none of the sounds includes any closure or friction noise. Indeed, you will not find any obstruction at all. It is this characteristic feature that distinguishes vowels from consonants. In contrast to consonants, vowels involve only a modulation, but not an obstruction of the airstream.

If there is no obstruction, then manner and place of articulation features as we introduced them for consonants cannot help us with vowels. Once we move away from our consonantal criteria, however, there are some things we can say about articulatory gestures in vowels. Consider the examples in (7a) above. Say the words out loud while standing in front of a mirror (or watch a partner saying them). You will notice that your tongue is fairly high for the vowel [iː] in *beat*, a little lower for [e] in *bet*, and lowest for [æ] in *bat*. Note that your jaw is open furthest for [æ], making space for the tongue. It seems that we have found a first aspect in which vowels can differ: the height of the body of the tongue.

Now take a look at the set of words in (7b), *beat* and *boot*. Try saying just the two vowels, [iː] and [uː], after each other and see whether you can describe what happens. This time, there is no considerable change in the degree of jaw opening. Your lips change their position, but we will ignore this for a moment. There is something else that distinguishes the two vowels, and figure 1.4. reveals what causes the distinctly different sound qualities.

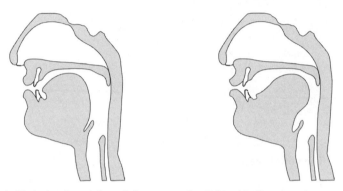

Figure 1.4. Estimated position of the tongue for [iː] and [uː]

As the pictures show, the body of the tongue is much further front for [iː] than it is for [uː], so that, if you say the two vowels after each other, you can feel a backward movement for [uː]. Thus, we can arrange the two vowels on a kind of scale ranging from front to back.

By now we have arrived at two dimensions which seem to play a role in characterising and distinguishing vowels: first, the high-low dimension, and second, the front-back dimension. We can thus classify vowels according to the two criteria of **vowel frontness** and **vowel height**. But how do we determine whether a given vowel should be categorised as high or low, front or back, or maybe somewhere in between — and if so, where in the space in between? The problem is that we are dealing with continua: front and back, high and low are all relative measures. They are defined in relation to each other, not independent of alternative options. Thus, if we hear, for instance, that [iː] is a high vowel, we automatically assume that [iː] occupies a space close to the upper end of the high-low scale for vowels. Similar reasoning applies to other vowels and their classification. In view of these problems of relativity we usually distinguish three levels in each of the two dimensions: high, mid (sometimes further divided into mid-high and mid-low), and low on the high-low continuum and front, central, and back on the front-back continuum.

For an overview of the English vowel inventory, we could use a table similar to the one we set up for the consonants. However, more common, and more useful, is a so-called vowel chart. The chart roughly represents the space in the oral cavity in which the tongue moves for the production of different vowels. The quadrangle in figure 1.5. illustrates this space:

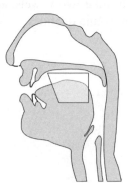

Figure 1.5. The vowel space

Inside the chart, vowels are plotted according to the tongue's highest point during the production of the respective vowel. The horizontal axis indicates differences in the relative frontness or backness of the tongue during vowel production, whereas the vertical axis reflects tongue height. Figure 1.6. below shows how this works for the vowels of RP.

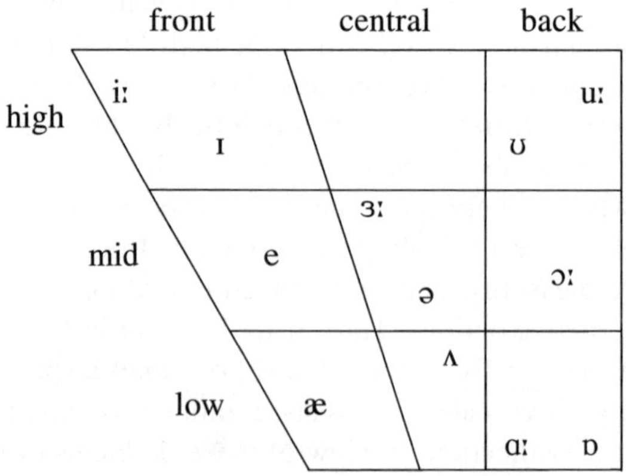

Figure 1.6. Vowel chart: the vowels of RP; IPA symbols

The grid lines divide the vowel chart into the different areas according to which vowels are classified as high, mid, central, back, and so on. You can see that the vowel [iː] is placed in the grid cell that is labelled both high and front. Thus, we say that [iː] is a high front vowel. Analogously, [e] can be classified as a mid front vowel, [æ] as a low front vowel, [ɑː] as a low back vowel, and so on. The mid central vowel represented by the symbol [ə] is usually considered the most neutral vowel as it occupies a position that is roughly in the middle of the chart in both dimensions and therefore as far away as possible from any extreme quality. This particular vowel is called 'schwa' [ʃwɑː], a term that originated in the name of the Hebrew letter for that particular sound.

We can sort our vowels nicely into groups according to frontness and height now. The vowel chart also shows, however, that this cannot be all there is to the description of vowels. In many of the squares we still find more than one vowel symbol, which up to now our criteria cannot distinguish. (7c) from above gives you sample words for one pair of sounds which meet the same frontness and height criteria, the two high front vowels [iː] and [ɪ], as in *beat* and *bit*, respectively. What is it that distinguishes the two sounds? One difference is revealed by the vowel chart: you can see that the two vowels are placed in slightly different positions, [iː] being a little higher and further front than [ɪ]. Unfortunately, our descriptive tools for vowels are not yet fine-grained enough to capture this qualitative difference. However, there is one additional difference between the two sounds which we can state much more easily. When saying *beat* and *bit*, you will surely have noticed that, although the sound quality appears rather similar, there is a clear difference in length: it takes longer to say the vowel in *beat* than it does to say the vowel in *bit*. We can thus distinguish [iː] from [ɪ] by saying that [iː] is a long high front vowel, whereas [ɪ] is a short high front vowel. Long vowels are indicated in IPA transcription by a colon after the vowel symbol. You can see in the chart above that there is no symbol which appears both with and without a colon. This means that in English we do not find pairs of long and short vowels which have exactly the same quality (and therefore the same symbol). Nonetheless, we have seen that including length as a descriptive criterion can help us classify English vowel sounds. Interestingly, the distinction in length strongly correlates with another difference between these sounds. This difference lies in the strength of the muscular activity needed to produce the two respective sounds. For [iː] and [uː] there is stronger muscular tension necessary than for [ɪ] and [ʊ]. Technically-speaking, the former set is characterised as 'tense', the latter as 'lax' vowels. You will find that sometimes only the tense-lax distinction is used in the literature, with no additional length marks included. For an example of such a notation, compare the American transcription conventions for General American vowels in (4) above.

So far we have covered the position of the tongue in two dimensions as well as the length/tenseness of the vowel sound. We ignored one other variable in our discussion of [iː] and [uː], however: the position of the lips. If you watch yourself in the mirror saying the two vowels, you can see the difference clearly: The lips are spread for [iː], but pursed for [uː]. Vowels which are produced with this lip "rounding" are called **rounded**, vowels that you pronounce with your lips spread are termed **unrounded**. In English, the former group includes [uː], [ʊ], and [ɔː], the latter group all remaining vowels. You might wonder at this point whether we really need lip rounding as a feature of vowel classification. After all, English does not appear to have two vowels which contrast only in this feature. There are no unrounded mid or high back vowels in the English vowel inventory, which could be paired with the rounded vowels. (Check the vowel chart to see that this is true.) In other words, none of the three rounded vowels has an unrounded counterpart. While this may be true for English, the situation is different in other languages. German, for instance, has two long high front vowels, [iː] and [yː], which occur in the words *Kiel* [kiːl] 'keel' and *kühl* [kyːl] 'cool', respectively. Here, unroundedness versus roundedness is the distinctive criterion that allows us to keep the two sounds apart in our classification. Taking the position of the lips into account, we can thus describe [iː] as a long high front unrounded vowel and its counterpart [yː] as a long high front rounded vowel.

We have arrived at four criteria to refer to and classify vowel sounds: vowel length, height, degree of frontness of the tongue, and position of the lips. The categories we have established allow us to describe all vowels plotted in the RP vowel chart and many more. However, if you compare the symbols that occur in the vowel chart in figure 1.6. to the complete list of symbols for RP vowels at the beginning of the chapter in (3), you will notice that there are a couple of symbols missing in the chart: We have not yet dealt with vowel sounds such as the ones that occur in *day, buy, boy*, and so on. In (8) we again list the vowels from (3) above. In what way are the vowels in the right-hand column different from the ones in the left-hand column that we have already discussed?

(8) | IPA symbol | example | IPA symbol | example |
|---|---|---|---|
| [iː] | beat | [eɪ] | day |
| [ɪ] | bit | [aɪ] | buy |
| [e] | bed | [ɔɪ] | boy |
| [æ] | bad | [əʊ] | boat |
| [ɜː] | bird | [aʊ] | how |
| [ə] | along | [ɪə] | here |
| [ʌ] | cut | [eə] | hair |
| [uː] | boot | [ʊə] | tour |
| [ʊ] | book | | |
| [ɔː] | bought | | |
| [ɒ] | what | | |
| [ɑː] | bath | | |

If you compare the vowel sounds in the two words *beat* and *day* (or *see* and *say*, for example), one thing you will notice is that in *day* (or *say*), there is a change in vowel quality within the syllable: it starts out somewhere mid front and then changes to a high front vowel. For the vowel in *beat* (or *see*), on the other hand, you have no such change.

What happens in the former case is that the tongue moves from the position for one vowel sound (mid front) to the position of the second vowel sound (high front). Thus, the vowel sound in *day* combines two articulations and consequently two different sound qualities. This is also reflected in the symbols we use in the phonetic representation of *day* [deɪ]. Does this mean that we should consider *day* as consisting of one consonant [d] and two separate vowels [e] and [ɪ]? Of course, the same question applies to all other remaining two-part symbols in the right-hand column in (8), namely [aɪ], [ɔɪ], [aʊ], [əʊ], [ɪə], [eə], and [ʊə]. Why would we want to treat them as one unit if, in effect, we have two different vowel qualities? However, treating them as two separate units would imply that [e] and [ɪ] in *day* are merely one of a multitude of possible combinations of English vowels. The examples in (9) reveal that there might be a problem with the latter interpretation. An asterisk indicates that the given combination of sounds is not attested in English within one syllable.

(9) [aʊ] as in *how*   *[ʊa]
    [ɔɪ] as in *boy*   *[ɪɔ]
    [ɪə] as in *here* *[əɪ]
    ...   *[ɔa], *[ʊɔ], ...

The left-hand column gives you sample words for some of the symbols from our list above. By contrast, the combinations in the right-hand column are not valid sound combinations in English. Apparently, it is not the case that anything goes in the combination of vowels. If you recall our discussion of consonants, and in particular, manner of articulation, this reminds us strongly of the situation we found for the affricates [tʃ] and [dʒ]. For these consonantal sounds we solved the problem in assigning them single-unit status, thus separating them from other combinations of consonants, which are either unattested or more restricted than [tʃ] and [dʒ]. We can do the same for the two-part vowel articulations. These particular vowel sounds in which there is a change in auditory quality within a single syllable are called **diphthongs**. The contrasting term that can be used for simple vowels which show no such change in quality is **monophthong**.

In order to appropriately describe a diphthong, we need to include a statement concerning the change in sound quality. We therefore specify both the starting and the end point of the articulation, using the height and frontness criteria we introduced for vowel classification. For instance, the diphthong [aʊ] is characterised by a movement from low central to high back position, the change in [ɔɪ] can be described as mid back to high front, and so on. An interesting question at this point is how to represent diphthongs in the vowel chart. We need to recognise two different sound qualities as well as to indicate which of the two is the starting point and which the end point. You can see the solution to this problem in the three vowel charts below, which show all RP diphthongs.

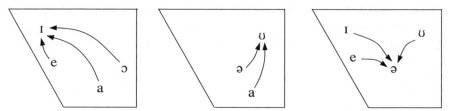

Figure 1.7. The diphthongs of RP

For each diphthong, the vowel symbols corresponding to the starting and end points respectively are given in the chart. The direction of the movement is indicated by an arrow from one symbol to the other. Note that some of the IPA symbols used in diphthongs differ from those we use for the simple vowels. For example, you find [aɪ] (as in e.g. *buy*) and not [ɑɪ] or [ʌɪ], as you might expect. Since we are dealing with phonetic symbols, a different symbol corresponds directly to a different sound quality, of course. Therefore, the choice of [aɪ] tells you that the first element of the diphthong has a quality that is distinct from the vowel in *father* as well as the vowel in *cut*. [a] is slightly further front than [ɑ], but lower than [ʌ].

You may have noticed that the diphthongs in the three charts are not grouped together randomly. In each chart, the diphthongs have a common second element: [ɪ] in the leftmost chart, [ʊ] in the middle and [ə] in the vowel chart on the right. The former two groups can be contrasted with the diphthongs ending in [ə] according to the direction of the movement: the fact that the second element, [ə], is a central vowel, gives the latter group its name, 'centering diphthongs'. By contrast, diphthongs ending in the high vowels [ɪ] or [ʊ] are usually termed 'closing diphthongs'.

In the above discussion we have seen that we can find criteria for the description of vowel sounds which make reference to the position of the articulators. However, it has also become obvious that statements of these positions are approximations rather than fixed values. The fact that places of articulation in vowels are not so discrete makes vowels much more accessible to variation in pronunciation than consonants. It is therefore not surprising that varieties of English show considerable differences mainly in the vowels (compare the lists of RP and General American sounds in (3) and (4) that we looked at earlier). The sample words below illustrate how varied the pronunciation of one and the same word can actually be across speakers of different varieties of English. Here, the IPA phonetic transcription is given for RP, General American, and Standard Scottish English. Examples are adapted from Giegerich (1992).

(10)		**RP**	**General American**	**Standard Scottish English**
	boat	[bəʊt]	[boʊt]	[boːt]
	make	[meɪk]	[meɪk]	[meːk]
	bird	[bɜːd]	[bɜɹd]	[bɪɹd]
	heard	[hɜːd]	[hɜɹd]	[hɛɹd]
	cot	[kɒt]	[kɑt]	[kɔt]

The examples show that there is variation in three different aspects: firstly, words which have diphthongs in RP may have monophthongs in other varieties. For instance, Standard Scottish English has monophthongs in both *boat* and *make*. Secondly, vowel length can vary. Some varieties of English may have a short vowel where RP has a long vowel (cf. *bird* or *heard*). Finally, there is also variation in vowel quality. All three varieties above have a short monophthong in the word *cot*, but we find three different vowel qualities: [ɒ], [ɑ], and [ɔ].

1.5. Conclusion

In this chapter we have seen that languages construct their words from their own, individual, sound inventories, which are subsets of all possible speech sounds. We have also seen that it is crucial to distinguish between sounds and letters, and a system for the representation of speech sounds, phonetic transcription, has been introduced.

Focussing on English, we have learned how different types of consonants and vowels are produced and how we can describe distinct sounds with respect to their articulatory properties. For consonants, we have established voicing, place, and manner of articulation as relevant criteria, whereas we found that vowels are more appropriately described with reference to length, frontness, vowel height, and lip rounding.

Additionally, in the discussion of English affricates and diphthongs, we have already hinted that languages impose restrictions on the combinations of sounds in their respective inventories. Not every sound can occur in every theoretically possible position. We will come back to this last issue in the next chapter, which deals with the organisation of speech sounds into a more abstract system.

Further reading

A standard reference for the pronunciation of English words is Jones' (2006) *English Pronouncing Dictionary*, which includes British and American pronunciations. For those interested in a general and accessible approach to phonetics, we recommend Ladefoged (2006), which introduces beginners in some detail to articulatory and acoustic phonetics. The book includes numerous exercises, among them also some highly useful performance exercises. For a practical guide to acoustic data analysis use Ladefoged (2003). Johnson (2003) is more theoretically based and covers acoustic as well as auditory phonetics. Readers looking for a more thorough and advanced treatment of principles of phonetics are referred to Laver (1994).

Exercises

Basic level

Exercise 1.1.: Articulatory classification of speech sounds

In (10) you find a list of phonetic symbols without a description, as well as descriptions without the corresponding symbol. Supply the missing information in each case.

(10) a. [h] _____
     b. [ŋ] _____
     c. [tʃ] _____
     d. [ʌ] _____
     e. [ʊə] _____
     f. [ɔː] _____
     g. [   ] voiced palato-alveolar affricate
     h. [   ] voiced dental fricative
     i. [   ] short low back unrounded vowel
     j. [   ] diphthong; low central to high front

Exercise 1.2.: The position of the articulators

The figures below show the position of the articulators for different sounds. For each illustration, identify the corresponding sound or sounds (articulatory description) and give the phonetic symbol(s).

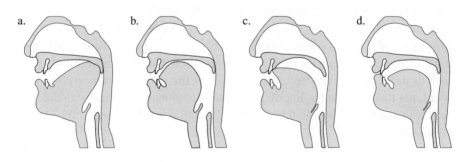

a.   b.   c.   d.

Exercise 1.3.: Comparing sounds

Consider the pairs of sounds in (11). What distinguishes the sounds in each pair? Give the kind of feature and specify. Note that the given sounds may differ in more than one feature.

(11) a. [d] and [n]   e. [æ] and [ɔː]
     b. [ʒ] and [z]   f. [aɪ] and [eɪ]
     c. [ŋ] and [k]   g. [ʊ] and [ɒ]
     d. [w] and [ɹ]   h. [ə] and [e]

Exercise 1.4.: Phonetic transcription

Find the errors in the transcription of sounds in the words below (using RP as a reference accent). In each word, there may be one or two errors. Indicate the error and provide a corrected version of the phonetic transcription.

(12) a. *singer*   [sɪngə]   e. *wife*   [waiv]
     b. *calling*   [kɔːllɪŋ]   f. *along*   [ælɒŋ]
     c. *speak*   [spik]   g. *cool*   [cuːl]
     d. *run*   [run]   h. *these*   [θiːz]

Advanced level

Exercise 1.5.: Comparing sound inventories

The table below lists all the consonants of (RP) English.
a. Find out in which position(s) each sound can occur in English: at the beginning of a word (word-initially), at the end of a word (word-finally), or both. Give one example for each possible position. Since we are talking about sounds here, the relevant reference for you is the phonetic transcription of a word, not its orthography. In order to make sure you are working with the correct transcription, consult the *English Pronouncing Dictionary* by Daniel Jones (2006).

Exercises

Example:

IPA symbol	word-initial position	word-final position
[d]	[deɪ] *day*	[bed] *bed*

IPA symbol	word-initial position	word-final position
[p]		
[t]		
[k]		
[b]		
[d]		
[g]		
[m]		
[n]		
[ŋ]		
[f]		
[v]		
[θ]		
[ð]		
[s]		
[z]		
[ʃ]		
[ʒ]		
[h]		
[w]		
[l]		
[ɹ]		
[j]		
[tʃ]		
[dʒ]		

b. Choose one other language that you know well and prepare an analogous list of its consonants. Proceed in the same way as you did for the English sounds: identify the positions in which each consonant can occur and give examples. Use a good dictionary of the language to check the pronunciation of your sample words.

c. Compare the two consonant inventories: Which consonants do the two languages share? Do these sounds occur in the same positions in both languages? Are there any consonants which occur in only one of the two languages? Make a list of differences between the two consonant inventories.

Chapter 2
The sound system: phonology

2.1. Introduction

Spoken English does not simply consist of the sound waves that we perceive or produce when using the language. Instead, the sounds of language are grouped into a system of abstract categories in the minds of speakers and listeners. Being able to speak and understand a language means mastering this sound system; it is part of the language system. **Phonology** is the study of the abstract categories that organise the sound system of a language. These abstract categories comprise individual speech sounds as well as the way in which speech sounds are grouped into larger phonological units, such as syllables and words.

The chapter is structured as follows. Using the English r-sound as an example, section 2.2. will explain why we need to introduce abstract categories to describe the sound system of a language. In a second step (section 2.3.) we will introduce the methodology that we can use to find out which sounds are grouped into which categories in English. On the basis of this, we will analyse a sample of interesting English phonemes (section 2.4.). Section 2.5. will then be concerned with the syllable as a unit that organises sounds in spoken language into higher-level phonological units.

2.2. Introducing order into the chaos: the phoneme

Consider the sound [ɹ] in the following three words: *rip, wrap, rope*. In the phonetics chapter of this book you have learned that English [ɹ] is a voiced alveolar central approximant. The picture in (1) shows you what [ɹ] in *rip, wrap*, and *rope* looks like in a so-called **spectrogram**. A spectrogram is a graphic representation of the frequency distribution of the complex jumble of sound waves that give the hearing impression of speech sounds. The speaker who produced the words *rip, wrap*, and *rope* for our spectrograms is an adult male native speaker of Northern British English. The part of the spectrogram that represents [ɹ] is highlighted.

30 *The sound system: phonology*

(1) a. rip

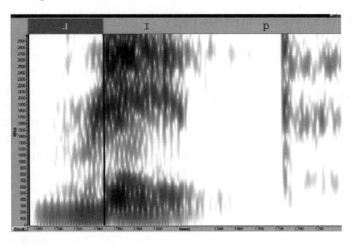

b. wrap

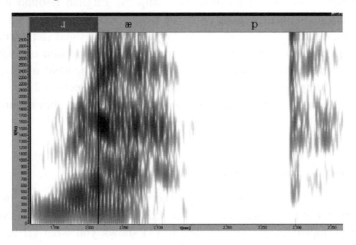

c. rope

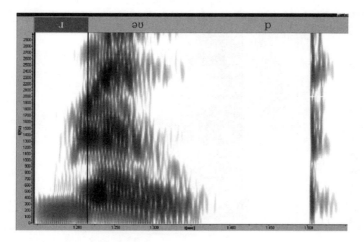

Although you may not be an expert in spectrogram reading, you see that the part representing [ɹ] looks very similar in all three spectrograms in (1). Now consider three words which are very similar to *rip, wrap,* and *rope*: *trip, trap,* and *trope*. If you had to transcribe these three words, you would probably — and correctly! — assume that, like *rip, wrap* and *rope*, they contain an [ɹ]: [tɹɪp], [tɹæp], [tɹəʊp]. What, however, makes you think that there is an [ɹ] in *trip, trap,* and *trope*? In (2) you find the pertinent spectrograms, spoken by the same speaker as in (1). Again, the area representing [ɹ] is highlighted.

(2) a. trip

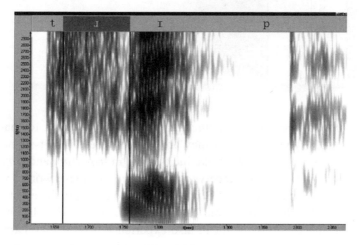

b. trap

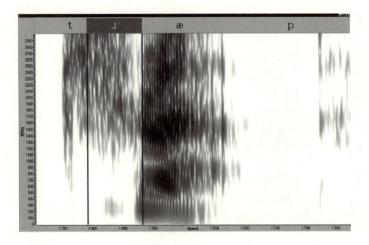

c. trope

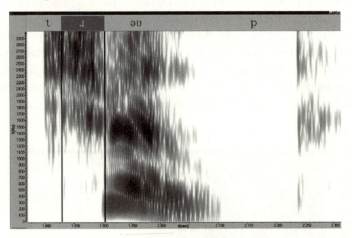

If you compare the spectrographic image of these r-sounds to that of the r-sounds in (1), you notice that they are very different. The r-sound in *rip*, *wrap*, and *rope* does not sound like the r-sound in *trip*, *trap*, and *trope*! So if up until now, you used to perceive an r-sound in all these words, you now know that, without being aware of it, you grouped two very different acoustic impressions into the same sound category. You can see this difference not only in the spectrograms, you can also experience it in a small experiment: Say only the first sound of *rip*, *wrap* or *rope* while touching your larynx with your fingers. You should be able to feel vibration. Now say the first two sounds of *trip*, *trap*, and *trope*, making sure you stop after the second sound. I predict that your larynx does not vibrate. Why? Because what we perceive as the r-sound in *trip*, *trap*, and *trope* is not a voiced consonant. Whereas the r-sound in *rip*, *wrap*, and *rope* is a voiced alveolar central approximant, the r-sound in *trip*, *trap*, and *trope* is a voiceless alveolar central approximant. We must then conclude that our idea of the English r-sound is an abstract, mental category, rather than a phonetic fact. We call such a category a **phoneme** (a more detailed definition of the term 'phoneme' will be given in section 2.3.1.). A physical realisation of a speech sound like the voiceless or the voiced alveolar approximant is a **phone.** Phones which function as alternant realisations of the same phoneme are called **allophones of the phoneme**. In notation, we will henceforth use slashes ('/ /') if we talk about phonemes. Thus, the abstract category comprising the r-sounds in *rip*, *wrap*, *rope*, *trip*, *trap*, and *trope* is the phoneme /ɹ/. In all other cases we will use square brackets ('[]'). For example, the phone which functions as an allophone of /ɹ/ in *rip*, *wrap*, and *rope* is [ɹ], whereas the phone which functions as an allophone of /ɹ/ in *trip*, *trap*, and *trope* is [ɹ̥]. The symbol [̥] indicates that the sound is voiceless. Our findings about /ɹ/ are summarised in (3).

(3)

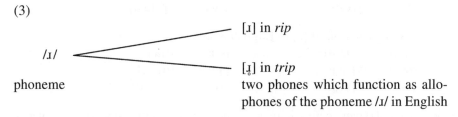

phoneme

[ɹ] in *rip*

[ɹ̥] in *trip*

two phones which function as allophones of the phoneme /ɹ/ in English

With respect to transcription, you now see that the symbols which you learned in chapter 1 are the symbols needed to represent English phonemes. Our example shows that if we want to analyse allophones of a particular phoneme, it is sometimes necessary to include additional articulatory details in the transcription (such as, for example, [̥] in [ɹ̥]). Such a transcription is called a **narrow transcription**. In this chapter I will only use narrow transcription if knowing articulatory details is necessary for the analysis. For all other transcriptive purposes, the symbols you learned in chapter 1 fully suffice — this is the level of detail that you will also find in the major dictionaries of English.

The categorisation of [ɹ] and [ɹ̥] as allophones of /ɹ/, however, immediately opens up yet another problem. Why do we assume that [ɹ] and [ɹ̥] are realisations of the same phoneme? Maybe you are tempted at this point to use the spelling of *trip*, *trap*, and *trope* and of *rip*, *wrap*, and *rope* as an argument, which in all cases contains <r>. However, recall from the discussion in chapter 1 that in English there is no one-to-one correspondence between the letters and the sounds that make up a word. Orthography is thus not a reliable representation of sound structure.

Instead, we can use two types of evidence to support the idea that [ɹ] and [ɹ̥] belong to the same phoneme. One of them, quite straightforwardly, is that [ɹ] and [ɹ̥] are phonetically very similar. They differ only in terms of a single articulatory feature, voicing. The second, and more important, line of argumentation is based on the **distribution** of [ɹ] and [ɹ̥] in English words. The term 'distribution' refers to the different positions in which a speech sound can occur or cannot occur in the words of a language. We can describe the distribution by stating in which position (henceforth: phonetic context) a particular sound can occur in the words of the language, and, crucially, in which phonetic context it cannot occur. The data in (4) and (5) do this for [ɹ] and [ɹ̥]. Ill-formed words are marked by an asterisk.

(4) The distribution of [ɹ] in English words
    wrap   [ɹæp]   trap   *[tɹæp]
    room   [ɹuːm]   pray   *[pɹeɪ]
    very   [veɹiː]   crude *[kɹuːd]

(5) The distribution of [ɹ̥] in English words
    wrap   *[ɹ̥æp]   trap   [tɹ̥æp]
    room   *[ɹ̥uːm]   pray   [pɹ̥eɪ]
    very   *[veɹ̥iː]   crude [kɹ̥uːd]

We see that [ɹ] can occur wherever [ɹ̥] is not allowed to occur, and vice versa. [ɹ] occurs at the beginning of words and between two vowels whereas [ɹ̥] occurs only after voiceless consonants. There is no context in which both [ɹ] and [ɹ̥] are possible. Two sounds which are distributed in such a way that one can only occur where the other cannot occur are said to be in **complementary distribution**.

The distributional facts make it very likely that [ɹ] and [ɹ̥] belong to the same phoneme in the sound system of English. Why is this so? Because the assumption of an abstract category /ɹ/ will allow us to explain the regularity which we observed in the distribution of [ɹ] and [ɹ̥]. The interesting thing about the complementary distribution of [ɹ] and [ɹ̥] is that it allows us to predict for every English word, which of the two allophones it will contain. Predictable alternations like those between [ɹ] and [ɹ̥] are usually expressed in linguistics in terms of 'phonological rules'. We can thus formulate a rule for

English which states that /ɹ/ will be realised as [ɹ̥] after voiceless consonants and as [ɹ] in all other contexts that we looked at. This rule is part of the grammar of the language, just like any other morphological or syntactic rule that you will get to know in the course of this book.

Complementary distribution is not only used in linguistics to postulate the existence of abstract categories. Other sciences as well as our everyday line of reasoning make use of exactly the same concept. Consider, for example, the chemical molecule H_2O. It is part of our general world knowledge that H_2O can appear in at least three different states, a liquid state ('water'), a frozen state ('ice') and a gaseous state ('steam'). How do we know that water, ice, and steam are states of a single molecule, H_2O, and not independent molecules? The answer is that they appear in complementary distribution. Additionally we can predict which of the three states of H_2O will occur on the basis of the surrounding temperature. Water, ice, and steam are alternant realisations of H_2O in much the same way as [ɹ] and [ɹ̥] are alternant realisations of /ɹ/. Alternant realisations of speech sounds are called allophones, whereas the three alternant realisations of chemical molecules are termed states of matter.

We now turn to the problem of how we, as linguists, can investigate the phoneme system of a particular language. Given that the systematic nature of the sound system is not something speakers are aware of: how can we determine which phones are realisations of which phonemes in the sound system of English?

2.3. The key to finding the order

2.3.1 Minimal pairs

We have three strategies at our disposal to investigate how a language categorises phones into a system of phonemes. The first strategy looks at the system of phonemes and asks what distinguishes this system from the 'unordered' jumble of phones. The answer is that in a language, no phoneme can be used to replace another phoneme without running risk of changing meaning. As an example, consider the English phoneme /ɹ/, which occurs, for example, in the word *wrap* (/ɹæp/). If we replace /ɹ/ in *wrap* by a different phoneme in English, we are likely to get a different word. The data in (6) provide examples.

(6) | phoneme to replace /ɹ/ in /ɹæp/ | resulting form in phonetic transcription | resulting form in regular orthography |
|---|---|---|
| /l/ | [læp] | lap |
| /m/ | [mæp] | map |
| /n/ | [næp] | nap |
| /t/ | [tæp] | tap |
| /k/ | [kæp] | cap |

By contrast, if we replace one allophone by a different allophone, we never get a different word. We have seen this exemplified already in the data in (4) and (5) above. What we did there was taking the English words *wrap*, *room*, *very*, *trap*, *pray*, and *crude*, and replacing one allophone of /ɹ/ ([ɹ] and [ɹ̥], respectively) by another allophone of /ɹ/ ([ɹ̥] and [ɹ], respectively). The results were ill-formed words. Thus, we see that within the sound system of English, the difference between allophones like [ɹ] and [ɹ̥] is of a fundamentally different nature from the difference between phonemes like /ɹ/, /l/, /m/, /n/, /t/, and /k/. Phonemes can distinguish words; allophones cannot. On the basis of this insight, linguists define the phoneme as the minimal distinctive unit in the sound system of the language. Phonemes are distinctive in the sense that they enable speakers to distinguish between words.

Apart from reflecting the function of phonemes, this phoneme definition provides us with a useful diagnostic tool for differentiating phonemes in a language. If a phoneme is a category that can distinguish words, then there must be words which can be distinguished through the use of different phonemes. As has been shown in (6) above, this is the case for /ɹ/ and our example word *wrap*. The existence of the word *lap* shows that the phones [ɹ] and [l] can distinguish different words in English and hence belong to different phonemes, /ɹ/ and /l/. Likewise, the existence of the word *map* shows that the phones [ɹ] and [m] can distinguish different words in English and hence belong to different phonemes. An analogous argument can be made for every word listed in (6). Word pairs like *wrap* and *lap* or *wrap* and *map* are called **minimal pairs**. A minimal pair is a pair of words which differ in only one sound, but differ in meaning. The data in (7) provide you with a small selection of minimal pairs in English.

(7) | [tɪp] | vs. | [hɪp] | tip | vs. | hip |
|---|---|---|---|---|---|
| [məʊ] | vs. | [səʊ] | mow | vs. | so |
| [tʃiːp] | vs. | [tʃɪp] | cheap | vs. | chip |
| [bed] | vs. | [bɪd] | bed | vs. | bid |
| [ɹəʊd] | vs. | [ɹəʊp] | road | vs. | rope |

The data show that [t] and [h], [m] and [s], [iː] and [ɪ], [e] and [ɪ], and [d] and [p] belong to different phonemes in English; they are not allophones of the same phoneme.

2.3.2. Distributional characteristics of allophones

The second strategy that can be used to investigate how language categorises sounds into phonemes and allophones focuses on the properties of allophones. We already saw one such property in section 2.2., complementary distribution.

However, not all allophones are in complementary distribution. As an example, consider the pronunciation of /p/ in the word *clap*, as heard in many British varieties of English. The spectrograms in (8) show you two possible realisations of *clap* by an adult male speaker from Manchester. The part which represents /p/ is highlighted.

You notice that /p/ is realised differently, or, to be precise, you really see /p/ only in spectrogram (8a), whereas in spectrogram (8b) you see mostly white space instead, i.e. silence. If you relate the pictures to what you learned about the phonetic characteristics of plosives in chapter 1, then you may deduce that the 'nothing' which you see in both spectrograms corresponds to the phase in which air pressure is built up in the oral cavity, as is expected during the first phase of the realisation of plosives. The difference between the two spectrograms then lies in the fact that in spectrogram (8a), after the building-up phase, something else follows – the release of the air that has been built up. This does not happen in spectrogram (8b) – the air pressure is not released. The realisation in (8a) is thus termed a **released** consonant ([p]), whereas the realisation in (8b) is termed **unreleased**. For released realisations of /p/ we use the symbol [p], whereas for unreleased realisations we use the symbol [p̚].

Our question now is: What is the status of [p] and [p̚] in the sound system of English, and how does this status relate to what we learned about phonemes and allophones in this section? First of all it is clear that [p] and [p̚] are realisations of a single phoneme, /p/, because they do not distinguish meaning. [kl̥æp] has the same meaning as [kl̥æp̚]. We should thus categorise [p] and [p̚] as allophones of /p/. In contrast to the allophones [ɹ] and [ɹ̥], however, [p] and [p̚] are clearly not in complementary distribution. We conclude that allophones do not have to be in complementary distribution. The distribution of [p] and [p̚] is termed **free variation**: Speakers can choose which allophone they use. Note, however, that the term 'choose' is not meant to imply a conscious decision on the part of the speaker. Whether [p] or [p̚] is used depends on a variety of factors, most of which are extralinguistic in nature, with pres-

(8) a. clap 1

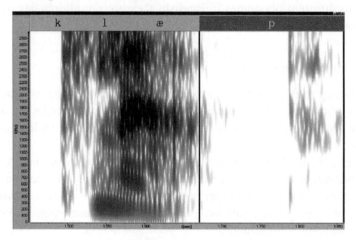

b. clap 2

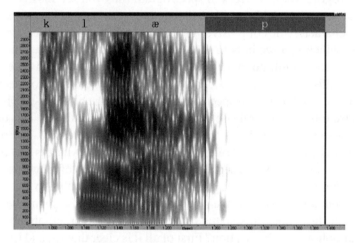

tige and social status among them (cf. chapter 7.3. for examples of how extra-linguistic factors can influence variability in language).

Understandably, the important function of distributional arguments in the analysis of phoneme systems makes it necessary that analysts are very clear about how they define the pertinent phonetic context, and which of all possible phonetic contexts they consider. Up until now we have only loosely defined contexts as, for example, 'word-medial' or 'after voiceless consonants'. At this point, however, I would like to introduce a more systematic definition as well as the notational conventions that go with it.

In most of this chapter, we will use the word as a reference category. Within words, we make a principled distinction between the beginning, the middle, and the end of a word. In notation, we use the symbol '#' to designate a word boundary, and a line ('__') to designate the position which interests us. Thus, for example, the word-final context in which we find unreleased [p˺] is symbolised as '__ #': 'The sound we are interested in occurs in the position ('__') before a word boundary ('#')'. Conversely, the word-initial context, in which we find, for example, voiced [ɹ], is symbolised as: '# __': 'The sound we are interested in occurs in the position ('__') after a word boundary ('#')', i.e. at the beginning of a new word. If we want to talk about word-medial contexts, we need to clarify which sounds surround the position we are interested in. Thus, for example, in our discussion of [ɹ̥] the relevant medial context was that a voiceless consonant precedes [ɹ̥]. We use the symbol 'C' for 'consonant' and a subscript to specify which type of consonant. The context 'after voiceless consonants' is thus '$C_{[-voice]}$ __', where $_{[-voice]}$ reads as 'minus voice' and is a shorthand for 'voiceless'. Another important word-medial context is the position between two vowels in a word. We use 'V' for 'vowel'; 'V __ V' now symbolises our intervocalic position. In this position we find, for example, the allophone [ɾ] of /ɹ/ in a word like *very*. Note that the four contexts that we have now formalised are by far not the only phonetic contexts which are relevant for phonemic analysis. For didactic reasons, however, I will limit the discussion of most phenomena in this chapter to those contexts.

We have seen in this section that we can identify two given phones as allophones of a given phoneme if we can show that they are either in complementary distribution or in free variation. Verifying one of these two distributions then automatically means showing that the two phones cannot distinguish meaning in the language. We have furthermore introduced the major phonetic contexts which we will consider in this chapter: # __, __ #, C __, and V __ V.

2.3.3. Observing allophonic alternations in different word forms

Another cue to how language categorises sounds into phonemes and allophones can be found if we look at different forms of a single word. Here we base our analysis on the fact that the phonetic context determines which allophone of a given phoneme will appear. Specifically, we will manipulate phonetic context in order to see different allophones appear. Consider an example. We saw above that the unreleased allophone of English /p/ can only occur word-finally. Furthermore, note that the example word that we used above was a verb, *clap*. As you know, it is a general characteristic of (most) English verbs that they can appear in the *-ing* form. This is also true for *clap*, which then becomes *clapping*. What interests us here is that by transforming *clap* into *clapping*, we alter the phonetic context of /p/ from a word-final context in *clap* to a word-medial context in *clapping*. If [p̚] is confined to the word-final context, we should see different allophones of /p/ appearing in *clap* and *clapping*. The data in (9) provide examples. I use the symbols introduced in section 2.3.2. to designate the relevant phonetic contexts.

(9) | | **base form, __ #** | | | *-ing* form, V __ V | | |
|---|---|---|---|---|---|---|
| *clap* | [klæp] | or | [klæp̚] | [klæpɪŋ] | but not | *[klæp̚ɪŋ] |
| *hop* | [hɒp] | or | [hɒp̚] | [hɒpɪŋ] | but not | *[hɒp̚ɪŋ] |
| *tap* | [tæp] | or | [tæp̚] | [tæpɪŋ] | but not | *[tæp̚ɪŋ] |
| *keep* | [kiːp] | or | [kiːp̚] | [kiːpɪŋ] | but not | *[kiːp̚ɪŋ] |

Different word forms here show us the alternation between the released and the unreleased allophones of /p/. Whereas word-finally the free variants [p] and [p̚] may both occur, only the released variant, [p], is possible word-medially. Methodologically, we see in the example that we can use different word forms to observe the alternation between different allophones in real-time. In other words, changing word forms can help us to identify allophones of a phoneme. This is so because by changing word forms we change the phonetic context — word-final sounds end up in word-medial position. It goes without saying then that this strategy of identifying allophones can only be used if one of the relevant phonetic contexts is the word-final position.

Another, slightly more complex, example comes from German. Consider the following two German words and focus on the word-final sound.

(10) *Rad* [ʁaːt] 'wheel' vs. *Rat* [ʁaːt] 'council'

Both words end in [t]. This is true in spite of the fact that in the case of *Rad* the spelling may suggest otherwise. Note that some native speakers of German may, for reasons that will become clear soon, find it hard to believe that both *Rad* and *Rat* should end in the same sound. In this case I suggest you conduct a small experiment. If you can find a group of native speakers of German, select one of them as your 'informant' and then ask the others to write down the word that the informant is going to tell them. Then have your informant say either *Rat* or *Rad* without speaking too carefully, and without context, and check what the rest of the group have written. I predict that some of them will have written *Rat*, whereas some will have written *Rad*. Why is this so? Because, if your informant is a native speaker of Standard German, her or his pronunciations of *Rat* and *Rad* will be the same.

So what does this have to do with identifying phonemes and allophones by means of different word forms? The answer is that, if we change the word forms of *Rad* and *Rat*, we will see that [t] in *Rad* and [t] in *Rat* belong to different phonemes. The relevant forms are given in (11); *Rad* and *Rat* are nouns, so we can use the plural form as a different word form here.

(11) **singular, __ #**   **plural, V__V**
 a. *Rad* [ʁaːt]   *Räder* [ʁɛːdɐ] 'wheel(s)'
 b. *Rat* [ʁaːt]   *Räte*   [ʁɛːtə] 'council(s)'

The sound that is [t] in *Rad* is realised as [d] in the plural, which is *Rä[d]er*, not **Rä[t]er*. By contrast, the sound that is [t] in *Rat* is not realised differently if moved to the word-medial position. The plural is *Rä[t]e*, not **Rä[d]e*. This shows that the t-sounds that appear in word-final position, although sounding the same, belong to different phonemes. [t] in *Rad* is an allophone of /d/, whereas [t] in *Rat* is an allophone of /t/. The voiceless allophone of /d/, however, is confined to appearing in word-final position. Word-medially, /d/ is realised as [d].

Apart from illustrating how we can use different word forms to investigate a sound system, the German example illustrates yet another important general property of phonemes and allophones. A contrast between different phonemes can be neutralised. **Neutralisation** here refers to the fact that in a particular context, a contrast between phonemes becomes invisible. The schema in (12) summarises our findings for German /d/ and /t/.

(12) neutralisation of the voicing contrast in German: /d/ and /t/

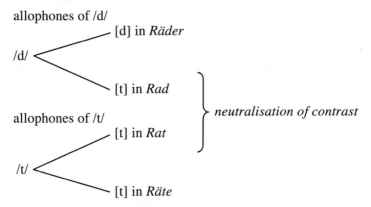

The fact that a voiced phoneme has a voiceless allophone in word-final position is known in the literature as **final devoicing**. In German, final devoicing is widespread; it does not only affect /d/, but also other plosives and fricatives. For German learners of English, final devoicing provides one of the most notorious pitfalls when learning the pronunciation of the new language. In contrast to German, English does not have final devoicing. Thus, for example, the two words *mat* and *mad* are pronounced [mæt] and [mæd]. German learners face the difficult task of having to 'unlearn' final devoicing in order to master the difference in pronunciation between *mat* and *mad*.

One more aspect is missing from our analysis of German final devoicing. We have assumed that /d/ and /t/ are different phonemes. However, we have not provided evidence that this is indeed the case. Phoneme status is to be diagnosed in terms of the minimal pairs test. So here is a selection of minimal pairs for /d/ and /t/, which confirms our assumption that /t/ and /d/ are different phonemes.

(13) German voicing contrast: minimal pairs
Dank [daŋk] 'thanks' vs. *Tank* [taŋk] 'tank'
Deich [daɪç] 'dyke' vs. *Teich* [taɪç] 'pond'
Seide [zaɪdə] 'silk' vs. *Seite* [zaɪtə] 'side'

In this section we have provided the methodological ground for investigating how the sounds of language are categorised into a phoneme system. Relevant categories, phonemes, are defined in terms of their ability to distinguish meaning. We can employ the minimal pairs test to diagnose phoneme status. Allophones, by contrast, exhibit specific distributional characteristics, which we can again use as diagnostics. They are either in complementary distribution or in free variation. We usually find their distributional characteristics by comparing the realisation of a phoneme across different phonetic contexts in different words of the language. In some cases, however, we are in the lucky position to observe the alternation between different allophones of a phoneme in different forms of a single word. In what follows we will use our newly-gained knowledge to learn more about the phoneme inventory of English.

2.4. More about the sound system of English

2.4.1. Allophones of /l/

The data in (14) show different realisations of /l/ in different phonetic contexts, as they occur in RP as well as in many other British and North American varieties of English.

(14) #__   C[-voice]__V   V__V   __#
[lɪp] lip   [kl̥ɪp] clip   [mɪlə] miller   [pɪɫ] pill
[leɪ] lay   [kl̥eɪ] clay   [sɪliː] silly   [eɪɫ] ale
[liːn] lean [kl̥iːn] clean [niːlə] kneeler [niːɫ] kneel

/l/ has three different realisations: [l], [l̥], and [ɫ]. From our discussion of /ɹ/ in section 2.2. you already know that the symbol [̥], if added to a sound symbol, means that the relevant sound is voiceless. Thus, like /ɹ/, /l/ has a voiced and a voiceless allophone ([l] and [l̥]). The distribution of [l] and [l̥] mirrors that of [ɹ] and [ɹ̥]. [l] occurs in words like *lap*, i.e. at the beginning of words, whereas [l̥] occurs in words like *clap*, i.e. after voiceless consonants.

The third realisation of /l/ found in (14), [ɫ], is what is called a **velarised** realisation of /l/, also termed **dark l**. The non-velarised realisation [l], i.e. the one which you know from the introduction of English consonants in chapter 1, is termed **clear l**. So before we consider the distribution of clear and dark l, let us clarify what the new variant, 'dark l', is. The terms 'clear l' and 'dark l' refer to the auditory impression of [l] and [ɫ], in that the latter somehow sounds darker. The term 'velarised l' refers to the articulatory properties of [ɫ], which may in fact be more helpful here. 'Velarised' comes from 'velum', which is, as you know, the very soft, back part of the so-called soft palate. But what has the velum, which is located far beyond the alveolar ridge, got to do with an l-sound, which is an alveolar sound? Figure 2.1. illustrates the answer to this question, by comparing the position of the tongue in clear and dark l.

You see that, whereas the tip of the tongue touches the alveolar ridge, the back of the tongue is still free to do something. So both [l] and [ɫ] are alveolar sounds. But during the production of [ɫ] the back of the tongue is raised towards the velum (which it does not touch). When producing 'clear l', by contrast, the back of the tongue is relaxed and remains in a lower position.

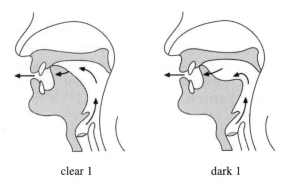

clear l   dark l

Figure 2.1. Clear l and dark l (from: Davis (2004: 22), printed with permission)

We are now ready to investigate the distributional characteristics of the allophones of /l/. The distribution of [l̥] is fully parallel to the distribution of [ɹ̥], discussed at length in section 2.2. I will thus focus on the more interesting parts of the /l/ allophony, [ɫ] and [l]. The data in (14) above show that [ɫ] can occur in word-final position, whereas [l] can occur in word-initial position and between two vowels. However, we have not yet tested whether [ɫ] and [l] belong to a single phoneme, and, if yes, whether they are allophones in complementary distribution or in free variation. In order to test this, we must follow the methodology outlined in section 2.3. The data in (15) and (16) show where [ɫ] and [l] can occur and, crucially, where they cannot occur.

(15) The distribution of [ɫ]

# __		V __ V		__ #	
*[ɫɪp]	lip	*[mɪɫə]	miller	[pɪɫ]	pill
*[ɫeɪ]	lay	*[sɪɫi:]	silly	[eɪɫ]	ale
*[ɫi:n]	lea n	*[ni:ɫə]	kneeler	[ni:ɫ]	kneel

(16) the distribution of [l]

# __		V __ V		__ #	
[lɪp]	lip	[mɪlə]	miller	*[pɪl]	pill
[leɪ]	lay	[sɪli:]	silly	*[eɪl]	ale
[li:n]	lean	[ni:lə]	kneeler	*[ni:l]	kneel

[ɫ] and [l] are in complementary distribution: There is no phonetic context in which both sounds can occur. This finding automatically means that [ɫ] and [l] are not in free variation, and that they do not belong to different phonemes (the latter is true because there can be no minimal pairs). Dark [ɫ] is restricted to word-final position, whereas clear [l] occurs word-initially and between two vowels.

Furthermore, we can observe the alternation between [ɫ] and [l] with the help of different word forms, along the lines outlined in section 2.3.3. What we need are sample words in which a change of word form moves /l/ from an intervocalic word-medial to a word-final position. Verbs and their *-ing* forms are again our first choice. Examples are provided in (17), with the allophones of /l/ shown in bold print.

(17)

	base form, __ #		***-ing* form, V __ V**	
kneel	[ni:ɫ]	*[ni:l]	[ni:lɪŋ]	*[ni:ɫɪŋ]
craw l	[kɹɔ:ɫ]	*[kɹɔ:l]	[kɹɔ:lɪŋ]	*[kɹɔ:ɫɪŋ]
tell	[teɫ]	*[tel]	[telɪŋ]	*[teɫɪŋ]

We can summarise the regularities that we found in the distribution of allophones of the English phoneme /l/ in terms of a phonological rule, which tells us in which phonetic contexts which allophone of /l/ will occur. This rule is given in (18); note, however, that it will be further refined in section 2.5.3.

(18) phonological rule predicting allophonic realisations of /l/
/l/ is realised
— as [l̥] after word-initial voiceless consonants,
— as [ɫ] in word-final position, and
— as [l] elsewhere.

Note that, in addition to the findings presented in this chapter, the rule also claims that the voiceless allophone [l̥] and dark [ɫ] are in complementary distribution. You may test this claim, using the same methodology we applied for [ɫ] and [l].

2.4.2. Stop phonemes

Another set of allophones involves the voiceless stops of English, /p/, /t/, and /k/. We already know two of the allophones of /p/: unreleased [p̚] and released [p], which are in free variation in word-final position (cf. section 2.3.2.). Like /p/, also /t/ and /k/ have unreleased allophones, [t̚] and [k̚], which bear the same phonetic and distributional characteristics as [p̚]. They are restricted to the word-final context, and they are in free variation with the released variant. Examples are provided in (19).

(19) a. /p/
    clap [klæp] or [klæp̚]
    stop [stɒp] or [stɒp̚]
  b. /t/
    hat [hæt] or [hæt̚]
    hot [hɒt] or [hɒt̚]
  c. /k/
    stack [stæk] or [stæk̚]
    duke [djuːk] or [djuːk̚]

As with the unreleased allophone of /p/, the choice between the released and the unreleased realisation does not alter the meaning of the relevant words. Hence, the word pairs in (19a—c) are not minimal pairs, but exemplify two allophones in free variation.

The second type of stop allophony to be discussed in this section manifests itself in stops that occur word-initially before stressed vowels. Note that stress is not one of the factors defining phonetic context that we want to consider in this chapter. Thus, to keep matters simple, we will restrict the present discussion to words that have only one syllable, and to words with two syllables in which the initial syllable is stressed. For a more detailed account of the role of stress in allophonic variation among English stops you may want to consider the account in Spencer's (1996: 206—210) phonology textbook.

As an example, read out the following pairs of monosyllabic words, focussing on whether you hear a difference between the stops in bold print.

(20) /p/ in   *p*in   vs.   /p/ in   *sp*in
 /t/ in   *t*eam   vs.   /t/ in   *st*eam
 /k/ in   *k*in   vs.   /k/ in   *sk*in

Depending on the degree to which you are accustomed to hearing subtle acoustic differences, you may have had difficulties perceiving differences in (20). In this case, you may again resort to a small experiment. It works best with words involving /p/. Take a thin sheet of writing paper and hold it in such a way that the edge of the sheet is very close to your mouth. Now say *pin* and *spin*, focussing on what happens to the sheet of paper in your hand. You should now notice that when you say *pin*, the paper vibrates in your hand. By contrast, if you say *spin*, the paper will vibrate to a far lesser degree, or not at all. If the experiment does not work at once, try moving the paper closer to your mouth, or try using a thinner sheet.

So what causes vibration of the paper in words like *pin*, but not in *spin*? Both realisations of /p/ are voiceless bilabial stops. But in *pin*, something else happens in addition to the articulation of that stop. In addition to letting the air pressure escape that has been built up with the help of the bilabial closure of the oral cavity, you press even more air through your larynx, where it produces a friction noise when passing through the glottis. In other words, speakers articulate a bilabial stop and, at the same time, an [h]-like sound, i.e. a glottal fricative. As a result, the release burst of the plosive is enhanced. This extra puff of air causes the sheet of paper to vibrate. The variant of /p/ that occurs in *pin* is called an **aspirated** stop, the process of aspirating stops is called **aspiration**. The term is derived from the Latin word *spiritus*, which means something like 'a breath of air'. An aspirated stop is a stop that is produced with an extra 'breath of air'. We mark aspirated stops in narrow phonetic transcription by adding a superscript ^{h} to the symbol: [p^h], [t^h], [k^h].

Let us now investigate the distribution of aspirated and non-aspirated stop allophones in English. We will again limit the discussion to the bilabial stop, but an analogous argument can be made for alveolar and velar voiceless stops. The data in (21) and (22) employ the now familiar procedure of illustrating where [pʰ] and [p] can occur in English. Note, however, that, as we said earlier, we will be looking only at words with a specific stress configuration. As usual, the relevant sounds are in bold print.

(21) The distribution of [pʰ]

# __ V	#[s] __ V	V __ V	__ #
[**pʰ**ɪn]	*[sp**ʰ**ɪn]	*[swiː**pʰ**ə]	[hɪ**pʰ**]
[**pʰ**ɪ̵]	*[sp**ʰ**ɪ̵]	*[ɹæ**pʰ**ɪd]	[ɹæ**pʰ**]
[**pʰ**eə]	*[sp**ʰ**eə]	*[ʃiː**pʰ**ɪʃ]	[kiː**pʰ**]

(22) The distribution of [p]

# __ V	#[s] __ V	V __ V	__ #
*[**p**ɪn]	[s**p**ɪn]	[swiː**p**ə]	[hɪ**p**]
*[**p**ɪ̵]	[s**p**ɪ̵]	[ɹæ**p**ɪd]	[ɹæ**p**]
*[**p**eə]	[s**p**eə]	[ʃiː**p**ɪʃ]	[kiː**p**]

The allophones [pʰ] and [p] are in complementary distribution in three contexts: word-initially, after [s], and between vowels. By contrast, in the word-final context, [pʰ] and [p] are in free variation. Although they can both occur in the same context, they do not distinguish meaning. Listening to native speakers, you will notice that speakers tend to use word-final [pʰ] in more careful, slow speech.

There is one more interesting aspect about aspiration in English. Aspirated voiceless stops are perceived by native speakers of English as the typical voiceless stops of their language. This perception is so strong that non-aspirated stops, if heard in isolation, are typically confused with voiced stops, in spite of the fact that they are voiceless, only not aspirated. If you are a native speaker of English, you can test this on your computer, with the help of a speech analysis program (such as, for example, the SIL (2007) *Speech Analyzer*, a simple demo version of which is available free of charge at http://www.sil.org/computing/speechtools/SATdownloads2.htm). You can then use a microphone to record yourself saying the word *spin*. Now 'cut off' the [s]-sound of the word, and play the rest. What you will hear will seem to you to be much closer to *bin* than to *pin*. This is so because you as a native speaker of English expect the typical voiceless stop to be aspirated. If a stop is not aspirated, you will classify it as voiced.

The fact that speakers of English are normally unaware of differences in aspiration is not problematic because in this language, presence or absence of aspiration does not lead to phonemic contrast. This is, however, not the case in all languages. Mandarin Chinese, for example, does not have voiced stops. Instead, it distinguishes phonemically between aspirated and non-aspirated stops. There are numerous minimal pairs; one of them consists of the two words [pa] and [pʰa], both spoken with a rising tone on the vowel. [pa] means 'to tear out', whereas [pʰa] means 'to climb'. *[ba], by contrast, is an impossible word in Chinese. There are even languages in which both voicing and aspiration are important to distinguish between different phonemes. Hindi is a case in point. The data in (23) show you minimal pairs for both the voicing and the aspiration contrast.

(23) Aspiration and voicing contrast in Hindi (data from Kenstowicz (1994: 38))
  a. Voiceless stops: non-aspirated vs. aspirated

Hindi word	gloss	Hindi word	gloss
[pal]	'to take care of'	[pʰal]	'edge of knife'
[tan]	'mode of singing'	[tʰan]	'role of cloth'
[kan]	'ear'	[kʰan]	'mine'

  b. Voiced stops: non-aspirated vs. aspirated

Hindi word	gloss	Hindi word	gloss
[bal]	'hair'	[bʰal]	'forehead'
[dan]	'charity'	[dʰan]	'paddy'
[gan]	'song'	[gʰan]	'kind of bundle'

We see that English makes a distinction with respect to voicing, but not with respect to aspiration. This, however, is an arbitrary characteristic of the English sound system. Other languages, such as Mandarin Chinese or Hindi, choose to set up different categories.

To return to English, there is yet one more kind of stop allophony that we would like to explore in this section. Unlike the allophones that we have discussed so far, which are pretty widespread among varieties of English, this class of allophones is often described as being specifically characteristic of North American varieties. Consider the data in (24) for illustration and try to determine in which phonetic context they deviate from what we have learned about the allophony of /t/ in this section. The pronunciation given is from the variety of North American English known as General American.

(24)
word	General American pronunciation
team	[tʰiːm]
tier	[tʰɪɹ]
steam	[stiːm]
stole	[stoʊɫ]
writer	[ɹaɪɾəɹ] or [ɹaɪtəɹ]

metal	[meɾəɫ] or [metəɫ]
hit	[hɪt], [hɪt˺], [hɪtʰ]
boat	[boʊt], [boʊt˺], [boʊtʰ]

In (24) we recognise allophones of /t/ that have already been discussed in this section: Word-initially (# __), after [s] (#[s] __V), and word-finally (__ #) we find the familiar alternation between aspirated [tʰ], non-aspirated [t], and unreleased [t˺]. However, in one phonetic context we see a difference between General American pronunciation and RP pronunciation, which has served as our reference accent so far. In word-medial, intervocalic position (V __ V), General American has an allophone of /t/ that RP does not have: a voiced alveolar flap, represented as [ɾ] in IPA transcription. A flap is a sound in which the tongue very quickly taps the alveolar ridge once. Many very fast successive flaps form a trill, a sound that you may be familiar with from r-sounds in other languages like, for example, Italian, Spanish, or Russian. In General American this flap is in free variation with [t].

What is interesting about the distribution of the phone [ɾ] in General American is that it does not only occur where other varieties have [t]. Consider the data in (25).

(25)
word	**General American pronunciation**
deem	[diːm]
dear	[diɹ]
rider	[ɹaɪɾəɹ] or [ɹaɪdəɹ]
medal	[meɾəɫ] or [medəɫ]
hid	[hɪd]
bode	[boʊd]

The data confirm our assumption from above that [ɾ] only occurs in word-medial, intervocalic position. What is new, however, is that in the data in (25) other varieties have [d] where General American optionally has [ɾ]. So what is the status of [ɾ] in General American? Is it an allophone of /t/? Or of /d/? Or is it a separate phoneme? The answer is already given by the choice of sample words in (24) and (25). The data in (24) suggest that [ɾ], [tʰ], and [t] are in complementary distribution, except for one context, where [ɾ] and [t] are in free variation. Thus, we are justified in analysing them as allophones of the phoneme /t/. The data in (25) then suggest that [ɾ] and [d] are also in complementary distribution and, in one context, in free variation. Analogously, then, we can analyse [ɾ] and [d] as allophones of /d/. But, you may object, doesn't this mean that /t/ and /d/ are one and the same phoneme in General American? The data in (24) and (25) show you that this is not the case. If you compare the sample words given for word-initial and word-final contexts, you will find minimal pairs among them, such as, for example, *team* and *deem*, or *hit* and *hid*, respectively. The fact that such minimal pairs exist is important for our analysis of [ɾ] because it shows that, just like in RP and in other varieties, /t/ and /d/ are separate phonemes in General American. The phonemic contrast is, however, neutralised in intervocalic position. Here both /t/ and /d/ can be realised as [ɾ], a process which is also known in the literature as **t/d-flapping**. The situation is reminiscent of what we have already seen in section 2.3.3. when we discussed final devoicing in German. Both German final devoicing and General American t/d-flapping are processes in which the contrast between two phonemes is neutralised in a particular phonetic context.

To sum up, you have learned in this section that English voiceless stops as they appear in RP have three major types of allophones: an unreleased, an aspirated (released), and a non-aspirated (released) allophone. Again we can capture this in a phonological rule. This is done for /p/ in (26).

(26) phonological rule predicting allophonic realisations of /p/ in RP
 /p/ is realised
 — as [pʰ] in word-initial position before vowels,
 — as [p] between [s] and a vowel and between two vowels, and
 — as [pʰ] or [p] or [p̚] in word-final position.

There are two phonetic contexts in which only one of the allophones described can occur: the word-initial position and the position between [s] and a vowel. By contrast, word-finally we have free variation between aspirated, non-aspirated, and unreleased variants.

Furthermore, we have seen in this section that other varieties may differ from RP in their set of stop allophones. Thus, for example, the set of allophones of General American /t/ and /d/ includes a flap, [ɾ], which is confined to intervocalic contexts.

2.4.3. A slightly more complex case: /ɹ/

We already know that /ɹ/, like /l/, has a voiceless allophone, [ɹ̥] (cf. section 2.2.). In this section we will look at more allophones of /ɹ/, and we will limit our discussion to our reference variety of English, RP. The data in (27) illustrate how the words *very*, *sorry*, and *courage* are pronounced in RP. The symbol [ɾ] stands for an alveolar flap — it is already familiar to you from our discussion of flapped allophones of /t/ and /d/ in General American in the previous section.

(27) very   [veɾiː]   or   [veɹiː]
    sorry   [sɒɾiː]   or   [sɒɹiː]
    courage [kʌrədʒ]   or   [kʌɹədʒ]

We see that between two vowels, /ɹ/ has two possible realisations: a flap ([ɾ]) and [ɹ]. For example, for the word *very* you will hear the pronunciation [veɾiː] alongside [veɹiː] in RP. Crucially, however, [veɾiː] and [veɹiː] do not differ in meaning, but are variant pronunciations of a single word: *very*. This shows that the distinction between [ɹ] and [ɾ] does not have consequences for meaning; there is no minimal pair for [ɹ] and [ɾ]. We conclude that, between vowels, the two allophones [ɾ] and [ɹ] are in free variation. But what about the general distributional characteristics of [ɾ]? The data in (28) show where [ɾ] is permitted in RP English. The relevant sounds are in bold print.

(28) # __   C_[– voice] __ V   V __ V   __ #
     rip   *[ɾɪp]   trip   *[tɾɪp]   very   [veɾiː]   hear *[hɪəɾ]
     wrap *[ɾæp]   trap   *[tɾæp]   sorry [sɒɾiː]   care *[keəɾ]
     rope *[ɾəʊp]   trope *[tɾəʊp]   courage [kʌrədʒ] cure *[kjʊəɾ]

[ɾ] can only occur between two vowels. Comparing the distributional characteristics of [ɾ] with those of the two allophones we know already, [ɹ̥] and [ɹ], we find that [ɾ] is in complementary distribution with [ɹ̥]. With respect to [ɹ], we have to be more specific. Between two vowels, [ɾ] and [ɹ] are in free variation. In word-initial and word-final contexts, however, [ɾ] cannot occur. In word-initial position, we find [ɹ] instead. In word-final position, we find a more complex situation, to which we now turn.

The data in (29) illustrate how the words *hear, care, cure, pour, bar* and *purr* are pronounced in RP.

(29) hear [hɪə]   pour [pɔː]
    care [keə]   bar   [bɑː]
    cure [kjʊə]   purr [pɜː]

In none of the words in (29) will you hear an r-sound. Note that I deliberately use the vague term 'r-sound' here, because it is as yet an open question whether the phoneme /ɹ/ is present at all in the words in (29). The data illustrate one of the most well-known phonological features of RP and many other varieties of English (especially British and Australian). In these varieties, r-sounds do not seem to occur in word-final position. Such varieties are termed **non-rhotic** varieties of English. Conversely, then, **rhotic** varieties of English are those in which r-sounds can occur in word-final position. This is the case, for example, in many North American varieties as well as in Irish or

52   *The sound system: phonology*

Scottish English. However, we will see that the term 'non-rhotic' is in fact misleading. In RP, the phoneme /ɹ/ is not absent word-finally; it is simply not pronounced. How can we show this?

We need to resort to the strategy of phoneme analysis introduced in section 2.3.3., using different word forms to transform word-final contexts into word-medial ones. Most conveniently, all sample words in (29) are verbs. Thus, just like in section 2.3.3., we can use the *-ing* form. The relevant data are given in (30).

(30) **base form, __ #**   *-ing* **form, V __ V**

	base form		-ing form	
hear	[hɪə]	*[hɪɹ]	[hiːɹɪŋ]	*[hɪə_ɪŋ]
care	[keə]	*[keɹ]	[keɹɪŋ]	*[keə_ɪŋ]
cure	[kjʊə]	*[kjʊɹ]	[kjʊɹɪŋ]	*[kjʊə_ɪŋ]
pour	[pɔː]	*[pɔːɹ]	[pɔːɹɪŋ]	*[pɔː_ɪŋ]
bar	[bɑː]	*[bɑːɹ]	[bɑːɹɪŋ]	*[bɑː_ɪŋ]
purr	[pɜː]	*[pɜːɹ]	[pɜːɹɪŋ]	*[pɜː_ɪŋ]

We see that, whereas we cannot detect an r-sound word-finally, [ɹ] surfaces in word-medial position in all sample words. Furthermore, we see that [ɹ] is obligatory here — leaving out [ɹ] renders the form ill-formed. Given what we know about phonemes and allophones, this situation leads us to conclude that /ɹ/ is present in the verbs in (30). But then we are confronted with a puzzle: Where is /ɹ/ in the base forms?

In order to answer this question, we have to differentiate between two sets of cases in (30): those words which end in a centring diphthong (*hear*, *care*, *cure*), and those that end in a long vowel (*pour*, *bar*, *purr*). With respect to centering diphthongs, you need to know at this point that they have a most peculiar characteristic. They occur only in non-rhotic varieties of English, and they occur almost only in contexts like those in (30), in which we suspect the presence of the phoneme /ɹ/. But this is not the whole story. If we look at what happens to the centring diphthongs in the *-ing* forms in (30), we note that one part of the diphthong (namely [ə]) disappears in the *-ing* form. That is, [ə] in the simplex form alternates with [ɹ] in the *-ing* form. We have thus found the allophone of /ɹ/ that occurs in the words *hear*, *care*, or *cure*: [ə].

But what about the long vowels in *pour*, *bar*, and *purr*? Words like these indeed provide evidence that the allophone of a phoneme can be 'zero'. In other words, the phoneme /ɹ/ is present in these words (this we can prove with the *-ing* form), but it does not have a phonetic realisation. Given that we already know that phonemes are abstract in nature, the existence of a zero allophone should not come too much as a surprise. Furthermore, we can support our analysis with the very same distributional argument that we have just used for centering diphthongs. In the base and -*ing* forms of our example words, [ɹ] alternates with 'zero': Word-medially we find [ɹ], and word-finally after monophthongs we find 'zero'.

There is, however, one possible objection to the generalisation about the zero allophone just formulated. If we can have zero allophones, doesn't this mean that these zero allophones can be everywhere? Put differently, how can we determine where we find a zero allophone and where we don't? The answer to this question has already been given in our analysis, which makes, as we recognise now, quite a powerful prediction. We can only assume a zero allophone if we see that it alternates with a non-zero allophone. In the case of *pour*, *bar*, and *purr*, 'zero' in the base form alternates with [ɹ] in the -*ing* form. In other vowel-final verbs, however, it does not. As an example, you may want to construct the -*ing* forms of the following two verbs: *paw* [pɔː] and *oompah* [ʊmpɑː]. The latter verb will strike you as unusual; according to the *Oxford English Dictionary*, it means 'to play oompah music', as in the sentence: *Outside the station a band of jolly minstrels were oompah-ing a typically folklorique welcome ...* (*Sunday Times*, March 31, 1991). The relevant forms are in (31).

(31) **base form,** __ #   -*ing* **form, V __ V**
    paw   [pɔː]   [pɔː_ɪŋ]   *[pɔːɹɪŋ]
    oompah [ʊmpɑː]   [ʊmpɑː_ɪŋ] *[ʊmpɑːɹɪŋ]

Apparently, there is no zero allophone of /ɹ/ in *paw* and *oompah*. We now have proof that verb pairs like *pour* and *paw* (both [pɔː]) and *bar* and *oompah* (both end in [ɑː]) differ in their phonemic makeup: *pour* and *bar* have word-final /ɹ/, *paw* and *oompah* do not.

With the help of our analysis of [ə] and zero allophones of /r/, we can now define more precisely the difference between rhotic and non-rhotic varieties of English, without having to resort to the vague label 'r-sound' as we have done up until now: Non-rhotic varieties are varieties which have [ə] or zero allophones of /ɹ/ in word-final position. Rhotic varieties such as General American or Irish English, are varieties in which non-zero and non-schwa allophones of /ɹ/ appear in word-final contexts. The data in (32) compare rhotic and non-rhotic pronunciations of our sample words.

(32) | **spelling** | **RP** | **General American** |
|---|---|---|
| hear | [hɪə] | [hiɹ] |
| care | [keə] | [keɹ] |
| cure | [kjʊə] | [kjʊɹ] |
| purr | [pɜː] | [pɜɹ] |
| pour | [pɔː] | [pɔɹ] |
| bar | [bɑː] | [bɑɹ] |

In General American English the allophone of /ɹ/ that appears in word-final contexts is [ɹ]. Of course, presence of /ɹ/ in non-rhotic varieties of English is also mirrored in the spelling of the relevant words. Varieties of English which are non-rhotic nowadays have not always been non-rhotic, but have lost the consonantal realisation of /ɹ/ in the course of history. In RP the spelling still reflects that earlier stage of the language.

To summarise, we found in this section that the realisation of RP /ɹ/ is subject to a quite complex phonological rule. This rule is given in (33).

(33) phonological rule predicting allophonic realisations of /ɹ/ in RP
/ɹ/ is realised
— as [ɹ̥] after voiceless consonants,
— as [ə] word-finally after [ɪ], [e], and [ʊ] (i.e. in centering diphthongs),
— as 'zero' word-finally after long vowels,
— as [ɹ] or [r] in intervocalic position, and
— as [ɹ] elsewhere.

The last section of this chapter will be devoted to the syllable as a phonological unit. You will learn that the syllable is not only an intuitively plausible timing unit of words in English, but that it also has an internal structure. Furthermore, it constitutes a very important point of reference for the description of relevant contexts in allophonic alternations.

2.5. The syllable

2.5.1. The structure of the syllable

Spoken language does not only consist of loose sequences of speech sounds, but sounds are grouped into higher-level units. One such unit, which we have used in our discussion so far, is the word. But in between the sound and the word, there is an intermediate category: the syllable. You will already be familiar with the syllable from your school days, and you will also be able to use the syllable intuitively in the description of the phonological form of words. Consider, for example, the English and German data in (34) and (35). They exemplify a process that is very common in both English and German: the shortening (or truncation) of first names. In both languages speakers use truncated names as terms of address if they know someone really well. But what is the major difference between the English and German truncated names in (34) and (35)?

(34) *Alfred*   is shortened to *Al*
     Susan   is shortened to *Sue*
     Patricia is shortened to *Trish*

(35) *Manuela* [manuːeːla] is shortene d to *Manu* [manuː]
     Sabine [zaːbiːnə]   is shortene d to *Bine* [biːnə]
     Karolin [kaːʁoːliːn] is shortene d to *Karo* [kaːʁoː]

You will intuitively use the notion of syllable in order to describe the difference: The English truncated names consist of one syllable (i.e. are monosyllabic), whereas the German truncated names have two syllables (i.e. are disyllabic). This shows that we tend to 'measure' the size of words in terms of the number of syllables they contain. By doing so, we automatically assume that there is such a unit, which we call syllable.

But what is a syllable? In order to investigate this question, let us look again at the English data in (34), this time focussing on both the full and the truncated form of the name. Before reading on, try to determine where in the names you would place syllable boundaries, i.e. the place where one syllable ends and the other begins. In (36) I provide transcribed versions of the relevant data. Following standard conventions, I mark syllable boundaries by a dot.

(36) *Alfred*   [æl.fɹəd]   *Al*   [æl]
     Susan   [suː.zən]   *Sue*   [suː]
     Patricia [pə.tɹɪ.ʃə] *Trish* [trɪʃ]

Let us approach the question of what a syllable is by looking at what all syllables in (36) have in common. The first obvious thing is that every syllable contains exactly one vowel. Apart from the vowel, the syllable can also contain consonants; consonants can either precede the vowel (as in [suː.] in *Susan* and *Sue*) or follow it (as in [æl.] in *Alfred* or *Al*), or both (as in [zən] in *Susan*). So if we want to describe the structure of the syllable, we can say that it has three slots: one 'central' slot in which we find the vowels in (36), and two 'peripheral' slots which can — but need not — be filled by consonants. We can schematise this situation through a tree diagram, in which the top node represents the whole syllable (symbolised by 'σ'), and the branches represent the slots for vowels and consonants. Such a schema is given in (37) for the syllables we found in (36). Note that in its present version it is only our first approximation of the facts, and it will be refined in the subsequent discussion.

(37) The structure of the syllable — a first approximation

	C (*optional*)	V (*obligatory*)	C (*optional*)
Alfred, Al			
[æl]		æ	l
[fɹəd]	fɹ	ə	d
Susan, Sue			
[suː]	s	uː	
[zən]	z	ə	n
Patricia			
[pə]	p	ə	
[tɹɪ]	tɹ	ɪ	
[ʃə]	ʃ	ə	
Trish			
[tɹɪʃ]	tɹ	ɪ	ʃ

We have postulated that the syllable has three elements, one of which is obligatory, whereas the other two are optional. Like all elements of linguistic structure, the elements that make up a syllable are termed **constituents**. We have provisionally labelled the constituents 'slots for consonants' and 'slots for vowels'. (37), however, is still in need of refinement.

First of all, we need to test a prediction made by the schema: Given that our two consonantal constituents are optional, English should also have syllables which consist of only a vowel. Luckily, English has such syllables, as is shown, for example, by the two monosyllabic words *eye* and *awe* ([aɪ] and [ɔː]). At the same time, the example of *eye* shows that the vowel slot of the syllable can be occupied not only by simplex vowels such as [æ] or [uː], but also by complex vowels, i.e. diphthongs.

Secondly, the examples of [fɹəd] and [tɹɪʃ] in (37) show that more than one consonant can occur in the slot preceding the vowel. One obvious question is whether this can happen in both consonantal slots. Again we need to look for pertinent English words, and, again, we find them. Monosyllabic words like *hand, act* or *grasp* end in a sequence of two consonants: [hænd], [ækt], [grɑːsp], and therefore prove that, like the prevocalic constituent, also the postvocalic constituent can be occupied by more than one consonant.

A more problematic prediction of our schema is that it claims that constituents of the syllable are defined in terms of the categories vowel and consonant. This definition, however, does not hold for the 'vowel slot'. Consider the pronunciation of the final syllable of the following English words: *little, button*, and, in (rhotic) General American English, *cupboard*. You will agree that all three words consist of two syllables. But if you read them out aloud, do you really hear a vowel in the final syllable? In most native speakers' pronunciations, you will not. Instead, the central part of the final syllable is occupied by [l], [n], or [ɹ], respectively. Consonants which occupy the central part of the syllable are termed **syllabic consonants**. The three words are transcribed in (38). In order to mark syllabic consonants, the symbol [̩] is added to the transcription symbol of the relevant sound.

(38) little   [lɪtl̩]
     button   [bʌtn̩]
     cupboard [kʌbr̩d]

Thus, constituents of the syllable need to be identified independently from the segments which they can contain. Our 'slot for a vowel' is termed the **nucleus** of the syllable. In English, the nucleus can be filled by a vowel, a diphthong, or a syllabic consonant. Among our 'slots for consonants', the prevocalic slot is termed **onset**, and the postvocalic slot is termed **coda**. In English, both slots can be filled by one or more consonants; furthermore, neither the onset nor the coda is obligatory. The final version of our syllable schema is presented in (39).

(39) The structure of the syllable

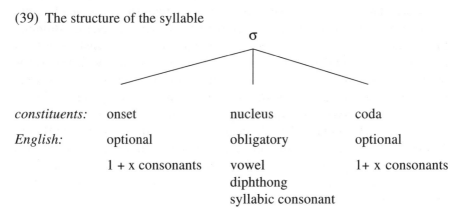

We now claim that the syllable as a structural unit consists of three (abstract) constituents. The question of how these constituents can be filled is answered by each language on an individual basis. And indeed, languages differ vastly in how they allow onset, nucleus, and coda to be filled. Japanese, for example, allows almost only nasal consonants in coda position. So what happens if Japanese borrows words from English which have non-nasal syllable codas? The data in (40) provide examples (from: Roca and Johnson 1999: 238). For reasons of readability, I use English spelling.

(40) **English word**   **borrowed into Japanese as**
     Christ.mas   ku.ri.su.ma.su
     text   te.ki.su.to
     disk   di.su.ko

Japanese systematically breaks up English consonantal codas and inserts vowels in such a way that each consonant ends up in the onset of a syllable of the borrowed word. The technical term for the insertion of vowels into syllables is **vowel epenthesis**.

Another example of different onset and coda restrictions in different languages comes from errors which German learners frequently make when learning English, illustrated in the data below.

(41) **English**   **erroneous pronunciation**
     psychology   [saɪkɒlədʒiː]   *[psaɪkɒlədʒiː]
     pseudonym   [suːdənɪm]   *[psuːdənɪm]
     knee   [niː]   *[kniː]
     knot   [nɒt]   *[knɒt]

For German learners, the errors exemplified in (41) are among the most frequent and most persistent. Why do they make them? Because the sequences <ps> and <kn> are present in the spelling of the English words, and because the learners have not yet mastered English syllable structure. Although English allows more than one consonant in the onset of its syllables, it bans certain sequences in that position, with [ps] and [kn] among them. The words in (41) are particularly problematic because they are related to similar German words (so-called **cognates**), which have [ps] and [kn]: [psyːçoːloːgiː] ('psychology'), [psɔɪdoːnyːm] ('pseudonym'), [kniː] ('knee'), and [knoːtən] ('knot'). In contrast to English, German allows the sequences [ps] and [kn] in its onsets. Historically, word pairs like English [saɪkɒlədʒiː] and German [psyːçoːloːgiː] have a common origin, which is still reflected in the spelling. However, the two words are subject to different restrictions on syllable structure in English and German.

2.5.2. Syllabification

Another problem that we need to tackle concerns the question of how consonants are distributed among syllables. Assigning syllable structure to words is called **syllabification**. We have established so far that every syllable must have a nucleus. But once we have identified the nuclei, how do we proceed to determine which consonant is in an onset and which consonant is in a coda? Why, for example, did we syllabify *Susan* and *Alfred* in (37) as [suː.zən] and [æl.fɹəd], and not as *[suːz.ən], *[ælfɹ.əd], *[ælf.ɹəd], or *[æ.lfɹəd]? Up until now we have used intuition to answer this question. Note, however, that the whole argumentation in that section was based on the assumption that, concerning syllabification, my intuitions as the author of this chapter are identical to your (numerous) intuitions as readers of this chapter. This alone shows that syllabification cannot be arbitrary, but must be regular and predictable. In order to see what that regularity consists of, I would like to consider a hypothetical example. Imagine there was a word *tatatatat* in English, pronounced [taːtaːtaːtaːt]. There are two principled possibilities of syllabifying *tatatatat*, given in (42). Which of them would you choose?

(42) a. ta.ta.ta.tat
b. tat.at.at.at

I predict you chose (42a), and indeed (42a) is the only possible syllabification of *tatatatat*, not just in English, but in all languages of the world. So what distinguishes the syllabification in (42a) from that in (42b)? The answer lies in syllable structure: Both (42a) and (42b) have only one syllable which has both an onset and a coda. But (42a) has three syllables which only have an onset, whereas (42b) has three syllables which only have a coda. The ill-formedness of (42b) thus shows that, if given a choice, we prefer to syllabify consonants in an onset rather than in a coda. Given a sequence of consonants and vowels, syllabification proceeds in such a way that as many consonants as possible end up in an onset, even if the language allows codas. This generalisation is termed the **Maximal Onset Principle**. Only if we do not have a choice, do we resort to syllabifying consonants in a coda. This is the case in the final syllable in (42a).

Transferring this insight from hypothetical *tatatatat* to our real English examples *Susan* and *Alfred*, we can now explain why *Susan* cannot be *[suːz.ən], and why *Alfred* cannot be *[ælf.ɹəd]. Both illegal forms syllabify consonants that could be in the onset or in the coda: [z] and [f], respectively. Using the Maximal Onset Principle, we can also explain why *[æ.lfɹəd] is an impossible syllabification of *Alfred*. The key here is the fact that the Maximal Onset Principle only calls for 'as many consonants as possible' to be syllabified in the onset. The syllabification of [lfɹ] in an onset in *[æ.lfɹəd] is, however, impossible because [lfɹ] is just not a possible onset. Why is this so? The reason lies in yet another principle of syllabification, to which we now turn. Curiously, this principle is respected in most languages of the world. It is based on the acoustic properties of the syllable.

If you take the perspective of a hearer, then you may say that a syllable is a group of sounds around a nucleus. The syllable nucleus, in turn, may be described as the 'most clearly audible' part of the syllable. The onset and the coda of a syllable, then, are 'less clearly audible' than the nucleus. In order to try out this definition, you may read out the following monosyllabic words, stopping after each constituent of the syllable: *boat* ([b-əʊ-t]), *fish* ([f-ɪ-ʃ]), *home* ([h-əʊ-m]). You will agree that in each of the syllables the vowel is the most clearly audible part, whereas the onset and coda consonants are less clearly audible than the vowels.

The technical term for the category that captures our acoustic impression of 'clear audibility' is **sonority**. According to *The Longman Dictionary of Contemporary English*, a sonorous voice is a 'pleasantly deep, loud voice'. Whereas everyday language may use categories like 'pleasantly deep', we cannot work with such categories in science. In linguistics, sonority has a more specialised meaning, which we find explained in specific dictionaries of linguistic terminology. For example, in the *Dictionary of Phonetics and Phonology* we find a definition of sonority as 'a measure of the output of periodic acoustic energy associated with the production of a particular segment, and hence its intrinsic loudness' (Trask 1996: s.v. *sonority*). You may notice that this definition is not too precise either, and indeed there is no general agreement among phoneticians as to what exactly the acoustic characterisation of sonority is. What is important for us here, however, is that sonority is a relative category. Speech sounds are more or less sonorous in relation to other speech sounds, never in absolute terms. A syllable is then a set of sounds which form a group around its most sonorous member (i.e. the nucleus). Using this definition as a basis, we can now draw a curve representing sonority in the constituents of our example syllables *boat*, *fish*, and *home*.

(43)

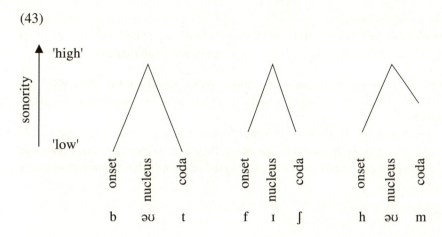

How can sonority help us to solve our initial problem, namely that [lfɹ] is an impossible onset and that, consequently, *[æ.lfɹəd] is an impossible syllabification of *Alfred*? The schemata in (43) make two interesting claims that bear on this issue. First of all, note that, instead of marking the relative sonority of syllabic constituents through isolated points, I have drawn a curve. This curve goes much further than just stating that sounds in onsets and sounds in codas must be lower in sonority than their respective nuclei. It claims that sounds preceding the nucleus (i.e. onsets) must rise in sonority, and sounds following the nucleus (i.e. codas) must fall in sonority. This principle is known as the **Sonority Sequencing Principle**.

Secondly, note that the sonority level that we have assumed in (43) for the coda [m] in *home* is much higher than that which we have assumed for other consonants like [b] in *boat*, for example. Likewise, the sonority level of the fricatives [f], [ʃ], and [h] is higher than that of [b]. This means that sonority differences cannot only be found between vowels and consonants. Also among consonants, we find more or less sonorous exemplars. You can again use your intuition to test this. How would you group the following consonants in terms of their relative sonority: [p], [k], [ŋ], [n]? You will probably say that it is hard to distinguish between [p] and [k], and between [ŋ] and [n]. By contrast, you will no doubt find that both [p] and [k] are less sonorous than [ŋ] and [n]. This shows us two things. First of all, sonority is a gradual notion, it forms a scale. Secondly, consonants differ in sonority if they differ in terms of manner of articulation – the plosives [p] and [k] differ from the nasals [ŋ] and [n]. In (44) I provide the full sonority scale for all speech sounds that exist in English. The symbol '>' means 'is more sonorous than'.

(44) Sonority scale
vowels > [w], [j] > [ɹ] > [l] > nasal > fricatives, > plosives
                                 consonants   affricates

At the highest end of the scale we find vowels, which are the most sonorous segments. The least sonorous sounds are plosives. All other consonants are in between.

All that is left to do now in order to find out why [lfɹ] is an impossible onset is to apply the Sonority Sequencing Principle to our case. The schema in (45) draws the sonority curve for the syllable [lfɹed], based on the sonority scale in (44).

(45)

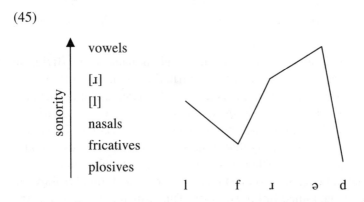

[lfɹ] does not consistently rise in sonority and, thus, the syllable violates the Sonority Sequencing Principle. This is why *[æ.lfɹəd] is an impossible syllabification of *Alfred*. We have discovered that the Sonority Sequencing Principle imposes a very rigid restriction on onsets and codas which consist of more than one consonant.

We therefore have to revise the generalisation that we found in section 2.5.1. for onsets and codas with more than one consonant. Discussing, for example, the impossibility of [kn] and [ps] in English onsets, we said that 'the question of how onsets and codas can be filled is answered by each language on an individual basis'. We now need to add an important provision to this generalisation. Languages can impose restrictions on how onsets and codas can be filled, but most languages do so only within the limits set by the Sonority Sequencing Principle. So [kn], [ps], and [lfɹ] are impossible English onsets, but for different reasons. Only [lfɹ] violates the Sonority Sequencing Principle. By contrast, [kn] and [ps] fulfil the principle. By not allowing [kn] and [ps], English poses additional restrictions on possible consonant sequences. These restrictions are language-specific, as is obvious from the fact that [kn] and [ps] are possible in other languages (as, for example, German).

Up to now, we have seen in our discussion of the syllable that syllables have a constituent structure, and that syllabification is predictable on the basis of two principles, the Maximal Onset Principle and the Sonority Sequencing Principle. What still remains to be seen is that the syllable constitutes an extremely useful category in the description of allophonic processes as discussed in section 2.2.

2.5.3. The syllable and allophonic processes: /l/ revisited

As an example, we will reconsider part of the discussion of the allophones of /l/ presented in section 2.4.1., the complementary distribution of clear [l] and dark [ɫ]. (46) repeats our previous findings. This time, however, syllable boundaries are marked in the example words. Note that in order to keep matters simple, we will omit syllabic l from the discussion.

(46) **clear l, # __**   **clear l, V__V**   **dark l, __#**
     lip   [lɪp]   pillow   [pɪ.ləʊ]   pill   [pɪɫ]
     lay   [leɪ]   halo   [heɪ.ləʊ]   ale   [eɪɫ]
     lean   [liːn]   kneeler   [niː.lə]   kneel   [niːɫ]

We found [l] word-initially and between vowels, whereas [ɫ] occurs word-finally. Given the syllable boundaries, we can reformulate this generalisation in such a way that it becomes much simpler: [l] occurs in syllable onsets, and [ɫ] occurs in codas. Interestingly, this formulation is not only shorter; it also makes strong and better predictions concerning the distribution of clear and dark l in contexts which we have not considered so far. Consider, for example, the words *Hilton* and *poultry*, as well as *Henley* and *hotly*. The contexts specified in (46) say nothing about which allophone of /l/ should appear here. But our syllable-based generalisation does so: In *Hilton* and *poultry*, /l/ is in coda position and should thus be realised as [ɫ]. In *Henley* and *hotly*, by contrast, /l/ is in onset position and should thus be realised as [l]. This prediction is borne out. The relevant structures are illustrated in (47) and (48). The relevant sounds are in bold print.

(47) Syllabification and /l/ in *Hilton* and *poultry*

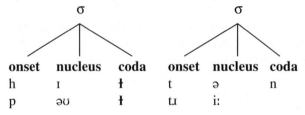

(48) Syllabification of /l/ in *Henley* and *hotly*

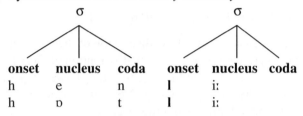

The rule that governs the distribution of clear and dark l has not only become simpler than the one that was postulated in section 2.4.1., it has also become more comprehensive, covering all contexts in which /l/ can occur in English. In addition to the word-medial contexts discussed above, we can now also explain why dark [ɫ] appears in words like the following: *cold* [kəʊɫd], *realm* [ɹɛɫm], *elk* [eɫk]. Again our generalisation from section 2.4.1. says nothing about these words: /l/ is not word-final. By contrast, our syllable-based generalisation predicts dark [ɫ] for these words — [ɫ] is in coda position in *cold*, *realm*, and *elk*.

Of course our rule is still subject to an important qualification. We have not yet incorporated the third allophone, [l̥]. Recall that we said that [l̥] occurs in word-initial contexts following voiceless consonants (#C$_{[-\text{voice}]}$ ___). We can now describe this context as an onset which contains more than one consonant, and in which /l/ follows a voiceless consonant. We therefore need to include a proviso for this special case in the formulation of our generalisation. Our final version of the phonological rule predicting the distribution of /l/-allophones is thus the one given in (49).

(49) phonological rule predicting allophonic realisations of /l/
 /l/ is realised
  — as [l̥] in complex onsets in which it is preceded by a voiceless consonant.
  — as [l] in all other onsets, and
  — as [ɫ] in non-onset positions.

Reanalysing /l/, we saw that the syllable is a very important unit in phonological analysis. Rules governing the distribution of allophones can be captured elegantly with reference to the category of the syllable. This does, of course, not mean that every allophonic rule does so.

2.6. Conclusion

In this chapter we have looked at two of the central aspects that phonology is concerned with: the system of speech sounds and syllables. We saw that speech sounds are organised into abstract categories, phonemes, and that phonemes, in turn, are grouped into syllables and words in spoken language. We also developed a systematic methodology with which to investigate phoneme systems. The minimal pairs test for phonemes is based on the definition of phonemes as distinctive units, whereas the two tests for allophones use the distributional characteristics of allophones to determine allophonic status. Applying this methodology in a systematic fashion, we have conducted exemplary studies of three English consonant phonemes and their allophony: /l/, /ɹ/, and stop phonemes.

With respect to the syllable, you learned that the syllable cannot only be identified and used on an intuitive basis. We can define syllables in terms of their internal structure. Furthermore, we saw that syllabification follows straightforwardly from a rule which makes reference to this internal structure. Finally, our reanalysis of clear and dark l has shown that the syllable plays a major role as a reference context in allophonic processes.

In the next chapter, you will study phenomena which can be observed on a higher level of representation than speech sounds and syllables: words.

Further Reading

Giegerich (1992), Kreidler (2003), or Collins & Mees (2008) can be recommended as textbooks on English phonology. Roca and Johnson (1999) and Spencer (1996) are very readable introductions to phonology that do not deal with English exclusively but cover many phenomena also from other languages. If you are interested in phonological differences between varieties of English, have a look at *The Handbook of Varieties of English, vol. 1: Phonology* (edited by Kortmann and Schneider (2004)). The handbook is accompanied by a CD-Rom, which, among other things, enables you to journey through sound samples from different varieties. If you want to know more about spectrogram reading, consult Ladefoged and Maddieson (1996).

Exercises

Basic level

Exercise 2.1.: Phonemes and allophones

Consider the sounds in bold print in the word pairs in (50). Do they belong to different phonemes, or are they allophones of the same phoneme? Give reasons for your analysis.

(50) *beat* vs. *bit*   [biːt] vs. [bɪt]
    tall vs. *stall*   [tʰɔːl] vs. [stɔːl]
    mill vs. *plot*   [mɪɫ] vs. [pl̥ɒt]
    sing vs. *sin*   [sɪŋ] vs. [sɪn]
    bed vs. *bad*   [bed] vs. [bæd]

Exercise 2.2.: Phonemes and allophones

Explain the notion of phoneme and allophone, using the word pairs in (51) as an example:

(51) *pin* vs. *spin*
    pin vs. *kin*

Exercise 2.3.: The syllable

In section 2.5.3. we saw that /l/ allophony is better explained if we use the syllable as the relevant context than if we use the word as a reference category. The key examples discussed were the words *Hilton, poultry, Henley,* and *hotly.* At the end of the section, however, we said that if we use the syllable as a context, we can 'also explain why dark [ɫ] appears in words like the following: *cold* [kəʊɫd], *realm* [ɹeɫm], *elk* [eɫk].'
    Show that this statement is true. Proceed as follows:
1. Recapitulate the relevant generalisation about dark [ɫ].
2. Provide a schema of the syllable structure of the three example words.
3. Apply the generalisation to the example words.

Advanced

Exercise 2.4.: Comparing [l] and [ɫ] in English and Russian

a. English: Are [l] and [ɫ] different phonemes or allophones of the same phoneme? Explain, using the examples below for illustration.

(52)　leave　　　miller　　　real　　　bulb

b. Russian: Are [l] and [ɫ] different phonemes or allophones of the same phoneme? Explain, using the examples below for illustration ([ɨ] is a short, high, unrounded, central vowel)

(53) [bɨɫ]　　　'(he) was'　　　[bil]　　　'true story'
　　[poɫka]　　'shelf'　　　　　[polka]　　'polka'
　　[jeɫ]　　　'(he) ate'　　　 [jel]　　　'pine-tree'
　　[meɫ]　　　'chalk'　　　　　 [mel]　　　'shoal'
　　　　　　　　　　　　　　　　　　　　　　　　　(an area of shallow water)
　　[pɨɫ]　　　'passionateness'　[pil]　　　'dust'
　　[ɫuk]　　　'onion'　　　　　 [luk]　　　'hatch'
　　[gaɫka]　　'jackdaw' (a bird) [galka]　 'pebble'

c. Compare the distributional characteristics of [ɫ] in English and Russian.

Exercise 2.5.: Clear l vs. dark l — an experiment

Recall what we said about the distribution of clear l and dark l in this chapter. This was true for our reference accent RP as well as for a large number of other varieties of English. However, it is also a fact that not all varieties of English have an alternation between clear l and dark l as described in this chapter. Your task will be to conduct a small empirical study (a reading experiment with 10 speakers of your local variety) to find out whether or not your own local variety of English behaves like RP. Proceed as follows:

　　1. Recapitulate the phonological rules that determine the distribution of clear l and dark l in RP.

　　2. Devise a list of test words that you will ask your experimental subjects to read out loud. The list should comprise words containing /l/, which should meet the following criteria:
- There should be two words for each phonetic context that is relevant for the distinction between clear l and dark l.
- The words should be given in ordinary spelling (no transcription!).
- The order in which the words appear on the list should be a random order.

Print out ten copies of this list.

3. For yourself, use a spreadsheet programme to prepare a table in whose columns the test words appear in exactly the same order as in your word list. The table should have four columns, one for each variable, i.e. one for the speaker, one for the word that is being spoken, one for the word's phonological context, and one for how the l is pronounced. It should look as follows:

speaker	word	context	realisation of l
speaker 1	leave	#___	
speaker 1	pill	___#	
speaker 1	low	#___	
...	...	...	
...	...	...	
speaker 2	leave	#___	
speaker 2	pill	___#	
speaker 2	low	#___	
...			
...			

4. Ask ten speakers of your local variety of English to read the word list for you — one speaker at a time. It is important that you explicitly tell them that they should read at their own speed, and that they should speak as naturally as possible. Also, make sure you do not tell them what exactly this experiment is about.

5. Record the reading of the word list. If you use a computer for the recording, make sure you use an external microphone, since you'll be needing a decent sound quality to hear subtle details of the subjects' pronunciation.

6. Listening to your recorded data, fill in the table on your computer with the realisations of /l/ for every word in your word list. Use three different categories: 'clear l', 'dark l', and 'unclear/other'.

7. Use your spreadsheet programme to count the number of occurrences of each allophone of /l/ in the different phonetic contexts in your word list. Then report on similarities and differences between RP and your local variety with respect to the distribution of clear and dark l.

8. Report on potential problems you may have encountered during your experiment. If you had to redo the experiment: What would you do differently? Why? What would you pay special attention to? Why?

Exercise 2.6.: Phonology and the acquisition of difficult sounds of English

German learners of English face many difficult tasks when learning the pronunciation of English. Among them are learning to differentiate between clear l and dark l, and 'unlearning' final devoicing. Although, of course, both learning tasks are important, it is often pointed out in the didactic literature that unlearning final devoicing is more important than learning the difference between clear [l] and dark [ɫ].

Why is this so? Use your knowledge about phonemes and allophones in English to defend this position. Illustrate your argument with the erroneous learner pronunciations below.

(54) learners missing the distinction between [l] and [ɫ]

word	English	erroneous learner pronunciation
sell	[seɫ]	*[sel]
pill	[pɪɫ]	*[pɪl]
help	[heɫp]	*[help]

(55) learners failing to 'unlearn' final devoicing

word	English	erroneous learner pronunciation
bed	[bed]	*[bet]
heed	[hiːd]	*[hiːt]
nod	[nɒd]	*[nɒt]

Chapter 3
The structure of words: morphology

3.1. Introduction

Knowing words is such an intrinsic part of our knowledge of a language that we often do not consciously think about how words are created or structured. However, once we take a closer look at words, many questions arise. For instance, what elements does the word *antiglobalisation* consist of? And can we subdivide the word *step* into any further parts? In general, how can we analyse the structure of words? Besides, we might ask why some words, such as *dishonest*, are attested in English, whereas other words, such as *honestdis* or *discar* are unattested. In other words, are there any rules that determine possible and impossible combinations of elements within words? Another array of questions we might be interested in when dealing with words is how we can create new words whenever we need a name for a new object, person, or process. Imagine, for instance, that you need a word to describe the process of removing old shelves from your flat. What word would you use to refer to this process? *Unshelfing*, *shelf-removing*, or something else?

There is a special sub-discipline of linguistics that deals with all these questions, **morphology**, which is the study of the internal structure of words, the rules that govern it, as well as the ways of creating new words. Interestingly, the term 'morphology' is originally not a linguistic term. It was invented by Johann Wolfgang von Goethe to designate the study of the structure of living organisms. Linguists borrowed it from biologists in the nineteenth century and used it to denote the study of linguistic 'organisms': words.

In the present chapter we will learn the basic notions necessary for the morphological analysis of words and take a closer look at different morphological phenomena.

3.2. Minimal building blocks: morphemes

We have mentioned above that morphology deals with the internal structure of words. But how can we analyse this internal structure? And what are the elements words can consist of? We will deal with these questions below.

If I asked you to determine intuitively the structure of the word *dreamless*, you most likely would say that it consists of two parts, *dream* and *-less*. But what about *dream*? Again, quite intuitively, you would say that this word cannot be subdivided into further parts. But why not? Why don't we say, for instance, that the word *dream* can be subdivided in the following way:

(1) [d-ɹ-iː-m]

We might say that the subdivision in (1) deals with sounds, and therefore is of interest for phonology or phonetics, but not so for morphology. Indeed, we should not confuse the morphological structure of words with their phonetic or phonological structure. But what is the difference between morphological and phonological or phonetic structure? This will become clear if you compare the division you made for *dreamless* and the division in (1). You will agree that the two analyses are fundamentally different. But why? The matter is that the elements *dream* and *-less* are meaningful, i.e. they have a certain meaning. For instance, *dream* means 'a series of images appearing in the mind during sleep' and *-less* means 'without'. By contrast, the separate sounds [d], [ɹ], [iː], and [m] do not have any meaning. Remarkably, the same holds for any other subdivision of this word, as the examples in (2) show.

(2) a. [dɹiː-m]
     b. [dɹ-iː-m]
     c. [dɹ-iːm]

Obviously, even the sound combinations in (2) cannot be regarded as meaningful units. Indeed, in the word *dream* only the whole unit, [dɹiːm], has a meaning, 'a series of images appearing in the mind during sleep'. We can say that morphology deals with the analysis of words into meaningful units.

The generalisation that emerges from the discussion above is that words can be analysed into meaningful units. Such meaningful units are called **morphemes**. Another important generalisation we can make is that since sounds or even combinations of sounds in the word *dream* are not meaningful units, *dream* cannot be subdivided any further into meaningful parts. This means that *dream* is the smallest meaningful unit in the word *dream*. So we should elaborate our definition of morpheme by saying that 'morpheme' is the smallest meaningful unit.

Finally, our discussion leads us to yet another insight. Consider what happens to the word *dream* if you remove a part of it. For instance, if you remove [dɹ], you get [iːm], which is meaningless, because it is only the whole sequence [dɹiːm] that carries meaning and is therefore a morpheme. We can conclude that a word must consist of at least one morpheme, there are no 'morphemeless' words.

The question that arises next is how we can identify which part in a word is meaningful and what meaning it has. Consider the word *shyness*. How can we establish what meaningful units it consists of? We know that there is the word *shy* in English, and we can check what it means in a dictionary, for instance in the *Longman Dictionary of Contemporary English*: 'nervous and embarrassed about meeting and speaking to other people'. So we can say that *shy* in *shyness* is a meaningful unit and therefore a morpheme. But what about *-ness*? There is no such word as *ness* in English. However, it may come to your mind that there are many words in English that contain the unit *-ness*, such as *sadness, loudness, boldness, happiness*, etc. We can assume that since this unit occurs in quite a number of words, it might be a morpheme. To verify this, we should find out whether it has any meaning. How can we do this? We can paraphrase different words containing *-ness* to see whether *-ness* contributes any meaning to the overall meaning of these words. To find this out, we should do the paraphrase by using the words to which *-ness* is attached, because then the remaining part of the paraphrase would be the meaning of *-ness*. Such paraphrases are shown in (3):

(3) *shyness*   'the state or property of being shy'
    loudness 'the state or property of being loud'
    sadness   'the state or property of being sad'
    happiness 'the state or property of being happy'

As the data in (3) show, the meaning of *-ness* is 'the state or property of being X', where 'X' stands for the meaning of the word it is attached to. Therefore, *-ness* is a morpheme in the data in (3). Note that another property of morphemes that we found in *dream* also holds for the morpheme *-ness*: It cannot be subdivided any further into meaningful components. If we divide this morpheme into [n] and [əs], for instance, these parts do not carry any meaning.

We can now make another important generalisation. If we compare the words *dream* and *dreamless*, or *shy* and *shyness*, we can say that the words *dream* and *shy* consist of only one morpheme, whereas the words *dreamless* and *shyness* consist of more than one morpheme. Words consisting of only one morpheme are called **monomorphemic** or **simplex words**, those that contain two and more morphemes are called **polymorphemic** or **complex words**.

So far the identification of morphemes and the analysis of words into morphemes presented little difficulty. Sometimes, however, this analysis is not equally straightforward. Consider the element *cran-* in *cranberry*. This element cannot stand alone in English, it occurs only in combination with the morpheme *berry*. Moreover, it is attested only in this one word. If you consult a dictionary for this element, you will most likely find no entry for it. To identify its meaning we cannot apply the method we used above, i.e. finding other words with the same element, because the element occurs in one English word only. However, we can use a similar strategy. We can try to collect other words containing the element *berry* in order to see how the meaning of *cranberry* differs from the meanings of other words denoting berries:

(4) *cranberry* 'berry which is red and sour'
   strawberry 'berry which is red, soft and has tiny seeds on its surface'
   blackberry 'berry which is black or purple and grows on a thorny bush'
   blueberry 'berry which is blue'

In contrast to *strawberry*, *blackberry*, or *blueberry*, *cranberry* denotes a 'red sour' berry, and not a 'red soft' or a 'black/purple' or a 'blue' berry. We can say therefore that the meaning of *cran-* is what makes 'cranberry' different from 'strawberry' or 'blackberry', i.e. that it is a 'red sour', and not a 'red soft' or 'black' berry. This difference in meaning must then be the meaning of *cran* in *cranberry*. To summarise, despite the fact that *cran-* does not occur independently in English, and also despite the fact that it occurs in only one English word, we are able to ascribe a meaning to it and thus to regard it as a morpheme. Such morphemes are called **unique morphemes** because of their sole occurrence in only one word of a language.

Now consider the data in (5) and decide whether the words in (5) consist of one or of two morphemes.

(5) *sustain* 'to keep something going'
   pertain 'to relate to something'
   contain 'to have inside'
   obtain 'to get or achieve something'

At first sight, you might identify the element *tain* in the words above as a morpheme, since it surfaces consistently in a number of words, similarly to the morpheme *-ness* above. To support this hypothesis, we should be able to prove that the element *tain* has a certain meaning. If you know Latin you would possibly suggest that *tain* comes from Latin *tenere* and has the same meaning as in Latin, namely, 'to hold', and that the words in (5) are therefore complex. However, the average native speaker of English might not have this etymological knowledge. Besides, if we compare the paraphrases of the words in (5), they do not follow the same pattern as it was the case with the morphemes *-less* and *-ness* above. In other words, the meaning 'hold' is not readily traceable. In fact, it is unclear from the point of view of today's English, what the meaning of *tain* in these words might be. This means that although etymologically the words in (5) are complex, they are simplex in

74   *The structure of words: morphology*

today's English. In general, we can conclude that when we do morphological analysis, morphology should not be confused with etymology.

So far we have assumed that morphemes have a certain meaning. But is meaning the only thing necessary for the identification of morphemes? Let us go back to our example of the morpheme *dream*. When you identified its meaning, how did you know that we were dealing with the morpheme *dream* and not *harm*, or *cake*, or *connect*? Definitely because you had access to the word's orthographic form (i.e. the way it is written): <dream>, and its phonetic form (i.e. the way it is pronounced): [dɹiːm]. In a similar way, you were able to discuss the meaning of *-ness* in *shyness* because it has a certain orthographic and phonetic form: <ness> and [nəs], respectively. In fact, meaning is something abstract: You cannot see or feel it, and we can generally access it only if it materialises in a certain 'physical' form. We can conclude that, usually, a morpheme has a certain form and a certain meaning. Note that the general term used in morphology to refer to the form is **morph**. We will use both terms, morph and form, throughout this chapter. The relation between morph/form, meaning and morpheme is depicted in (6):

(6)   The morpheme *dream*

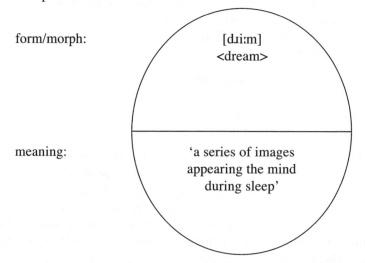

Identifying the form might seem to be fairly unproblematic for morphemes such as *dream* or *-less*, but less straightforward in other cases. We have seen some of such cases above, for instance *cran-* and *-tain*, and will now deal with yet another problematic case. Consider the data in (7) and think about whether the plural forms *teeth*, *geese*, *mice* consist of one or of two morphemes. To answer this question concentrate on the meaning of the plural forms:

(7) tooth [tuːθ]   teeth [tiːθ]   'more than one tooth'
    goose [guːs]   geese [giːs]   'more than one goose'
    mouse [maʊs]   mice [maɪs]   'more than one mouse'

As the paraphrases show, the meanings of the words *teeth*, *geese*, *mice* actually all contain two meanings: the basic meanings 'tooth', 'goose', 'mouse', and the meaning 'more than one'. We might therefore assume that the words *teeth*, *geese*, *mice* consist of two morphemes: the morphemes *tooth, goose, mouse*, and the morpheme with the meaning 'more than one'. But what is the form of this morpheme? As you know, in most English words the plural meaning, i.e. the meaning 'more than one', is created by adding a form, i.e. *-s* as in *dogs, beds, ideas*. In contrast, nothing is added in the examples in (7). What we see instead is that *teeth* is related to *tooth*, and *geese* to *goose*, by changing the vowel from [uː] to [iː]. In the pair *mouse-mice*, we observe a change from [aʊ] to [aɪ]. Thus, the plural meaning is not expressed by adding some form, but by a change in the vowel. The technical term for this type of process is **vowel change**, or **vowel alternation**.

The English word *sheep* also presents a puzzle for identifying the plural form. The plural of this word is created without any change in form: *one sheep* vs. *many sheep*. However, by analogy to the examples *tooth-teeth* above, we know that in *many sheep* the word *sheep* should be analysed as consisting of two morphemes: one morpheme meaning 'a farm animal that has thick curly hair', and another morpheme meaning 'more than one'. However, the form of this plural morpheme is physically neither visible nor audible, i.e. it is not marked overtly. Forms that are not marked overtly are often called **zero forms** or **zero morphs**.

In this section, we have seen that we split up words into meaningful units called morphemes. Morphemes usually have a certain form and a certain meaning. However, sometimes the identification of form and/or meaning is problematic, and needs a more careful investigation. In the next section we will see how we can classify morphemes in terms of their properties.

3.3. Types of morphemes

Until now we have treated morphemes as a group of homogeneous units. However, morphemes may differ from each other in a number of characteristics, as we will see in this section. To capture these differences, morphologists group morphemes together into certain types.

The first type can be identified if you consider the behaviour of the morphemes *mother* and *-ment* in the sentences below. Try to capture the difference between the morphemes *mother* and *-ment*. Awkward sentences are marked by a question mark.

(8) a. **Mothers** usually take too much care of their children.
    b. It is difficult to combine a career with **motherhood.**
    c. Sandra is a **mother** of three young children.

(9) a. This **settlement** consists of just ten houses.
    b. **Management** of an electronics firm is not an easy task.
    c. ?I saw a **ment** yesterday.

Both *mother* and *-ment* can appear in combination with other morphemes: *mother* can combine with the plural morpheme *-s*, or with the morpheme *-hood* meaning 'state of being X'. Similarly, *-ment* can also combine with other morphemes, such as *settle* and *manage*. However, the morpheme *mother* differs from *-ment* in that it can also stand alone, without any other morpheme attached to it, as in (8c), whereas the morpheme *-ment* cannot, as becomes evident in (9c). Consequently, the difference between the two morphemes lies in their ability or inability to stand alone. Morphemes such as *mother*, which can occur on their own, without any other morphemes attached to them, are called **free morphemes**. Morphemes that appear only in combination with other, usually free, morphemes are called **bound**. For instance, in the example *motherhood* above, the bound morpheme *-hood* appears attached to the morpheme *mother*. Similarly, in the word *management* the morpheme *-ment*, which is bound, appears attached to the morpheme *manage*, which is free. Morphemes like *mother* in *motherhood* and *manage* in *management* are called **bases** since they serve as the basis for attaching other, usually bound, morphemes, such as *-hood* and *-ment*. There is also another term, **stem**, which is used to denote bases to which bound morphemes carrying grammatical meaning, such as 'plural', attach. However, since the use of the terms 'base' and 'stem' is not always consistent in the morphological literature, we will not employ the term 'stem' here to avoid confusion.

So far we have clarified that in the word *motherhood*, *mother* is the base and *-hood* is a bound morpheme. But you might wonder whether there is any special term for the word *motherhood* itself, i.e. the word derived from the base. This term is **derivative**. Let us now take a closer look at bases. For this purpose, try to figure out the differences between the words in (10a–c):

(10) a. agree   b. disagree   c. disagreement
       construct   construction   constructional
       cheer   cheerful   cheerfulness
       create   recreation   recreational
       structure   poststructural   poststructuralism

As you may have noticed, (10a) gives the bases for the derivatives in (10b), which in turn contains the bases for the derivatives in (10c). The bases in (10a) differ from those in (10b) in one crucial respect: They do not contain any further morphemes and therefore cannot be analysed any further into constituent morphemes. We can say that these bases are simplex, and we call them **roots**. Roots are the core elements of words, and normally a word cannot exist without a root. In contrast to the simple bases in (10a), the examples in (10b) and (10c) can be further analysed into constituent morphemes. For instance, the base *disagree* can be analysed into two constituent morphemes: *dis-* and *agree*, and the base *recreation* into three: *re-, create* and *-ion*. Such bases are therefore regarded as complex. We can generally conclude that bases can be simplex or complex.

Now let us deal in greater detail with bound morphemes. We will use some of the examples mentioned in (8) and (9) and add some new data. What is the difference between the bound morphemes in (11a) and those in (11b)?

(11) a. unhappy   b. management
       dislike   motherhood
       mispronounce   settlement
       malnutrition   cupful

Generally, bound morphemes, such as *un-* and *-ment*, which appear only attached to other, usually free, morphemes are termed **affixes**. The difference between the two groups of affixes in (11) is that those in (11a) are attached before the base, whereas those in (11b) appear after the base. They are called **prefixes** and **suffixes**, respectively. We can therefore conclude that affixes can differ in their position with respect to their bases.

Prefixes and suffixes are the two most common types of affixes. There are, however, other types. Consider the following data taken from Tagalog, the official language of the Philippines (data from McCarthy and Prince 1993: 101–105), and try to figure out how they differ from the affixes in (11) above:

(12)   **base and its meaning**   affix   **derivative and its meaning**
   a.   *gradwet*   *-um-*   →   *gr-um-adwet*
        'graduate'   'one who graduated'
   b.   *sulat*   *-um-*   →   *s-um-ulat*
        'write'   'one who wrote'

In the examples in (12) the affix is not attached before or after the base, as was the case with the examples above, but inserted into the base. Affixes of this type are called **infixes**. English does not have infixes of a type similar to Tagalog. What we do find in English is a kind of infixation where whole words can be inserted into a base to indicate a negative attitude which a speaker holds towards something, as in *abso-bloody-lutely*, *kanga-bloody-roo*, *Kala-ma-goddam-zoo* (the last two examples cited from Katamba and Stonham 2006: 45).

To summarise, we have seen that there is a variety of morpheme types. The knowledge of these types allows us to do an accurate morphological analysis of every complex word in a language. In the next section, we will take a more detailed look at how such an analysis works.

3.4. Morphological analysis of words

To understand how morphological analysis of words works, we should deal with the question: What aspects are worthwhile mentioning in order to describe the morphological structure of a word? Let us consider the complex word *blender*. What can we say about its morphology? One aspect we can mention is that it consists of two morphemes, *blend* and *-er*. Besides, we can say that *blend* is the root, since it is not further analysable, and at the same time the base to which the suffix *-er* is attached. To conclude, if we carry out morphological analysis, we usually show what morphemes a word consists of and describe these morphemes in terms of their type. We can also present the structure of this word by way of a tree diagram, as in (13):

(13)   blender

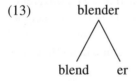

      blend   er

Let us now turn to a more sophisticated case, such as *globalisation*. We can say rather straightforwardly that it contains the root *globe* and three suffixes: *-al*, *-ise*, and *-ation*. But what bases can be identified in this word, and which suffix is attached to which base? Since the suffixes in *globalisation* appear in sequential order, we can assume that each suffix has been attached successively to that part of the word after which it appears. For instance, *-al* appears after *globe*, therefore *globe*, in addition to being the root, also serves as the base for the suffix *-al*. The suffix *-ise* appears after *global*, and therefore *global* is the base for this suffix, and so on. We can nicely illustrate this analysis graphically by drawing a tree diagram of this word as in (14). Note that spelling changes may occur if affixes are attached to a base.

(14)
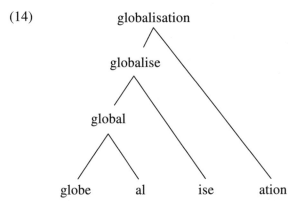

We can now summarise our analysis of the word *globalisation* in the following way:

(15) *globe*   is the root and the base for the suffix *-al*
    global   is the base for the suffix *-ise*
    globalise   is the base for the suffix *-ation*
    globalisation is the resulting derivative

In general, we can conclude that in a morphological analysis, we need to identify not only the morphemes and their types, but also the order in which the morphemes are combined with each other.

So far we have examined words that contained only suffixes. You might now be tempted to ask how words containing both suffixes and prefixes can be analysed. Consider, for instance, the words *unfearful*, *removable*, or *unreadable*. At first sight, the morphological analysis of these words seems to present no difficulty. We can say that all the three words consist of three morphemes: one prefix, one root, and one suffix. However, if we start to identify the bases for each affix, which is a crucial part of morphological analysis, the whole matter is no longer clear. Is, for instance, *fear* the base for the prefix *un-* in *unfearful*, or the base for the suffix *-ful*, or for both simultaneously? In other words, in which order are the morphemes in these words attached to each other? We will take a closer look at the word *unfearful*. As it may have become clear from the discussion above, we can think of three potential analyses of this word:

(16) a.

b.

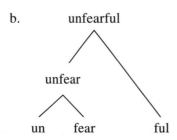

c.

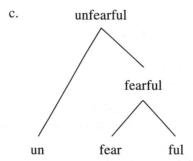

The diagram in (16a) suggests that the two affixes are added simultaneously to the base *fear*. According to the diagram in (16b), first the prefix *un-* is attached to the base *fear*, and then the suffix *-ful* is attached to the base *unfear*. Finally, the analysis in (16c) shows yet another variant: First the suffix *-ful* is attached to the base *fear*, and then the prefix *un-* is attached to the base *fearful*. But which of the three variants is the most appropriate one?

One way of answering this question is to examine the meaning of the word *unfearful* in order to find out which of the three potential constellations of morphemes given in (16) yields this meaning. The meaning of the word *unfearful* can be paraphrased as 'not fearful' or 'not full of fear'. This meaning suggests two steps in the formation of the word *unfearful*. First, the meaning 'full of fear' is created by means of attaching the suffix *-ful* to the base *fear* and then this meaning is negated by means of attaching the prefix *un-* to the base *fearful*. Given this overall meaning, we might suggest that possibly the variants in (16a) and (16b) should be abandoned. The analysis in (16a) seems to be incorrect since it presupposes that both affixes are attached simultaneously to the base *fear*, and this is improbable since, as suggested above, the meaning of the noun *unfearful* is created in steps. Similarly, the analysis in (16b) is problematic since it forces us to say that the prefix *un-* in *unfearful* first forms the noun *unfear*, which then must mean something like 'not fear' and adding the suffix *-ful* then renders the meaning 'full of not fear', which is not the meaning of *unfearful*. Besides, in this case it is also unclear what meaning the noun *unfear* might have in English. In contrast, the analysis in (16c) yields exactly the meaning 'not fearful'.

Another argument in favour of the analysis in (16c) comes from the formal behaviour of affixes. Usually, affixes attach to bases of special word-classes, i.e. nouns, verbs, adjectives, etc. Consequently, the question we should pursue now is to which bases the affixes *un-* and *-ful* attach. For this purpose, we could make a list of other words containing the same affixes and note the word-class of the base. This is done in (17) where A stands for 'adjective' and N for 'noun':

(17)
base	*un*-derivative	base	*-ful*-derivative
usual (A)	*unusual*	*respect* (N)	*respectful*
pleasant (A)	*unpleasant*	*regret* (N)	*regretful*
clear (A)	*unclear*	*pity* (N)	*pitiful*
happy (A)	*unhappy*	*tact* (N)	*tactful*

The conclusion that can be drawn on the basis of (17) is that the prefix *un-* attaches primarily to adjectives. Cases in which it is attached to nouns are rare, and in fact the word *unfear* is unattested in English. This again strongly suggests that the analysis in (16b) is problematic since it presupposes the creation of the noun *unfear*, which is not readily possible according to the formal properties of the prefix *un-*. The suffix *-ful*, by contrast, does attach readily to nouns, which supports the idea of the suffix *-ful* being first attached to the noun *fear*. The formal analysis also speaks against the variant in (16a): The tree diagram in (16a) suggests that both *un-* and *-ful* are simultaneously attached to the noun *fear*, which is improbable, since we now know that *un-* does not normally attach to nouns. We can therefore assume on the basis of this formal evidence, that first, the suffix *-ful* is attached to the noun *fear*, and then the prefix *un-* is attached to the adjective *fearful*.

We can conclude so far that both the formal analysis and the analysis based on meaning yield the same result. In the case of the complex word *unfearful*, the suffix *-ful* is attached to the noun *fear* first, and then the prefix *un-*

is attached to the adjective *fearful*. In general, we can say that both semantic (i.e. meaning-related) and formal arguments are useful in defining the structure of complex words. Another important generalisation that emerges from the analysis above is that when a word contains several affixes, they are not attached to the root or a base all at once, but in a certain order. Having learned a number of crucial properties of morphemes, we will deal with different ways of realising the same morpheme in the next section.

3.5. Realisations of morphemes: allomorphs

We have defined morphemes as units that usually have a certain meaning and a certain form. For most of the examples we have regarded so far we postulated one meaning and one phonetic form. This might be true for some morphemes, such as the morpheme *dream*, which we discussed in section 3.2. However, with most morphemes there is no one-to-one relation between form and meaning. Instead, it is often the case that one and the same meaning is expressed by more than one form.

Consider, for instance, the articles set in bold in the data in (18). Note that there is one more article in (18c), *the*, which we will ignore in our discussion. In the phonetic transcription, the symbol "'" indicates that the following syllable is stressed.

(18) a. There is **a** dog over there.
          [ə 'dɒg]
     b. He is recovering from **an** illness.
          [ən 'ɪlnəs]
     c. I said '**a**' dog, not 'the' dog.
          ['eɪ dɒg]

We can identify three different phonetic forms of the articles in (18): [ə], [ən], and [eɪ]. The question that arises now is: Do these forms represent three different morphemes, or one and the same? Since the meaning of these forms is the same, we can suggest that all three forms should be regarded as instances of the same morpheme. And this morpheme is known as the indefinite article. Following established conventions, we will present this morpheme by putting it in braces: {INDEFINITE ARTICLE}.

We are presented with the rather amazing fact that one and the same morpheme may have different physical realisations. To make sure that we are not dealing with random exceptions, let us collect some more data with the same morpheme. They are given in (19):

(19) a cup [ə'kʌp]   an arm [ən'ɑːm]   'a' cup, not 'the' cup   ['eɪ kʌp]
     a lake [ə'leɪk]   an egg [ən'eg]   'a' lake, not 'the' lake ['eɪ leɪk]
     a face [ə'feɪs]   an apple [ən'æpl] 'a' book, not 'the' book ['eɪ bʊk]

The data in (19) confirm our preliminary conclusion that the indefinite article has three different physical forms in English, [ə], [ən], and [eɪ]. As we have already seen above, the term used in morphology to refer in general to the form of any morpheme is 'morph'. However, when the same morpheme is realised through different morphs, we speak of **allomorphs**. Allomorphs are different morphs representing the same morpheme. The parts of the term 'allomorph', *allo* and *morph*, come from Greek and mean 'different' and 'form', respectively. In the case of the indefinite article above, we can say that [ə], [ən], and [eɪ] are allomorphs of the morpheme {INDEFINITE ARTICLE}.

But how come that we understand the meaning of this morpheme despite its different physical shapes? Obviously, we classify what we hear into abstract categories. The morpheme is such an abstract category that exists in our minds. This abstract mental category is realised physically, i.e. concretely, in a certain way or a number of ways. For instance, in the case of the indefinite article, the different allomorphs that we hear represent one abstract category, the morpheme {INDEFINITE ARTICLE}. The relation morpheme-allomorph is similar to the relation phoneme-allophone we learned about in the previous chapter. Both allophones and allomorphs are concrete physical realisations of some abstract categories. However, whereas allophones are realisations of an abstract phonological category, i.e. the phoneme, allomorphs are realisations of an abstract morphological category, i.e. the morpheme.

Let us now take a closer look at the distribution of the allomorphs in (19). Is it totally random or governed by some rule? Concentrating on the sounds following the indefinite article in the examples in (19) we can make an interesting observation. The allomorph [ə] appears only if the following word begins with a consonant, as in [ə 'dɒg]. The allomorph [ən] surfaces if the following word begins with a vowel, as in [ən 'eg]. Finally, when the article is stressed, the allomorph is [eɪ]. This type of conditioning, in which the distribution of allomorphs is governed by the sound structure, is called **phonological conditioning**.

We can conclude from our observations above that the distribution of the allomorphs of the indefinite article is by no means random. Quite on the contrary, it is totally predictable. We can predict, for instance, when the morpheme {INDEFINITE ARTICLE} will be realised as [ə], and when as [ən] or [eɪ]. And since the distribution is predictable, we can capture the distribution as in (20):

(20)

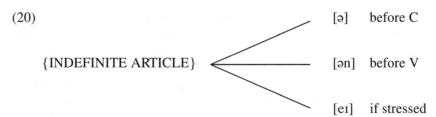

{INDEFINITE ARTICLE} [ə] before C
   [ən] before V
   [eɪ] if stressed

There are several other interesting cases of allomorphy in English. Consider, for instance, the different realisations of the English plural morpheme in (21):

(21) a. lip   [lɪp]   lips   [lɪps]
        rib   [ɹɪb]   ribs   [ɹɪbz]
        case [keɪs]   cases [keɪsəz]
     b. tooth [tu:θ]   teeth [ti:θ]
        sheep [ʃi:p]   sheep [ʃi:p]
        ox   [ɒks]   oxen   ['ɒksən]

The words in the rightmost column consist of two morphemes: the base and the morpheme {PLURAL}. As you might have noticed, the morpheme {PLURAL} is realised in a variety of ways in (21). For instance, in the examples in (21a) it is realised by adding a suffix that has three different phonetic forms: [s], [z], and [əz]. Since the majority of English nouns form their plural in this way, these realisations are called 'regular'. In the examples in (21b) the plural morpheme is realised differently. Since there is a rather small number of nouns that do not form the plural in the way shown in (21a), the realisations of the plural morpheme exemplified in (21b) are called 'irregular'. We will now take a closer look at regular and irregular realisations of the plural morpheme.

Let us first analyse the regular realisations. It has already been mentioned above that there are at least three different regular realisations of the plural morpheme: [s], [z], and [əz]. However, to substantiate this claim, we need more data. These are provided in (22). It would be useful for you to mark those parts in the words of the rightmost column which in your opinion express the plural.

(22) a. lip   [lɪp]   lips   [lɪps]
        rat   [ɹæt]   rats   [ɹæts]
        stick [stɪk]   sticks [stɪks]
        cliff [klɪf]   cliffs [klɪfs]
        path   [pɑ:θ]   paths   [pɑ:θs]

b.	rib	[ɹɪb]	ribs	[ɹɪbz]
	bed	[bed]	beds	[bedz]
	bug	[bʌg]	bugs	[bʌgz]
	claim	[kleɪm]	claims	[kleɪmz]
	star	[stɑː]	stars	[stɑːz]
c.	case	[keɪs]	cases	['keɪsəz]
	nose	[nəʊz]	noses	['nəʊzəz]
	lash	[læʃ]	lashes	['læʃəz]
	stitch	[stɪtʃ]	stitches	['stɪtʃəz]
	judge	[dʒʌdʒ]	judges	['dʒʌdʒəz]

The data in (22) confirm our observation that the plural morpheme has three different regular allomorphs: [s], [z] and [əz]. But what is their distribution, i.e. what causes the allomorphy? In the case of the indefinite article we examined the sounds that followed the different allomorphs. Since nothing follows the allomorphs of the plural morpheme in (22), we may try to concentrate on what sounds precede them. In this case, it would be useful to list all the different sounds after which each allomorph occurs in the data:

(23) [s] occurs after: [p], [t], [k], [f], [θ]
   [z] occurs after: [b], [d], [g], [m], [ɑː]
   [əz] occurs after: [s], [z], [ʃ], [tʃ], [dʒ]

The lists in (23) give us a good idea of the environments in which each of the allomorphs occurs. However, mere listing is not a very helpful procedure because lists lack the power of generalisation which is necessary for a systematic description of linguistic phenomena. Therefore, in a next step, our task is to find out whether the sounds listed for each allomorph have something in common. Their phonological features might be an obvious choice. And indeed, all sounds after which the allomorph [s] occurs have one feature in common, they are voiceless. In contrast, the voiced allomorph [z] occurs after voiced consonants (e.g. [b], [d], [g], [m]) and after vowels (e.g. [ɑː]). In other words, the voiced allomorph [z] occurs after voiced sounds. The sounds after which the allomorph [əz] occurs seem to have nothing in common at first sight. However, if we consider their articulatory features, we discover an interesting similarity between them. [s], [z], [ʃ], [tʃ], [dʒ] are alveolar (or palato-alveolar) fricatives or affricates that are characterised by a particular hissing noise. Phonologists have shown that these sounds behave similarly in many languages and have therefore assigned them to a class of their own, called **sibilants**. Hence, we can generalise that the allomorph [əz] occurs after sibilants. And we can draw the conclusion that, like the allomorphs of the indefinite article, the regular allomorphs of the English morpheme {PLURAL} are phonologically conditioned. Their distribution is again predictable and can be formalised as follows (the symbol 'I' means 'in the following context:'):

(24)

{PLURAL}
- [s] I C $_{[- voice]}$ __ #
- [z] I C $_{[+ voice]}$ __ # or V __ #
- [əz] I C $_{[sibilant]}$ __ #

The representation in (24) reads as follows: the morpheme {PLURAL} is realised as [s] after voiceless consonants, and as [z] after voiced consonants or after vowels, and as [əz] after sibilants.

Now let us turn to the irregular realisations of the plural morpheme. We will repeat the examples from (21b) and add more data.

(25) a. tooth   [tuːθ]   teeth   [tiːθ]
          goose   [guːs]   geese   [giːs]
          mouse   [maʊs]   mice   [maɪs]
      b. sheep   [ʃiːp]   sheep   [ʃiːp]
      c. ox   [ɒks]   oxen   [ˈɒksən]
      d. child   [tʃaɪld]   children [ˈtʃɪldɹən]

As can be inferred from (25), the morpheme {PLURAL} has a number of different irregular realisations. In (25a) it is realised by a vowel change: In *tooth — teeth* and *goose — geese* the base vowel changes from [uː] to [iː], in *mouse — mice* from [aʊ] to [aɪ]. Therefore, we can say that in the words in (25a), the allomorphs are the root vowels [iː] and [aɪ] that substitute the root vowels [uː] and [aʊ], respectively. In the case of the noun *sheep* the morpheme {PLURAL} is realised by no overt change in form, i.e. by a zero form. In *oxen* the plural is expressed by adding a suffix whose phonetic form is [ən]. Thus, the allomorph is [ən]. Finally, in *children*, the plural morpheme is expressed by combining a vowel change from [aɪ] in *child* to [ɪ] in *children* and the suffixation of [ɹən].

We can say therefore that there are different irregular realisations of the morpheme {PLURAL}. The root vowels [iː] and [aɪ] substituting the root vowels [uː] and [aʊ], a zero form, [ən], and a combination of the root vowel [ɪ] (which substitutes the root vowel [aɪ]) and [ɹən]-suffixation. The challenging question now is what triggers each allomorph. In the case of phonological conditioning it was the sound that follows or precedes a given morpheme, but in the case of the examples above the shape of the morpheme does not depend on the sound structure. In fact, it depends on the individual word of which the plural should be formed. The plural form of each of the words must therefore be learned separately as the plural of that particular word. So, if the word is *sheep*, we know that the allomorph is 'zero'. If the word is *ox* then the allomorph is [ən], and so on. This type of conditioning is called **lexical conditioning**.

Now we can revise our schema of the allomorphy of the English morpheme {PLURAL} in (24) above by adding the irregular realisations to it:

(26)

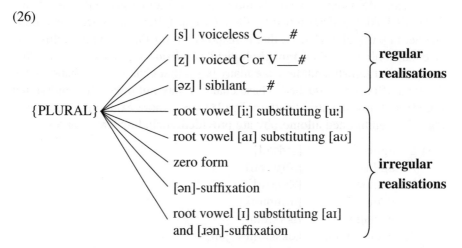

Let us now deal with another interesting case of allomorphy. Consider the bases [kənˈkluːd], [kənˈkluːʒ] and [kənˈkluːs] in (27) and think whether they represent the same morpheme. The symbol "ˈ" again indicates that the following syllable is stressed. For a better identification of the bases in the examples *conclusion* and *conclusive*, the suffixes in the phonetic transcriptions of the last two words are separated from the bases by a hyphen.

(27) *conclude*   [kənˈkluːd]
    conclusion   [kənˈkluːʒ-ən]
    conclusive   [kənˈkluːs-ɪv]

To test whether they represent the same morpheme, we have to check whether all three bases have the same meaning. Their meaning is indeed the same: 'to infer that something is true on the basis of the facts at hand', and we can therefore regard the forms in (27) as allomorphs of the same morpheme: {CONCLUDE}. Obviously, the three allomorphs differ only in the realisation of the final consonant: [d] in *conclude*, [ʒ] in *conclusion*, and [s] in *conclusive*. But what triggers the allomorphy in this case? Let us take a closer look at the morphological structure of the words in (27). *Conclude* is a simplex word, it consists of the base [kənˈkluːd] only. In contrast, *conclusion* and *conclusive* are complex words. They consist of the bases [kənˈkluːʒ] and [kənˈkluːs] and the suffixes [ən] and [ɪv]. We can observe so far that, if no suffix is added, the morpheme {CONCLUDE} has the form [kənˈkluːd], but when suffixes are added, this morpheme has different forms. When the suffix [ən] follows, it has the shape [kənˈkluːʒ] and when a different suffix, [ɪv], is attached, it has the shape [kənˈkluːs].

We can infer from the analysis above that the allomorphy of the morpheme {CONCLUDE} is determined by the affix that follows it. Since it is a morpheme, in particular a suffix, that is responsible for the alternation, this type of conditioning is called **morphological conditioning**. This type is rather common in English, and there are many bases that change their shapes when different affixes are attached. These changes may not only affect individual sounds, but also the stress pattern. In (28) some more examples of morphologically conditioned allomorphy are provided, including stress marks:

(28) a. agile   [ˈædʒaɪl]
      agility   [əˈdʒɪl-əti]
   b. demon   [ˈdiːmən]
      demonic   [dɪˈmɒn-ɪk]
   c. exclaim   [ɪksˈkleɪm]
      exclamation [ˌekskləˈm-eɪʃən]
   d. receive   [ɹɪˈsiːv]
      receptive   [ɹɪˈsept-ɪv]

The English morpheme {AGILE} has the allomorphs [ˈædʒaɪl] (when no affix is attached) and [əˈdʒɪl] (when the suffix *-ity* is attached). They differ from each other both in the quality of the vowels and in their stress pattern. Thus, in *agility*, the vowel [æ] changes into [ə], and the diphthong [aɪ] changes into the monophthong [ɪ], and the stress shifts from the first to the second syllable. A similar analysis can be applied to the words in (28b–d).

In conclusion, we have seen that morphemes are abstract units that have different concrete realisations, allomorphs. The distribution of allomorphs is usually predictable and can be conditioned by a number of different factors: phonological, lexical and morphological.

3.6. Morphological processes: inflection and derivation

We have learned so far that morphemes are minimal building blocks of words. But what exactly is the purpose of combining morphemes into words? To deal with this question, consider the reasons for using the suffixes *-s*, *-ed*, and *-er* in the words *bakes*, *baked*, and *baker* below:

(29) a. She **bakes** sweet-scented cakes on Sundays.
 b. She **baked** sweet-scented cakes last Sunday.
 c. She knows a good **baker**.

In (29a), we attach the present tense suffix *-s* to the verb *bake* because we must use this tense form to indicate that something, in this case the baking, is happening regularly and at the present time. Furthermore, the subject of this sentence is the third person pronoun *she*, which — in present tense sentences — requires the use of the suffix *-s* on the verb. So the reason for using the suffix *-s* in (29a) is grammatical in nature and is dictated by the grammatical rules of English. Similarly, in (29b) we have to use the suffix *-ed* on the verb *bake* if we want to say that the baking happened in the past. The suffix *-ed* is thus again determined by a grammatical rule of English and it expresses grammatical information, namely that the verb is in the past tense. In none of the two cases would we say that the meaning of the verb *bake* has changed, since in both cases it means something like 'cook in an oven'. The suffixes only specify the word grammatically. By contrast, the suffix *-er* in *baker* creates a completely new concept, i.e. 'person who bakes', and the occurrence of *-er* is not dictated by any grammatical rule of English. In fact, if you exchange the suffix *-er* for another suffix, e.g. *-ery*, you will do no damage to the grammar of this sentence. *She knows a good bakery* is as grammatically correct as *She knows a good baker*. What we change, however, is the meaning of this sentence, since the word *bakery* means something different from the word *baker*.

There is another important observation we can make on the basis of the data above. We have already observed that the words *bakes* and *baked* have the same meaning. The two words *bakes* and *baked* should therefore be regarded not as two different words, but as two different forms of a single word. At this point we need to be more careful about what we mean when we say 'word'. Obviously, we have been using the term for two entirely different things. On the one hand, we have used it to refer to grammatically fully specified forms, such as *bakes* and *baked*. On the other hand, we have used the notion of 'word' to refer to an abstract unit, the verb *bake*, which manifests itself in different forms, such as *bake, baking, baked, bakes*. To properly differentiate between these two uses of the notion of 'word', we need more terminology. For the notion of 'word as an abstract unit in the vocabulary of a language' we will use the term **lexeme**. Notationally, lexemes are indicated by means of small capitals, e.g. BAKE. The different grammatically specified forms of a given lexeme are called **word-forms** or **grammatical words**. Returning to our example *baker* vs. *bakes/baked*, we would not think of *baker* as a word-form of the lexeme BAKE, but regard it as a different lexeme, i.e. BAKER. This lexeme BAKER manifests itself again in different word-forms, such as the singular form *baker*, the plural form *bakers* and the genitive form *baker's*.

Based on our discussion, we can now draw the following conclusion concerning the purpose of the suffixes *-s*, *-ed*, and *-er*. The suffixes *-s* and *-ed* in *bakes* and *baked* are used to encode grammatical information and thus to create different word-forms of the same lexeme. Such affixes are called **inflectional**, and the morphological expression of grammatical information and categories is termed **inflection**. By contrast, *-er* is used for a different purpose, namely to create a new lexeme. Affixes that serve to create new lexemes are called **derivational**, and the creation of new lexemes by affixation is called **derivation**. Note that in this context 'new' does not mean 'never seen before in the language', but rather 'different in meaning from the base'.

Given the distinction between inflectional and derivational morphemes, two questions arise. First, you might be tempted to ask what other grammatical words, besides the past tense or third-person-singular forms, can be created by inflectional affixes. The inventory of English inflectional morphemes is provided in (30):

(30)
affix	function	examples
-s	creates the plural form of nouns	*cats, days*
's	creates the genitive form of nouns	*Peter's, John's*
-ed	creates the past tense form of verbs	*played, stopped, cared*
-s	creates the third person singular present tense form of verbs	*(he/she/it) plays, stops, cares*
-ing	creates the progressive form of verbs	*(is/are) playing, going, writing*
-er	creates the comparative form of adjectives	*warmer, colder*
-est	creates the superlative form of adjectives	*warmest, coldest*

Evidently, besides the plural form of nouns or the past tense form of verbs, inflectional suffixes can also create other grammatical forms. For instance, in

Claire's passion the suffix *-'s* creates the genitive form of the noun *Claire*. In *He is cooking the supper* the suffix *-ing* is used to create the progressive form of the verb *cook*. In general, however, we can say that the inventory of English inflectional morphemes is quite small.

Another question that arises is whether the difference in function is the only feature by which inflectional and derivational affixes can be distinguished. In fact, the two types of affixes also differ in a number of other features. The first difference can be established if we compare the position of the inflectional affixes listed in (30) above with respect to their bases with the position derivational affixes can occupy in English lexemes. All inflectional affixes in (30) are evidently suffixes. With derivational affixes, the situation is different. In addition to derivational suffixes, such as *-age* in *spillage*, or *-ish* in *reddish*, there are many derivational morphemes that are prefixes, such as *dis-* in *disorganisation*, *re-* in *remove*, or *anti-* in *antifreeze*. We can therefore conclude that in English, inflectional morphemes are only suffixes, whereas derivational morphemes can be both suffixes and prefixes.

Another interesting difference between the two types of affixes lies in the consistency of their meaning or function. Consider, for example, the meanings of the derivatives with the suffix *-ise* in (31a) and compare this state of affairs to that of the inflected words in (31b).

(31)   **example**   **word meaning**   **affix meaning/function**
    a. *computerise*   'put into a computer'   'put into X'
       hospitalise   'put into a hospital'   'put into X'
       modernise   'make (more) modern'   'make (more) X'
       regularise   'make (more) regular'   'make (more) X'
       brotherise   'provide with a brother'   'provide with X'
       gutterise   'provide with a gutter'   'provide with X'
    b. *cars*   'more than one car'   'more than one'
       tables   'more than one table'   'more than one'
       shoes   'more than one shoe'   'more than one'
       cottages   'more than one cottage'   'more than one'

Obviously, the function of the inflectional suffix *-s* is consistently the same in every word to which it is attached: It signals the plural. By contrast, *-ise* seems to have a number of different (though probably related) meanings. We can therefore conclude that inflectional affixes have consistently exactly the same meaning in all words they are attached to, whereas derivational affixes do not always exhibit this consistency. A given derivational affix may have different meanings. Note, however, that this raises the question whether the data in (31a) might show that we are actually dealing with three different *-ise* suffixes, instead of only one, with each of them having its own distinct meaning. This question leads us to the more general theoretical problem of how one should analyse words and morphemes that have more than one meaning. For example, should we assume the existence of two lexemes TREE$_1$ and TREE$_2$, one meaning the plant, the other meaning an abstract structural representation as the one in (14)? Or should we assume the existence of only one lexeme TREE that happens to have two closely related meanings? This problem will be discussed in detail in our chapter on meaning, in section 5.4.2. We have assumed here that we are indeed dealing with only one suffix *-ise*, which can have different, related meanings.

Inflectional and derivational affixes differ in yet another property. Let us consider whether the English past tense suffix *-ed* can be attached to every verb in English. In fact, it can be attached to every regular verb. Or take the third person singular suffix *-s*, as in *(he) writes* or *(he) carries*. There is no English verb (with the exception of BE) to which this suffix cannot be attached. We can thus say that inflectional affixes seem to be able to occur on most words of a given class. But how do derivational affixes behave in this respect? Let us examine the English derivational suffix *-ity*, which attaches to adjectives to create nouns. There are many adjectives on which it can occur, as in *sanity, clarity, stability, creativity, polarity*, etc. However, there are also many adjectives to which it cannot be attached. For instance, the derivatives **longity, *joyfulity, *freeity* are unattested in English. We can thus establish yet another important difference between inflectional and derivational morphemes, namely that inflectional morphemes can be attached to most or all words of a given class, whereas derivational morphemes have a more restricted usage.

Another difference between the two types of affixes concerns word-class. Consider what happens to the word-class of the base words in (32) below when the inflectional third person singular present tense suffix *-s* and the derivational prefix *-er* are attached.

(32)
	base	word-class of the base	suffixed form	word-class of the suffixed form
a.	*walk*	V	*walks*	V
	write	V	*writes*	V
	bake	V	*bakes*	V
b.	*walk*	V	*walker*	N
	write	V	*writer*	N
	bake	V	*baker*	N

Obviously, whenever we attach the third person singular present tense suffix *-s* to a verb, it remains a verb, as the examples in (32a) show. The same observation can be made for any of the inflectional suffixes listed in (30) above. The derivational suffix *-er*, however, behaves in a different way in this respect. It changes the word-class of its bases from verb to noun. This is also the case with many other derivational affixes, as, for instance, with the derivational suffix *-less*, which changes nouns into adjectives, as in *joy* (N) – *joyless* (A), or the derivational suffix *-en* which changes adjectives into verbs, as in *black* (A) – *blacken* (V), etc. Note, however, that very few English prefixes change the word-class of the base. They are nevertheless considered derivational because they create new lexemes, and not word-forms of the same lexeme, as, for instance, *semi-transparent, impossible, replay*. We can conclude that whenever an affix changes the word-class of the base, it is a derivational affix.

To summarise, we have seen in this section that affixes can be grouped into two different types according to their function: derivational affixes, which are used to create new lexemes, and inflectional affixes, which are used to express different word-forms of the same lexeme. The two types of affixes differ in a number of properties. We will summarise these properties in the following table:

(33) **inflectional affixes**
   – are always suffixes in English
   – have consistently the same grammatical function in every word they attach to
   – attach to every word of a given class
   – never change the word-class of the base

derivational affixes
   – can be suffixes and prefixes
   – can have different meanings in different words
   – attach to certain words of a given class
   – can change the word-class of the base

Using derivational affixes is only one of many possible ways of creating new lexemes. In the next section we will take a closer look at different processes by which new lexemes can be created.

3.7. Word-formation

3.7.1. What is word-formation?

It has already been mentioned above that, among other things, morphology deals with the ways of creating new lexemes. We have also seen in the previous section that one such way is adding derivational affixes to existing bases. However, there are many other ways by which speakers can create new lexemes and thus give names to new things, abstract notions, etc.

If, for example, a five-year-old child whose native language is English wants to invent a name for a flag decorated with moons, he or she might naturally call this type of flag a *moon-flag* because as a speaker of English the child knows that new concepts can be denoted just by putting several words together into one (example from Clark 1993: 148). Or imagine a situation in which a speaker is faced with the necessity to tell her interlocutor that she searched the internet auction *ebay* the day before. The strategy this speaker would possibly resort to is just using the name *ebay* to denote the process associated with this name: *Yesterday, I ebayed till late in the evening*. The speaker would do so probably because she is aware of the fact that one and the same form can be used to denote both objects and processes connected with these objects. Yet another situation would trigger the use of a different strategy. For instance, if the speaker is an experienced university student who has attended many lectures, she might refer to a lecture as *lec* in a conversation with her fellow-students one day. She will be able to do so because she has many words of the same type in her mind, such as *exam*, *lab*, and *prof*, and knows that such shortened words can be used to express familiarity with the concept they denote.

These and some other strategies of creating new lexemes are studied within a special area of morphology called **word-formation**. In the sections to follow we will take a closer look at different word-formation processes.

3.7.2. Affixation

We have already dealt with one common strategy of creating new words, namely adding affixes to existing bases. This is called 'affixation'. In English, we differentiate between **prefixation** and **suffixation**. The two strategies are illustrated in (34):

(34) a. disconnect   b. idolise
         malfunction   balloonist
         unstable   extremity
         pre-film   nursery

Both prefixes and suffixes exhibit a number of interesting properties, and we will take a look at some of them, starting with suffixes.

As we have seen earlier in this chapter, suffixes often cause a number of phonological changes. Besides, suffixes often trigger another kind of change just discussed, that of changing the word-class. (35a) provides more examples of this kind:

(35) a. forget   V → forgetful   A
         fiction   N → fictional   A
         elect   V → election   N
         solid   A → solidity   N
         speech   N → speechify   V
         black   A → blacken   V
     b. green   A → greenish   A
         devil   N → devilry   N
         professor   N → professorship   N

As becomes obvious in (35b), however, some suffixes do not change the word-class of their bases.

The data in (36) illustrate another pervasive fact about suffixes. Try to make observations on the differences between the affixes in (36) in terms of the word-class of their derivatives:

(36) **suffix base** **derivative**
   a. -ee   employ, divorce, refuge   employee, divorcee, refugee
   b. -al   fiction, tradition, culture fictional, traditional, cultural
   c. -en   black, broad, strength   blacken, broaden, strengthen
   d. -wise length, clock, street   lengthwise, clockwise, streetwise

Obviously, each of the suffixes in (36) creates derivatives of a certain word-class. For instance, the suffix *-ee* creates nouns, the suffix *-al* creates adjectives, the suffix *-en* creates verbs, and *-wise* creates adverbs. Therefore, depending on the word-class of the derivative they create, suffixes can be subdivided into nominal, verbal, adjectival, and adverbial suffixes. For instance, the suffix *-al* is regarded as an adjectival suffix, since it creates adjectives.

Another interesting generalisation can be made if we consider the bases to which the suffixes in (36) are attached. For instance, all bases to which the suffix *-al* is attached are nouns: *fiction, tradition, culture*. We can say that the suffix *-al* attaches primarily to bases of a particular word-class, such as nouns. In contrast, the suffix *-en* in (36c) can attach to adjectives, e.g. *black* and *broad*, but also to nouns, e.g. *strength*. We can conclude that some suffixes attach primarily to bases of a certain word-class, whereas other suffixes can attach to bases of different word-classes.

Suffixes can render a whole range of different meanings, and some of these meanings are illustrated below. Try to figure out the meaning of the suffixes in (37) on the basis of these data:

(37) **suffix**   **derivatives**
   a. -er   commander, preacher, wanderer
   b. -er   mixer, cutter, toaster, slicer
   c. -ette   kitchenette, towelette, theatrette
   d. -ess   millionairess, waitress, tigress, hostess
   e. -able   movable, changeable, navigable, readable
   f. -ly   fatherly, womanly
   g. -en   blacken, broaden, quicken, lengthen

The words with the suffix *-er* in (37a) can be paraphrased as 'person who Xes'. A *commander* is a person who commands, a *preacher* is a person who preaches, and so on. Therefore, the suffix *-er* is often called an **agentive suffix**. The same suffix can also be used to create words that denote instruments, as in *mixer, cutter,* etc. and is therefore regarded as an **instrumental suffix**. Derivatives with the suffix *-ette* have the meaning 'small X', therefore the suffix is called a **diminutive suffix**. The suffix *-ess* forms lexemes denoting female beings. A *tigress* is a 'female tiger', *-ess* is thus called a **gender-marking suffix**. The suffix *-able* often renders the meaning 'capable of being Xed', with *movable* meaning 'capable of being moved'. The derivatives containing the verbal suffix *-en* mean 'make (more) X'. These are just a few examples from a wide range of meanings that can be expressed by suffixes.

Let us now turn to prefixes. Consider the data below and try to establish the difference between the prefixes in (38a) and (38b):

(38) a. obey   V → disobey   V
        manage   V → mismanage   V
        store   V → restore   V
        rational A → non-rational A
        medical   A → premedical   A
        legal   A → illegal   A
        function N → malfunction   N
        member   N → non-member   N
     b. witch   N → bewitch   V
        large   A → enlarge   V
        forest   N → deforest   V
        courage   N → discourage   V

Obviously, in contrast to suffixes, many English prefixes do not change the word-class of the base. The data in (38b) show, however, that there are a few prefixes that can do so.

Prefixes can also render a variety of meanings. The following list provides some examples:

(39) **prefix**   **examples**
      non-   non-scientific, non-American, non-stop
      semi-   semi-desert, semi-conscious, semi-transparent
      mal-   malformation, malnutrition, maladministration
      pre-   pre-war, pre-historic, pre-arranged
      ultra-   ultra-light, ultra-conservative, ultra-thin

Evidently, the meaning of the prefix *non-* in *non-scientific* is 'not X'. Prefixes with such a meaning are called **negative prefixes**. The prefix *semi-* means 'half X', and *semi-conscious* can be paraphrased as 'half conscious'. *Malformation* means 'wrong formation', therefore the meaning of the prefix *mal-* is 'wrong'. The prefix *pre-* has the meaning 'before X', as in *pre-war* 'before war'. *Ultra-* is called an **augmentative prefix** because it creates words with the meaning 'very, extremely X' (*ultra-conservative* is 'very/extremely conservative').

Interestingly, some affixes are often used to create new lexemes, whereas others are not. The English agentive suffix *-er*, for instance, is used very frequently and gave rise to many new words in the 20th century, such as *fictioner, jazzer, kinker, legger, litterer, packager, pager, socialiser*. In contrast, the suffix *-th*, as in *length, strength, width*, is attached to a very limited number of words, and is hardly ever used to create new words. These examples show that affixes may differ considerably in their ability to coin new words. This ability of affixes to create new words is called **productivity**. Productivity is a relative notion, i.e. some affixes are more productive than others. For instance, the agentive suffix *-er* is more productive than the nominal suffix *-th*, since it is used more often to create new words.

The productivity of a given affix is determined by a number of factors. Of course, new words are only created when there is a need for them, e. g. when a new concept, object, or property must be named. Consider how the authors of the following sentences use the suffix *-ness* to give names to a number of new concepts (examples taken from the *Oxford English Dictionary*):

(40) An irreproachable state of clean-shirtedness, navy blue-broadclothedness and chimney pot-hattedness.
Dislike-to-getting-up-in-the-morningness.

However, not every 'useful' or potentially possible word is indeed created. Quite often, the formation of a new word with a given affix simply does not happen, as the following data show. Impossible words are marked by an asterisk.

(41) booking office   *ticketery
     thief   *stealer
     chairwoman   *chairess
     friendship   *friendhood

The data in (41) suggest that the formation of a new word with a given affix is apparently impossible if there is already a word that denotes the same concept. Thus, we do not use the place-forming suffix *-ery* to name a place where tickets are sold because there is already the word *booking office* that denotes this concept. This phenomenon is called 'blocking'.

Besides blocking, there are a number of structural restrictions on the productivity of a given affix. Try to figure out what restriction operates on the bases to which the person-forming suffix *-eer* is attached. Pay particular attention to the stress pattern of the base words.

(42) a. auction   auctioneer   b. stock   *stockeer
        pamphlet   pamphleteer   book   *bookeer
        mountain   mountaineer   instrument   *instrumenteer
        basket   basketeer   police   *policeer

The examples in (42) illustrate a rather complex phonological restriction: The agentive suffix *-eer* attaches primarily to disyllabic bases that are stressed on the second-but-last syllable.

A restriction of a different type can be stated on the basis of the data in (43):

(43) a. adjectivise   adjectivisation   *adjectivisement
        hospitalise   hospitalisation   *hospitalisement
        institutionalise   institutionalisation   *institutionalisement
     b. treat   treatment   *treatation
        adjust   adjustment   *adjustation
        accomplish   accomplishment   *accomplishation

The English nominal suffixes *-ation* and *-ment* are synonymous since both create nouns with the meaning 'process of Xing' or 'result of Xing' from verbs. However, only the suffix *-ation*, and not *-ment*, can be used to create nouns from the verbs listed in the first column of (43a). On the other hand, only the suffix *-ment*, and not the suffix *-ation*, can be attached to the bases in (43b). This means that there must be some difference between the bases in (43a) and (43b) that triggers the difference in the choice of the nominalising suffix. You might have noticed already that all bases in (43a) end in the suffix *-ise*. By contrast, the bases in (43b) do not end in *-ise*. Consequently, we can make the generalisation that the suffix *-ation* is attached only to those bases that end in the suffix *-ise*, whereas the suffix *-ment* attaches only to bases that do not contain the suffix *-ise*. We can therefore conclude that in the case of the suffixes *-ation* and *-ment* there is a morphological restriction at work, in that these suffixes are sensitive to the morphological structure of the bases to which they attach.

Yet another type of restriction is illustrated in (44). You may easily find out why the words in the third column are unattested in English.

(44) actor   actress   *bookess
     waiter   waitress   *airplaness
     heir   heiress   *theatress
     count   countess   *policess
     lion   lioness   *milkess

The English suffix *-ess* attaches primarily to bases that denote human beings or higher animals. Therefore, formations with nouns denoting things, such as *theatress*, are impossible. This kind of restriction is semantic in nature.

To summarise, in this section we have discussed derivational affixation, one of the common processes of creating new words in English. We have seen that suffixes and prefixes have a number of different properties. Suffixes often change the word-class of the bases to which they attach, whereas prefixes do so in few cases only. Besides, affixes can be used to create a wide range of different meanings, such as agentive, instrumental, diminutive, augmentative, etc. Finally, we have seen that affixes can differ in their productivity, i.e. the extent to which they can be used to create new words, and that the productivity of a given affix can be restricted by phonological, morphological, and semantic factors.

3.7.3. Compounding

Another way of creating new words, extremely productive in English, is illustrated in (45).

(45) moonlight, high-speed, overcoat, wildlife sanctuary, high-level expert group

As you may have guessed, all words in (45) are formed by combining two or more words to form a new word. This process is called **compounding**. Like affixed words, English compounds have a number of interesting properties, some of which we will investigate below.

One of the interesting features of English compounds is their variable orthography. Consider the following data:

(46) a. ashtray, windmill, hotline
b. income tax increase, education minister
c. fast-food, icy-cold, call-girl

Obviously, there are three ways of spelling English compounds. Some compounds are spelled as one word, as in (46a). Others, such as those in (46b), are spelled separately, and one group of compounds are written with a hyphen, as in (46c). Note that for some compounds, all three orthographic variants are attested (for instance, *breadbin*, *bread bin* and *bread-bin*). There are no hard and fast rules for compound orthography in English, but one important determinant of the spelling is frequency of occurrence. Compounds that are infrequent are unlikely to be spelled as one word or to be hyphenated.

Another interesting feature of English compounds is their stress pattern. Consider the difference in the stress pattern between the words in (47a) and in (47b). The stressed vowel is indicated by an accent.

(47) a. *a bláckboard*
'a board for writing on with chalk'

a blúebell
'a plant which has blue flowers in the shape of a bell'

a rédcoat
'a British soldier in the 18th and 19th centuries'

b. *a black bóard*
'a board which is black in colour'

a blue béll
'a bell which is blue in colour'

a red cóat
'a coat which is red in colour'

The constructs in (47a) are nominal compounds, i.e. nouns, and they are stressed on the left-hand member. In contrast, the constructs in (47b) appear to be syntactic constructs, not words, and they are stressed on the right-hand element. One can generalise therefore that compounds are regularly stressed on the left-hand element. However, one has to be careful since there are also sets of compounds that are stressed on the right-hand element. For example, compounds whose first element indicates a location (as in *Newton résidents* or *Boston márathon*) are often stressed on the right-hand element.

Let us now take a look at some other features of English compounds. Since many compounds we have investigated so far consist of two words, as, for instance, *law firm*, you may have the impression that compounds consist of two elements, a left-hand element and a right-hand element. However, we have also seen in (45) above that there are compounds that consist of more than two words, as, for instance, *wildlife sanctuary*, which we should then describe as consisting of three elements: *wild*, *life*, and *sanctuary*. But intuitively, you might also object to such an analysis by saying that *wildlife* is in itself a word and can be regarded as one element. Indeed, we can argue that when a compound like *wildlife sanctuary* is created, we first create the word *wildlife* and then combine this word with the word *sanctuary*. This analysis can be supported by our discussion of the order in which morphemes are combined with each other in section 3.4. We said that normally, morphemes are attached successively, and not simultaneously, to each other. Further support for this analysis comes from the meaning of this compound, which is 'a sanctuary for wildlife' rather than 'a sanctuary for the life in the wild' (or something similar). To generalise, we can represent the structure of the compound *wildlife sanctuary* in the form of a tree diagram:

(48)   wildlife sanctuary

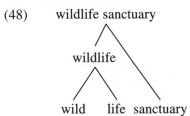

The tree diagram in (48) shows that compounds like *wildlife sanctuary* can be described as binary structures, i.e. as entities with two structural units ('constituents'). The compound *wildlife* consists of *wild* and *life*, and *wildlife sanctuary* of *wildlife* and *sanctuary*. This allows us to state that, in general, compounds can be described as containing two constituents, the left-hand constituent and the right-hand constituent. Each of these constituents can be complex in itself. Given this structure of compounds, we may now ask which role each constituent plays in a compound and whether the roles of both constituents are equally important. To deal with this question, we will take a look at what contribution to the meaning and to the grammatical features of a whole compound each constituent makes.

We will first deal with the contribution in terms of meaning. Consider the meaning paraphrases of the compounds provided in (49) below:

(49) a. plant house   'a kind of house'
     b. lawn tennis   'a kind of tennis'
     c. chairlift   'a kind of lift'

The data in (49) show that if we want to describe the meaning of a given compound, we can paraphrase it by using 'a kind of' and the right-hand element. Let us now try to do the same paraphrases using the left-hand elements. The asterisks indicate that the paraphrases do not render the meaning of the compounds correctly.

(50) a. plant house   *'a kind of plant'
    b. lawn tennis   *'a kind of lawn'
    c. chairlift   *'a kind of chair'

For instance, a *plant house* is not a kind of plant but a kind of house. This observation leads us to the insight that compounds can generally be interpreted in such a way that the whole compound denotes a subset of the entities denoted by the right-hand element. Thus, the right-hand element of a compound contributes the main information about the meaning, and can therefore be regarded as the more important element of the compound in terms of meaning.

In addition to being important in terms of meaning, the right-hand element is also important in terms of the grammatical information it contributes. Consider the data in (51):

(51) | **compound** | **inflected forms** | |
|---|---|---|
| message board | message boards | *messages board |
| windmill | windmills | *windsmill |
| crash-land | crash-landed | *crashed-land |

The data in (51) show that if a compound is inflected, the inflectional suffix is attached to the right-hand element, and not to the left-hand one. This shows us that the right-hand element is more important than the left-hand element in determining the grammatical features of a compound, such as, for instance, its number.

The right-hand element is more important in yet another way. Compare the word-classes of both elements to the word-class of the whole compound in the examples below:

(52) | **compound** | word-class of elements | word-class of the whole compound |
|---|---|---|
| *glasshouse* | N N | N |
| *colour-blind* | N A | A |
| *small talk* | A N | N |
| *deep-fry* | A V | V |

The comparison makes it clear that the word-class of the compound is always the same as the word-class of the right-hand element, no matter what word-class the left-hand element belongs to. This shows us that it is the right-hand element, and not the left-hand element, that determines the word-class of the whole compound.

We can conclude from our discussion above that generally, compounds have one element that is semantically and grammatically more important than other elements. This element is called the **head** of a compound. As the data above reveal, in English compounds, the head is usually the right-hand element.

Let us now examine the left-hand elements of compounds, using *windmill* as an example. What role does the element *wind* play in this compound? Evidently, it describes what kind of *mill* is meant if compared with other types of mills, such as *water mill, paper mill, powder-mill, coffee-mill*, or some other kind of *mill*. Hence we can say that the left-hand elements of compounds describe or specify the heads of compounds, i.e. provide additional information about them. The left-hand elements are called **modifiers**. In general, we can conclude that structurally, English compounds can be described as consisting of a modifier and a head.

Besides examining the structure of compounds in terms of the elements they contain, we can also investigate the structure of compounds with respect to the word-class of these elements. For a start, try to figure out the differences between the following compounds in terms of the word-classes of their heads.

(53) a. ash-tray b. colour-blind c. to housekeep
     fast-food   dark-blue   to deep-fry
     playground   to crash-land
     overweight

Obviously, the compounds in (53a) have nouns as their heads, whereas the compounds in (53b) have adjectives as their heads and those in (53c) verbs. Since we now know that the head of a compound determines the word-class of the whole compound, we can make the generalisation that mainly words of three word-classes can be produced by compounding in English: nouns, adjectives, and verbs. Therefore, we distinguish between three major types of compounds: **nominal, adjectival** and **verbal compounds**.

Another observation about the structure of compounds in (53) can be made if we consider the word-classes of their modifiers. You might have noticed that in nominal compounds, the modifiers can be nouns, adjectives, verbs and prepositions. By contrast, in adjectival compounds in (53b), the modifiers can be nouns and adjectives but not, for instance, prepositions. In general, within each type of compounds in (53), certain combinations of word-classes are attested, whereas other combinations are not. This is summarised in the following table, where the rows indicate the word-class of the modifiers of the compounds given, and the columns show the word-class of the heads of these compounds. The table shows, for instance, that there are compounds in English which consist of a noun and an adjective, such as *colour-blind*, where the noun *colour* is the modifier and the adjective *blind* is the head.

104   The structure of words: morphology

(54)

	Noun	Adjective	Verb
Noun	morning paper	colour-blind	to housekeep
Adjective	fast-food	dark-blue	to deep-fry
Verb	playground	—	to crash-land
Preposition	overweight	—	—

The examples in (54) represent the most common structural patterns of English compounds. However, the patterns in (54) differ considerably in terms of their productivity. Whereas NN compounding is the most productive pattern in English, VV compounding is extremely rare.

In the present section we have examined one common way of creating new words in English, compounding. We have seen that compounds have a number of interesting properties. Orthographically, they can be spelled together, separately, and with a hyphen. Phonologically, they exhibit a specific stress pattern. They are normally stressed on the left-hand element. Structurally, compounds generally consist of a head, the element that bears the crucial semantic and grammatical information about a compound, and a modifier, the element that describes the head. Finally, we have seen that the structure of compounds can also be described in terms of the word-class of the modifier and the head. According to the word-class of the head, English compounds can be subdivided into three major groups: nominal, adjectival, and verbal compounds. In the next section we will take a look at another productive word-formation process in English, conversion.

3.7.4. Conversion

The processes of compounding and affixation regarded so far are called **concatenative processes**, because they follow the principle of adding some morphological material to a given form. However, there are also processes that do not follow the principle of concatenation. One of the most productive **non-concatenative processes** in English, especially for the derivation of verbs, is illustrated in (55):

(55)

	base		derivative
a.	a cage	→	to cage
	a gesture	→	to gesture
	water	→	to water
b.	to coach	→	a coach
	to bore	→	a bore
	to flirt	→	a flirt

c. miserable → the miserable
professional → a professional
comic → a comic
d. pale → to pale
empty → to empty
clear → to clear

In (55), the words on the right are derived from the words on the left by means of changing the word-class, without any change in form. This word-formation process is called **conversion**. Some linguists call this process **'zero-derivation'** or **'zero-affixation'** because they suggest that in each of the cases in (55) a 'zero'-affix is added, i.e. an affix which is not expressed by any overt linguistic material. For reasons of space, we will not enter this debate here but will simply call this process 'conversion'.

The examples in (55) illustrate four major types of conversion in English: noun-to-verb conversion in (55a), verb-to-noun in (55b), adjective-to-noun in (55c) and adjective-to-verb in (55d). Pairs such as those in (55) raise the interesting question of how we know which word is the base and which is the derivative. Why do we say that in *cage* (N) – *cage* (V) the direction of conversion is from noun to verb and not vice versa? One way of finding out is checking the history of the language. Bases naturally appear earlier and give rise to derivatives. For instance, in the *Oxford English Dictionary*, the first date of attestation for the noun *cage* is 1225, whereas for the verb it is 1577. This means that the noun appeared considerably earlier, and must therefore be the base. The second clue for determining the direction of conversion is the meaning of the words. Derivatives usually have more complex meanings than their bases and rely on their bases for their meaning. Thus, to explain the meaning of the verb *to cage* we need the noun *cage* since the meaning of the verb is 'to put into a cage'. In such a case, we can argue that the verb is semantically more complex, and should consequently be regarded as the derived word. Another criterion can be frequency of occurrence. Derivatives are usually less frequently used in language because they are semantically more complex, hence more specialised, and therefore less versatile in usage. For instance, *cage* as a noun occurs 966 times in the *British National Corpus* (a 100 million word collection of English texts), whereas *cage* as a verb occurs only once.

In conclusion, we have seen that new words can also be created by changing the word-class of a base word without any change in form. In order to establish the direction of conversion, a number of different criteria can be used, such as the date of first attestation, the complexity of meaning, and the frequency of occurrence of a given derivative and its assumed base.

3.7.5. Shortening

In addition to conversion, there is a whole array of other non-concatenative word-formation processes. In these processes new items are formed by deleting linguistic material instead of adding it. Such processes are generally labelled as 'shortenings', but there are different types of shortening depending on what and how we delete. We will start with a process which you might well be familiar with, the shortening of names. Try to specify how the derivatives in (56) are created. The acute accent indicates on which syllable the main stress falls.

(56) **base**   **derivatives**
     Patrícia   →   Pat, Trish
     Alónzo   →   Al, Lon
     Augústus   →   Aug, Guss

Obviously, the words on the right in (56) are created by means of deleting a part of the base word. Such a process is called **truncation**. We can also make an important observation on the part of the base that survives truncation. As the data in (56) show, most truncated names retain either the first or the main-stressed syllable. As you probably know from your own experience, truncation is highly productive with names as a means of expressing familiarity.

Besides names, other words can be truncated as well. Usually, truncated words other than truncated names are called **clippings**. Consider the following data and try to make observations on which part of the base survives in the derivatives. Again, the acute accent indicates the syllable with the main stress.

(57) **base**   **derivative**
     dóctor   →   doc
     véterinary   →   vet
     labóratory   →   lab
     advértisement   →   ad
     examinátion   →   exám
     celébrity   →   celéb
     exécutive   →   exéc

Several interesting observations can be made on the basis of the data in (57). First, most clippings in (57) are monosyllabic or disyllabic words. Second, usually the first part of the base survives in the clipping. In many cases, it is just the first syllable that survives, as in *advértisement* → *ad*. In some cases, it is the first and at the same time the stressed syllable, as in *dóctor* → *doc* or *véterinary* → *vet*. Similarly to name truncations, clippings often express the speaker's familiarity with the concept they denote.

Another type of shortening is illustrated in (58):

(58) **bases**   **derivative**
    motor+hotel → motel
    breakfast+lunch → brunch
    smoke+fog → smog
    situation+comedy → sitcom
    parachute+troops → paratroops

The examples in (58) are created by two processes: deleting parts of both bases or of only one base, and combining the remaining parts into a new word. Such words are called **blends** since the remaining parts are 'blended', i.e. mixed together. Blending is similar to clipping since it involves deletion. However, in blends two bases are used, whereas in clippings only one base is used.

As you can infer from the examples, usually the first part of the first word and the last part of the second word are combined in a blend. Thus, in *brunch* it is *br-* from *breakfast* and *-unch* from *lunch*. In some cases, as in *paratroops*, parts of only one base are deleted (*parachute* → *para*), whereas the other base, *troops*, enters the blend without deletion.

The following words are also formed by shortening, although of a different type:

(59)   **bases**   **derivative**
  a. United Kingdom → *UK*
     Member of Parliament → *MP*
     portable document format → *PDF*
     digital video disc → *DVD*
  b. North Atlantic Treaty Organisation → *NATO*
     National Aeronautics and Space Administration → *NASA*
     Test of English as a Foreign Language → *TOEFL*
     lightware amplification by stimulated emission of radiation → *laser*

The examples in (59) are also formed by deletion and, similarly to blends, involve more than one word. In fact, most of them involve multi-word combinations. However, in contrast to blends and clippings, the deletion in the examples in (59) is not based on the phonological structure of words, but purely on orthography. Moreover, deletion is more radical, in that the bases in (59) are stripped down to their initial letters. Words formed by combining only the initial letters of multi-word combinations are called **abbreviations**. There are two types of abbreviations, as you can see in (59). In the examples in (59a), the initial letters are combined and pronounced as a sequence of letters, in the way in which you spell the letters in the alphabet: UK [juːˈkeɪ], MP [emˈpiː], etc. Such words are called **initialisms** (since the 'initials' are pronounced). The examples in (59b) are pronounced as regular words, i.e. following the regular reading rules of English, as, for example, NATO [ˈneɪtəʊ] or NASA [ˈnæsə]. The technical term for such words is **acronyms**.

In the present section we have seen that new words can also be created by shortening, a word-formation process involving deletion of linguistic material. It has been shown that shortening can be done in a variety of different ways. In clippings and name truncations, a part of a base word is deleted. Blending involves deletion of a part of one base or of two bases and combining the remaining parts. In abbreviations, multi-word combinations are shortened to their initial letters. In spite of its variability, shortening is not a random process but follows certain regularities.

3.8. Conclusion

In the present chapter we discovered another core area of linguistics: morphology. Morphology deals with the internal structure of words and ways of creating new words. We have seen that words can be divided into smallest meaningful units called morphemes. Morphemes differ in a variety of characteristics, such as their ability to occur independently (free vs. bound), their function (inflectional vs. derivational), their position with respect to each other (root, base, affix), and their position with respect to the base (prefixes, suffixes, and infixes). Using the inventory of different morpheme types, we are able to do a thorough morphological analysis of various complex words of a language. It was also shown that morphemes are abstract units that, depending on the context, acquire concrete shapes, called allomorphs. The distribution of allomorphs can be conditioned by a number of different factors, phonological, morphological, and lexical. Finally, it was demonstrated that a number of different strategies can be used for creating new words, such as affixation, compounding, conversion, and different shortening processes.

In the next chapter, we will move on to a higher level in the linguistic hierarchy and investigate how words are organised into sentences.

Further reading

For general introductions to morphology and morphological theory I recommend Aronoff and Fudeman (2005), Bauer (2003), Haspelmath (2002), and Katamba and Stonham (2006), which are all based on data from different languages, including English. Detailed introductions to English word-formation are provided in Bauer (1983) and Plag (2003). An overview of English word-formation processes can be found in Adams (2001) and Marchand (1969), both of which contain a great number of examples.

Exercises

Basic level

Exercise 3.1.: Types of morphemes

Analyse the words below into constituent morphemes and identify the type of each morpheme (free or bound, root, base, affix (prefix or suffix), inflectional or derivational (for affixes)).

(60) premodernism   uncivilised   demilitarisation   historicity
     simpler   manservant's   recreated   minimalists

Exercise 3.2.: Morphological analysis of words

Analyse the morphological structure of the words below. Draw tree diagrams and provide arguments for your analysis.

(61) deformation   removable
     disorganisation   interdependency

Exercise 3.3.: Allomorphs

Below you will find a number of English verbs in their past-tense form. Identify the allomorphs of the past tense morpheme. State the rules of their distribution and determine the type of conditioning.

(62) [stɑːtəd]   [kɔːld]   [pleɪd]   [mɪst]   [pækt]
     [stɒpt]   [pʊʃt]   [ædəd]   [ɹɒbd]   [dɹægd]
     [tiːzd]   [nɪtəd]   [beɪðd]   [feɪdəd] [snɔːd]

Exercise 3.4.: Word-formation processes

Identify the type of word-formation process by which the following words have been created. Explain in detail how they are derived.

(63) telebanking   rosewater   hush-hush   semi-circle
     to narrow   Bart   hunter-gatherer   postmastership
     radar   fire extinguisher Chaplinesque   deforestation
     job-hopper   PO   dorm   cosmonaut

The structure of words: morphology

Advanced level

Exercise 3.5.: Restrictions on the productivity of affixes

The data below contain possible and impossible derivatives with the English suffix *-en*. Try to figure out the restrictions that rule out the impossible formations in (64b) and (64c). (Hint: the restriction has nothing to do with meaning).

(64) a. brighten   bright
      harden   hard
      fatten   fat
      strengthen   strength
      weaken   weak
   b. *calmen   calm
      *freeen   free
      *greenen   green
      *smallen   small
   c. *easien   easy
      *vividen   vivid
      *curiousen   curious
      *obedienten   obedient

Exercise 3.6.: Directionality of conversion

The data below show some word-pairs created by conversion. For each word, the date of its first attestation in the English language, as documented in the *Oxford English Dictionary*, and its frequency of occurrence in the *British National Corpus* are given. Determine the directionality of conversion in each word-pair, using the criteria discussed in section 3.7.4. above. To do so, compare the two members of each pair in terms of a) their dates of first attestation as given in the OED, b) their frequency of occurrence in the BNC, c) their semantic complexity. Discuss on the basis of this comparison which member is more likely to be the base and which the derivative. If you encounter any problems, discuss them and their possible solutions.

(65)

	date of first attestation	BNC frequency		date of first attestation	BNC frequency
clean (A)	883	4591	to clean (V)	c1450	1576
sweet (A)	c825	2924	sweet (N)	1300	114
light (V)	c900	4357	light (N)	971	18853

Chapter 4
The structure of sentences: syntax

4.1. Introduction: rules and grammar

When people speak or write they do so usually in strings of words that are not arbitrary in their sequence. That is, we cannot form sentences by adding just any word to any word preceding it. And speakers of a language have rather clear intuitions about what is a possible string of words in their language, and what is not. For example, we know that the sentence in (1a) is a possible English sentence, while the sentence in (1b) is an impossible sentence. Following the usual conventions in linguistics, I mark impossible sentences by an asterisk:

(1) a. I don't like getting up early.
 b. *Up earlyn't getting do like I.

Likewise, in (2) speaker B may answer the question posed by speaker A in various ways, but not in others. Consider the answers in (2a-h):

(2)   A: Where did Jane put the stupid key for the garage?
 a. B: I have no idea.
 b. B: No idea.
 c. B: Right there.
 d. B: On the shelf.
 e. B: I said it's in the closet.
 f. B: *Have no.
 g. B: *Shelf the on.
 h. B: *Key in closet.

The answers (2f), (2g), and (2h) are not possible. Of the possible answers, (2a) and (2e) are full sentences, while (2b), (2c), (2d) are not. We see that the possible answers to the question can consist of a full sentence, or only a part of a sentence. The impossible answers in (2f), (2g) and (2h) show, however, that not just any part of a sentence is an acceptable answer. What is it then that makes a given string of words acceptable or unacceptable? First of all we need to realise that the impossibility or unacceptability of the answers is not really a matter of meaning or logic. While (2f) might be practically uninterpretable, the order of words in (2g) would be grammatically perfect and the answer fully comprehensible in other languages (e.g. Japanese). Hence, it seems that the interpretability of a given sentence depends on the types of rules that a given language provides. And even sentences that clearly violate these rules can be interpretable, as is the case with (2h), which, though certainly not in accordance with the rules of English grammar, is still meaningful for speakers of English. The reason why speakers of English don't like the starred sentences from above is because of grammar: we consider them 'ungrammatical', i.e. not in accordance with the grammatical rules of English. Obviously, these rules are concerned with the structure of sentences, i.e. their **syntax**.

Syntax is usually considered the core of a language's grammar, but what exactly do people mean when they speak of **grammar**? There are two important senses of the word 'grammar' that we should be aware of. In linguistics, the term 'grammar' refers to the complete system of phonological, morphological, syntactic and semantic information and rules that speakers of a given language possess. As you have already seen in the previous chapters, language is a very complex, well organised system of abstract entities and categories, and their realisation in speech. This system, or the speaker's tacit knowledge thereof, is called the 'grammar' of a language.

This scientific meaning of 'grammar' differs substantially from the everyday usage of the term you might be familiar with. In everyday language, 'grammar' simply refers to a special kind of book. And in this book one finds rules which one needs to obey in order to use a particular language correctly. Grammar books are not meant to be entertaining and are usually consulted (rather than read) if one is not sure about how to use a particular word or expression. In other words, the grammar book contains a description of the system of rules referred to by linguists as 'grammar'. The important point now is that, given the complexity of human language, the grammar book can only be an incomplete representation of the language system in question, i.e. an approximation of the vast knowledge that speakers actually have. As a natural consequence, many rules that one finds in grammar books can be shown to be not quite adequate, or simply wrong, since they are not in accordance with the reality of the language. Unfortunately, this is especially true for rules in grammar books that are written for less advanced second language learners. The reason for this state of affairs is that — for mainly didactic reasons — these grammars simplify the intricacies of pertinent rules considerably. Let us look at an example for illustration.

In a number of school grammar books for German learners of English, we find the rule that in a sentence with more than one expression of manner, place and time, expressions of manner should precede expressions of place, which in turn should precede expressions of time. This is encapsulated in the phrase 'manner before place before time' that many German learners of English memorise in their school lessons. A careful analysis of large numbers of naturally occurring sentences reveals, however, that this alleged 'rule' is more often violated than observed by native speakers of English. Native speakers are in fact much more inclined to place shorter expressions before longer ones, irrespective of their meaning (cf. Hawkins 1999). The inadequacy of the manner-place-time rule can be illustrated with a few sentences that do not obey the would-be rule but are nevertheless in accordance with English grammar (i.e. the language system):

(3) a. As promised,
        Joan met me at noon in the dark and terribly crowded station.
                     time   place

    b. Jaye played soccer last night like an Italian defender.
                            time   manner

How can we deal with the fact that native speakers do not follow the alleged rule? Tell the native speakers that their grammar (i.e. their language system) is wrong? Certainly not, since we can assume that native speakers have successfully internalised the real rules of their language. Furthermore, native speakers of English are quite uniform in not following the alleged rule, and employing instead a different strategy (roughly 'short before long', all other things being equal). Hence, the native speaker's rule-system is right, and the grammar book (or rather: its author) is wrong. We have to state that the manner-place-time-rule is not a rule of English. It may exist in grammar books and may be taught to German learners of English, but it does not exist in the minds of English native speakers and has nothing to do with the reality of the language. In general, it is the task of the linguist to describe this reality, and not to think up ill-founded rules and impose them on others.

To summarise, the authors of grammar books can only attempt to describe the language system, and they often fail to do so adequately, due to the complex nature of the language system, or due to their lack of expertise as linguists, or due to their desire to simplify matters for didactic purposes. Users of grammar books should therefore be very careful citing such books as evidence for what is 'correct' or 'incorrect' in a language.

Having clarified the notion of grammar, we may now return to our subject matter, the syntax of English, to see how sentences in this language are structured. What does it mean that a sentence has 'structure'? The *Oxford English Dictionary* defines 'structure' generally as an "organised ... combination of mutually connected and dependent parts or elements" (s.v. structure). The study of syntax is thus the investigation of the parts sentences consist of and their connections and dependencies. There are many theories of syntax around, with a lot of theoretical and technical apparatus. In this chapter we will largely ignore individual theories and instead try to get a feel for syntactic argumentation, i.e. the kinds of reasoning that can be adduced in favour of or against particular syntactic analyses. This will prepare the reader for the study of the more specialised syntactic literature.

In the following sections, we will first look at the building blocks of sentences and their internal structure, then turn to the functions of these structural units and finally discuss how the structural and functional levels of analysis can be related to each other.

4.2. The building blocks: words and phrases

4.2.1. Constituency tests and phrases

Let us start with the analysis of a rather straightforward sentence, and ask ourselves what parts or structural units we can detect that can combine to form the kind of 'organised combination' mentioned above. We will start our discussion by investigating the sentence in (4):

(4) Many people will go to the station every morning.

Simply using our intuition we might say that each word is a kind of building block for this and certainly many other sentences. The fact that in writing we use spaces between words is a reflection of that intuition. In addition to the words, you would perhaps also want to say that [*Many people*] belongs together and thus forms a structural unit, that [*to the station*] belongs together, and that [*every morning*] is also a larger structural unit within the sentence. In analogy to structural units in phonology and morphology, we will call syntactic units **constituents**, or, in more syntax-specific terminology, **phrases**. Obviously, words are also syntactic constituents, and we will later see that constituents or phrases may sometimes consist of only one word, for example a pronoun or a proper noun. In writing we use brackets to mark constituents. Returning to the analysis of (4), you may even hypothesise that [*will go*] might form a constituent, but that [*station every*] or [*people will*] are not constituents. We can represent our intuitions about this sentence in the form of a tree diagram. The tree in (5) shows us that, according to our hypotheses, the sentence

'S' contains four constituents which are all on the same level (for reasons of clarity we omit brackets around individual words inside larger constituents):

(5) a first tree diagram for [*Many people will go to the station every morning*] (to be revised as we go along)

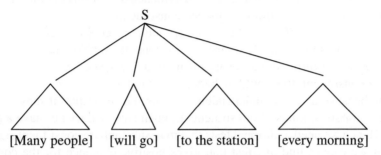

Note that the tree diagram so far does not say anything yet about the internal structure of the phrases [*Many people*], [*to the station*] and [*every morning*], which, for that reason, are represented by simple triangles without internal branches. Before dealing with the internal structure of phrases let us first turn to the obvious question of what kind of evidence we can find to support our intuitions about the constituency of the sentence. Syntacticians have developed a number of tests that can be applied to sentences in order to prove constituent status, some of which we will now discuss.

The first is **pronominalisation**, that is the substitution of a constituent by a pronoun. The reasoning runs as follows: if you can replace a string of words by a pronoun, this string must be a constituent. This seems easy for [*Many people*] and [*to the station*], still possible for [*every morning*], but less so for [*will go*]. This is illustrated in (6), with the pronouns appearing in bold print:

(6) a. **They** will go **there** every morning.
    b. They will go there **when**?
    c. **When** will they go there?

In (6a) *they* pronominalises [*Many people*], and *there* pronominalises [*to the station*]. Note that these examples show us that the term 'pronoun', if taken literally as 'replacing a noun', is somewhat misleading. The pronoun *they* does not stand for a noun, but for the whole phrase, and can in fact not be used to stand for only the noun *people* in that phrase (cf. *[*many they*]). Similarly, the pronoun *there* does not stand for a noun, but for a larger phrase. And so does the interrogative pronoun *when*. It would therefore be best to rename pronouns as 'pro-phrases' or generally 'pro-forms'. While the term 'pro-phrase' is (unfortunately) not in use in linguistics, the term **pro-form** is, and we will therefore use it interchangeably with the established term pronoun, keeping in mind that a 'pro-noun' is actually a pro-phrase. Returning to our pronominalisation test, we can see that in (6b) and (6c), the string [*every morning*] is replaced by a so-called **wh-pronoun**. Given that these pronominalisations work perfectly, we have good evidence that [*Many people*], [*to the station*], and [*every morning*] are indeed constituents.

But what about [*will go*]? There is no pronoun that could replace those two words. Does that mean that [*will go*] is not a constituent? Not necessarily, because we cannot turn around the argumentation. If a test does not work for a putative constituent, this could be because it is not a constituent, but it could also be because of other, independent reasons. For example, it may be the case that for some kinds of constituents English simply does not have a pronoun. Hence we need additional tests that may substantiate constituent status. Only if we cannot find *any* test that gives positive evidence for the constituency of a given string, can we conclude that our string in question is really not a constituent.

Another such test for constituency is **movement**. If a string of words can be moved to other sentential positions, it is proof of the string's being a constituent. This test works nicely for [*to the station*] and [*every morning*], but not really for [*many people*] and [*will go*], as is illustrated in (7). The original position of the moved string is marked by a gap indicated by underscores:

(7) a. [To the station] many people will go ___ every morning.
 b. [Every morning] many people will go to the station ___.
 c. *___ will go to the station [many people] every morning.
 d. *[Will go] many people ___ to the station every morning.

In the case of [*many people*], we can see why movement is impossible. [*Many people*] is the subject of the sentence, and the sentential position of subjects in English is severely restricted, in that they generally occur before the verb complex. Hence, although we have already good evidence that [*Many people*] is a constituent, there is an independent reason, i.e. a rule for subject position, that precludes successful application of the movement test. Note that the string *will go* fails this constituency test, just as it failed the pronominalisation test. Hence, there is no evidence so far that this string forms a constituent.

A third test is the so-called **coordination test**, according to which it is only constituents that can be coordinated by the coordinating conjunction *and*. This conjunction has the wonderful property of combining only constituents of the same kind. Such constitutents can be simple words (cf. *black and white, night and day, twist and shout, up and down*), but also phrases, as illustrated in (8):

(8) a. [[Many people] and [my friends]] will go to the station every morning.
   b. Many people will go [[to the station] and [into the woods]] every morning.
   c. Many people will go to the station [[every morning] and [every evening]].

So, if we can coordinate two expressions with *and*, this is good evidence for their being constituents. The coordination test can even show us that there is yet another constituent detectable, [*go to the station every morning*]:

(9) Many people will [[go to the station every morning] and [come home at night]].

That [*go to the station every morning*] is a constituent can be further substantiated by pronominalisation. English has a pronominal phrase that can replace constituents such as [*go to the station every morning*], namely [*do so*]:

(10) Many people will **do so**.

Our analysis of [*go to the station every morning*] as a constituent is further corroborated by the behaviour of this string when we add a tag question:

(11) Many people will [go to the station every morning], won't they ___?

The tag question leaves a gap, in which we could insert the missing string [*go to the station every morning*]. This **gapping** behaviour is a fourth kind of test, which works with certain types of phrases. Surprisingly, the coordination test can also be applied to [*will go to the station every morning*], as in (12):

(12) Many people [[will go to the station every morning] and [may stay there until 10 p.m. every night]].

This shows us that even this very large string forms a structural unit.

Finally, there is the so-called **sentence-fragment test**, which brings us back to the discussion of possible answers to the question in (2). We saw that only certain types of string can form possible sentence fragments which speakers can use to, for example, answer a question. If we apply this test to the constituents in our sample sentence (4), we could, for example, answer the questions in (13) with the respective sentence fragments given in (14). This provides good evidence for their being constituents.

(13) a. Who will go to the station every morning?
   b. Where will many people go every morning?
   c. When will many people go to the station?
   d. What will many people do?

(14) a. [Many people].
   b. [To the station].
   c. [Every morning].
   d. [Go to the station every morning].

Let us summarise our findings so far. We have found good evidence for the following constituents:

(15) [Many people]
   [will go to the station every morning]
   [go to the station every morning]
   [to the station]
   [every morning]

We did not find empirical evidence for our hypothesis that [*will*] and [*go*] together would form a separate constituent (in spite of the fact that your school grammar books may have suggested just that). We did find evidence, however, that [*will*] forms a constituent together with [*go to the station every morning*]. This means that we have to revise our tree diagram accordingly:

(16) revised tree diagram for [*Many people will go to the station every morning*]

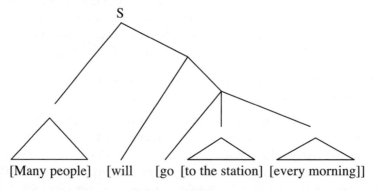

[Many people] [will [go [to the station] [every morning]]

We can now see graphically that the sentence consists of two major constituents, represented by the two lines branching off the top node 'S'. The right one of these two branches splits up further into two constituents, of which again the right one splits further into three constituents. Before we turn to the more detailed investigation of the internal structure of phrases, we should apply our tests to another sentence in order to see how the kind of syntactic reasoning developed so far works on another example. Take a look at the sentence (17) and set up some hypotheses about which strings of words might form a constituent. Before reading on, try to apply pronominalisation, movement, and coordination tests to test whether your hypothesis about the constituency is correct:

(17) My brother invited the girl to his party.

[*My brother*] can be replaced by *he*, [*the girl*] can be pronominalised by the personal pronoun *her*, [*to his party*] can be coordinated with a similar phrase, as in [[*to his party*] *and* [*to the excursion*]], and [*invited the girl to his party*] can be pronominalised by [*did so*]. Thus, we arrive at the following tree diagram:

(18)

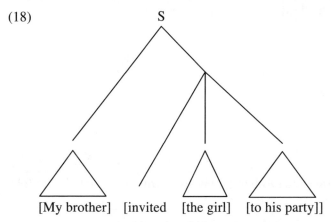

Now consider (19), which is a somewhat more complicated case:

(19) My sister will read the letter to John.

The application of our pronominalisation tests may first look straightforward. The status of [*my sister*] is uncontroversial, we can easily pronominalise this string by *she*. The string [*read the letter to John*] is also uncontroversial, it can be pronominalised with [*do so*]. The string [*will read the letter to John*] may be coordinated with, for example [*may regret it afterwards*], and is thus also a constituent. But what about *the letter to John*? Two possibilities suggest themselves. Under one interpretation of the sentence, this string refers to a letter that is directed to John, and this letter will be read by the speaker's sister. There is, however, also another interpretation, according to which it is my sister's reading of the letter (and not the letter itself) that is directed to John. In the second case, we could pronominalise *the letter* with the personal pronoun *it* or the wh-pronoun *what* and get the appropriate interpretation:

120   *The structure of sentences: syntax*

(20) My sister will read *it* to John.
      What will my sister read to John? — The letter.

If, in contrast, it is a letter addressed to John that is being read by my sister, [*the letter to John*] forms a constituent, as evidenced by the pronominalisation test, in which [*the letter to John*] is replaced by *it* or *what*:

(21) My sister will read *it*.
      What will my sister read? — The letter to John (not the e-mail from Jane).

The two interpretations with their respective constituency can be made visually more transparent by drawing tree diagrams. The respective interpretations are given in the third line below the trees in (22):

(22)

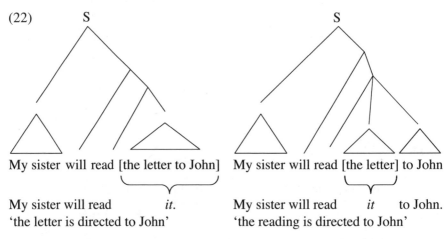

My sister will read [the letter to John]   My sister will read [the letter] to John
My sister will read   *it*.   My sister will read   *it*   to John.
'the letter is directed to John'   'the reading is directed to John'

The tree diagrams bring out the crucial structural difference between the two interpretations. In order to describe the facts represented in the two tree diagrams, some more terminology is helpful. Thus we can speak of 'mother' and 'sister' nodes when describing relationships in a tree. A mother node is defined as the node immediately above a given node, and sister nodes are nodes that share the same mother node. Using these terms we can say that in the left tree, [*the letter to John*] forms a single constituent and is the sister node of the verb, while in the right tree [*the letter*] and [*to John*] do not form one constituent. Instead, they are two constituents sharing the same mother node with the verb and thus are sisters to each other and each of them is also a sister to the verb.

For obvious reasons, in cases in which different interpretations arise through different sentence structures assigned to the same strings of words, we speak of **structural ambiguity**. Having clarified how we can find constituents in a sentence, we may now turn to the question of the internal make-up of multi-word constituents.

4.2.2. The internal structure of phrases

It seems that there exist different types of phrases, whose possible structures are somehow dependent on the most important word of the respective phrase. For example, in the phrases given below, the most important word is a noun, and the noun can be accompanied by certain types of words in certain positions. Have a look at (23):

(23) [his **sister**]
[their red-haired **brother**]
[a **letter** to John]
[the best **actor** in town]
[this good **student** from Washington]
[my last **friend** at school]
[**people** who knock on the door]

It seems that within a phrase certain types of words always occur in the same type of position. This becomes clear if we draw a table, as in (24):

(24)

slot 1	slot 2	slot 3	slot 4
his		sister	
their	red-haired	brother	
a		letter	to John
the	best	actor	in town
this	good	student	from Washington
my	last	friend	at school
		people	who knock on the door

There are four slots where certain kinds of elements can go. The central element of the phrase, the noun, is in slot 3, while slot 2 is optionally occupied by an adjective, and the first slot is occupied by an article (*the, a*), a demonstrative (*this*) or a possessive (*his, their*). Note that this slot can also remain empty, as for example in [*people who knock on the door*]. Slot 4 can either remain empty or may contain smaller or larger constituents.

We will call the most important element of a phrase its **head** and name the phrases after their heads. Thus, in (24) we have examples of **noun phrases** (abbreviated as 'NPs'), i.e. of phrases headed by a noun. As we can see in the following examples, other kinds of phrases have other kinds of head. The heads are given in bold, and the name of the phrase is given as a subscript label:

(25) a. [**to** the station]_PP
       [**at** school]_PP
    b. [**proud** of his results]_AP
       [extremely **expensive**]_AP
    c. [**go** to the station]_VP
       [**drink** a glass of milk]_VP

Following the practice of naming the phrase after its head, we can say that in (25a) we find a preposition to be the most important constituent of the phrase, in (25b) it is an adjective, and in (25c) it is the verb. Hence we have two **prepositional phrases** (PPs) in (25a), two **adjective phrases** (APs) in (25b), and two **verb phrases** (VPs) in (25c). Our examples also show that phrases can contain other phrases. For instance, the VP [*go to the station*] contains the PP [*to the station*], which in turn contains the NP [*the station*].

But how do we determine whether a given word is 'the most important element'? What makes it 'important'? One answer to this question would be semantic, i.e. the head is semantically the most important element. For example, the prepositional phrase [*to the station*] indicates a direction or goal, and this meaning is chiefly contributed by the preposition *to*, and not by the NP following the preposition. This is evidenced by the contrast between the directional preposition *to* and the preposition *at*, which indicates a location (cf. [*at the station*]). Similar semantic arguments hold for other kinds of phrases and their semantically central heads. For instance, in the adjective phrase [*very proud of his results*]_AP the adjective *proud* is semantically central, and in the verb phrase [*drink a glass of milk*]_VP it is the verb *drink*.

The other crucial cluster of properties of heads concern their structural relation to the other constituents. Thus, in verb phrases and prepositional phrases the head assigns case to the constituent to its right, which is the reason why we find *him* instead of *he*, and *her* instead of *she* in (26):

(26) a. I saw *him/*he* yesterday.
       I met *her/*she* yesterday.
    b. This was a surprise for *him/*he*.
       This was a surprise for *her/*she*.

Another indication for a word being the head of its phrase is that the head of the phrase, for example a noun, can have the same distribution as the phrase it heads. Having 'the same distribution' means that in all sentential positions where we can find a given phrase, we should also be able to find only the head of that kind of phrase. (27) illustrates this:

(27) a. [The two little **kids**] meet their friends regularly at the playground.
    a.' [**Kids**] meet their friends regularly at the playground.
    b. John meets [the two little **kids**] regularly at the playground.
    b.' John meets [**kids**] regularly at the playground.

The final indication that a word is the head of a phrase is that the phrase obtains its semantic and syntactic properties from its head. This can be seen in pronominalisation: the noun phrase [*my older sister*] can only be replaced by the personal pronouns *she* or *her*, but not by *it*, *he* or *they*. This is a consequence of the properties of the head *sister*, which is an animate noun, has feminine gender, and is singular. These properties call for the pronouns *she* or *her*, and these properties do not come from the non-head words *my* or *older*. Syntacticians say that the head **projects** its properties onto the phrase as a whole (which is also the reason why phrases are often called **projections** of their head).

Talking about heads and their properties raises the question of how we know whether we are dealing with a noun, a preposition, an adjective or a verb as head in a given example. Most of us have learned in school that there are things like adjectives, nouns, verbs, prepositions. These classes are variably referred to as **word-classes**, **syntactic categories**, **parts-of-speech**, or **lexical categories**. But what exactly *is* a noun and what distinguishes a noun from, say, a verb, a preposition etc.? Before discussing in more detail the internal structure of phrases, we should take a closer look at those syntactic categories.

Of course one can look up the word-class of a word in a dictionary, but this shifts the problem to the dictionary-makers. How do they arrive at their decisions? And how can we tell whether the dictionary-makers are right in their decisions? And what about new words that have not yet made it into dictionaries?

Generally, there are three types of criteria that are used to find out about the word-class of a given word: semantic, morphological, and syntactic. We will discuss each in turn, starting with the semantic classification. In elementary schools it is quite common to introduce the word-class distinctions by pointing out that different types of words express different kinds of meanings. In this line of reasoning one would, for example, say that nouns refer to things or persons, verbs to actions or events, that adjectives express properties or qualities, and prepositions express relations. While this may seem intuitively attractive, a closer inspection reveals that the semantic approach to word-classes is not entirely satisfactory. Nouns like *love, production* and *restlessness* show that nouns can also refer to feelings, actions and properties, respectively, not only to things. And not all verbs seem to refer to actions or events, as the verb *seem* itself illustrates. What is even more disturbing for a primarily semantic approach to word-classes is the fact that we can quite easily determine the word-class of words whose meaning we don't know at all. Consider the following sentence:

(28) John gnorbed the pirkness only twenty pripless skirps ago.

I think most readers would agree if I said that *gnorbed* is probably a verb, *pirkness* is a noun, *pripless* is an adjective and *skirps* is a noun. If so, this is proof that you can determine the syntactic category of *gnorbed, pirkness, pripless*, and *skirps*, even though you have no idea what these words mean. And you cannot have any idea what they mean because I invented these words only a minute ago, with no idea in mind what they could mean. So how do we know the word-class? Here our two other kinds of criteria come into play, morphological and syntactic. Let us begin with the morphological ones.

We know that words of a particular category have a specific morphological make-up. Thus only verbs take the past tense suffix *-ed*, the suffix *-ness* is only found on nouns, the suffix *-less* is restricted to adjectives, and *-s* is a suffix that expresses plural on nouns. From this it follows that *gnorbed* is probably a verb, *pirkness* is a noun, *pripless* is an adjective and *skirps* is a noun. But, you might be tempted to say, how can we know that *gnorbed* is not an adjective, since there are also adjectives with the suffix *-ed*, such as *beheaded, long-haired* or *blue-eyed*? And how do we know that the suffix *-s* on *skirp* is a nominal plural suffix and not a third person singular *-s* suffix? These are very good questions, and they show that, solely on the basis of the morphology, *gnorbed* could indeed just as well be an adjective and *skirps* a verb.

What speaks strongly against such an analysis is, however, the position of these words in the sentence. This brings us to the syntactic criteria for word-class membership. Given *John* as the first element of the sentence, we expect it to be the subject of the sentence, which, in English, should be followed by the verb, which in turn should be followed by its object. Assuming *gnorbed* to be a verb is in accordance with this expectation, while *gnorbed* as an adjective would be in the wrong place. Independent evidence for *pirkness* being a noun comes from it being preceded by the article *the*, which is quite common for nouns in English. Positional considerations also support the analysis of *pripless* and *skirps*. Adjectives often immediately precede nouns and nouns often immediately follow adjectives. Furthermore, if *skirps* was a verb, it would be in the wrong place and the sentence would be ungrammatical. We can support our analysis also by substituting *gnorbed* by an adjective (e.g. *bad*) and *skirps* by a verb (e.g. *entertains*). Given that we think that such an analysis would be wrong we would predict that the substitution would lead to an ungrammatical sentence. This is indeed the case, as (29) shows:

(29) *John *bad* the pirkness only twenty pripless *entertains* ago.

Having established the notion of word-classes and the methodology of how to figure out the word-class of a given item, let us briefly look at the set of word classes and their major properties. We have already mentioned nouns, verbs, adjectives and prepositions, but there are more word-classes around: adverbs (e.g. *extremely, often*), articles (e.g. *a, the*), demonstratives (e.g. *that, these*), possessives (e.g. *my, theirs*), conjunctions (e.g. *and, because, that*), etc. For reasons of space we cannot discuss all of these, but we will take a closer look at articles, demonstratives, and possessives. Looking at the syntactic distribution of these items, we find that they may occur in the first slot of noun phrases, as evidenced in (30):

(30)

slot 1	slot 2	slot 3
his	younger	sister
this	good	student
the	best	actor
determiner	**adjective**	**noun**

Uncontroversially, the words in slot 3 form a class (called nouns), and the words in slot 2 form a class (called adjectives). The words in each class share a specific syntactic position and also other properties, as discussed above. Along the same lines we can state that the words in slot 1, i.e. *my, this,* and *the*, form a larger class (with different subclasses, such as definite and indefinite articles, possessives and demonstratives). This larger class is called **determiners**.

Interestingly, demonstratives and possessives may not only occur in slot 1 of an NP, but also as words *replacing* a whole phrase, i.e. as pro-forms acting as the head (and only constituent) of the phrase. This is illustrated in (31):

(31) a. You met [your sister], I met [my sister], she met [her sister], he met [his sister].
You met [yours], I met [mine], she met [hers], he met [his].
b. [These cars] are very expensive, but [those cars] are not.
[These] are very expensive, but [those] are not.

As we can see in (31a), most possessive nominal heads have a form different from their determiner form (e.g. *my/mine, your/yours, her/hers,* also *our/ours, their/theirs*), but not all of them do. The possessive determiner *his* has the same form as the possessive pronoun *his*. And demonstrative determiners always have the same form as demonstrative heads.

We may now return to our tree diagrams from above and label the phrases and constituents accordingly, thereby enriching our tree structure with categorial, i.e. word-class, information. We take the phrases from (25) above and provide each node with a categorial label, depending on the kind of constituent this node represents. We use the following new abbreviations: N = noun, V = verb, A = adjective, D = determiner, P = preposition, Adv = adverb.

(32) a. prepositional phrases

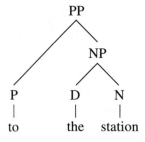 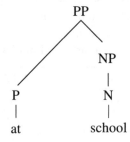

b. adjective phrases

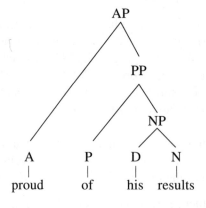 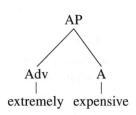

c. verb phrases

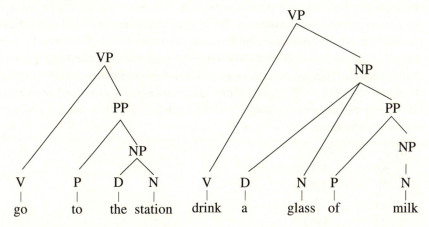

We can apply analogous labeling procedures to whole sentences, as illustrated in (33):

(33)

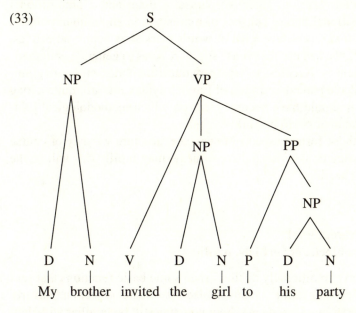

To summarise, we have seen that there is good empirical evidence for the internal structure of sentences. There are a number of different tests that can be employed to test hypotheses about constituency and the word-class membership of a given word. These tests can lead us to a detailed and well-motivated description of the internal structure of sentences and their constituents. Word-class membership was shown to be important for the construction of phrases, because phrase structure provides distinct slots which can only be occupied by certain types of constituents. These considerations have led syntacticians to develop whole grammars on the basis of rules that build syntactic structures. These so-called phrase structure grammars use so-called **phrase structure rules** to generate sentences. In (34) this is demonstrated with some rules that can be stated on the basis of our sentences and phrases from above. Note that some constituents appear in parentheses because they are not obligatory in the given phrase:

(34) S → NP VP
    NP → (D) (AP) N (PP)
    PP → P NP
    VP → V (NP) (PP)
    AP → (Adv) A

The above rules can be read as 'a sentence consists of an NP and a VP, an NP consists of a determiner, an adjective phrase, a noun and a prepositional phrase, a prepositional phrase consists of a preposition and a noun phrase', and so on. And if we then have a list of words marked as nouns, adjectives, determiners, etc., we can use the phrase structure rules to generate grammatical English sentences. Needless to say, from our little phrase structure grammar to a full and adequate description of English syntax it is still quite a long way to go, but it should have become clear on which methodological principles such a grammar could be built.

Apart from these formal aspects of sentence structure we may of course also look at the functions sentential constituents may fulfill. This will be the topic of the next section.

4.3. The functional level: subjects, objects, adverbials, predicates

Grammarians have traditionally distinguished some basic functions that sentential constituents can fulfill, namely subject, predicate, object and adverbial. From your grammar lessons in school you may still be familiar with definitions of these notions. For example, subjects are usually said to represent the entity which the sentence is about, or to represent the 'doer of the action', while objects represent the entities that are affected by the action denoted by the verb. Adverbials are constituents that are said to give the circumstances of the event denoted by the rest of the sentence (such as time, place, manner, reason, etc.). In sentence (33), for example, we would say that [*My brother*] is the subject of the verb *invited*, [*the girl*] is the object of the verb *invited*, and [*to his party*] is an adverbial. The term **predicate** is used in a number of different ways in traditional grammar, school grammar books, and formal linguistics. For example, in ancient grammar 'predicate' refers to everything in a sentence apart from the subject. In this frame of thought, a predicate is that part of a sentence that says something about the subject. In contrast, some school grammars use 'predicate' to refer to auxiliary and main verbs in a sentence, while others use the term 'predicator' for the main verb and the term 'predicate' in the ancient sense. To avoid terminological confusion, we will not use the terms 'predicate' or 'predicator', and simply employ the term 'verb'. Having clarified the potential terminological problems surrounding the notion of predicate we will now focus our discussion on the nature of the other sentence functions (subject, object and adverbial), because these are often felt to be much more problematic.

Although intuitively appealing, the definitions of these notions need to be refined in order to be really useful in the analysis of sentences. Let us begin with the notion of subject. One construction that is a challenge for the above-mentioned definition of subject is the passive. In sentences in the passive voice the subject is not the 'doer' of the action, but refers to an entity that is affected by an action. Consider the passive sentences in (35), in which the subject is given in bold:

(35) a. [**The house**] was bought by someone from Boston.
 b. [**The textbook**] was read by generations of students.
 c. [**The graduate students**] were trained in computational linguistics.

Why do we consider the NPs in bold in (35) subjects in spite of their not referring to the 'doers of the action'? One reason is their structural behaviour. Subjects trigger so-called **subject-verb agreement**, a syntactic process which requires subject and verb to share the same person and number features. If the subject is, for example, third person singular, the verb has to be marked as third person singular, too. This is the case in (35a) and (35b). Or, if we have a third person plural subject, the verb must agree with it in its features, i.e. must occur in its third person plural form, as in (35c).

Another structural criterion for subjecthood is the sentential position. Apart from some special types of sentences, the position of the subject in English is rather fixed. Subjects occur immediately before the verb phrase, with only certain adverbials being allowed to intervene. This is different from many other languages, where also other kinds of sentence functions are permitted in preverbal position. These facts are illustrated with data from English in (36) and data from German in (37), with English glosses given below each German word:

(36) a. [**She**]_{subject} [loves being outdoors]_{VP}.
　　b. [**We**]_{subject} [often] [go skiing in the nearby mountains]_{VP}.
　　c. [**They**]_{subject} [never] [came home so late]_{VP}.
　　d. *[So late]_{adverbial} came [**they**]_{subject} never home.
　　e. *[This man]_{object} know [**I**]_{subject} not.

(37) a. [Draußen zu sein]_{object} liebt [**sie**]_{subject} über alles.
　　　　outdoors to be　　　loves　she　　　above all
　　b. [Den Mann]_{object} kenne [**ich**]_{subject} nicht.
　　　　that man　　　know　I　　　not
　　c. [Oft]_{adverbial} gehen [**wir**]_{subject} Skifahren in den nahen Bergen.
　　　　often　　go　we　　　skiing　in the nearby mountains
　　d. [So spät]_{adverbial} kamen [**sie**]_{subject} nie nach Hause.
　　　　so late　　　came　they　　never home

The data in (36) show that in canonical English sentences the pre-VP position is reserved for subjects and that subjects are normally not allowed to appear in a different position, for example post-verbally, as in (36d) and (36e). In German, however, the first position of the sentence can be occupied also by other kinds of functions (i.e. objects and adverbials), as in (37a-d), and subjects can occur also in other positions, e.g. after the inflected verb.

Another interesting fact about subjects is that in English, subjects are obligatory. This is not true for all languages, as the following sentences from German illustrate:

(38) a. Hier darf　　　　getanzt werden.
　　　　here is-allowed　dance-passive-infinitive
　　b. You may dance here./Dancing is allowed here./*Here may danced be.

(39) a. Mir　　　ist　　　kalt.
　　　　1sg-dative　be-3sg　cold
　　b. I am cold./I feel cold./*Me is cold.

In (38a) there is no constituent in sight that would resemble a subject, and in (39a) the NP corresponding to the subject in English is in the dative case. In German the dative is, however, not the case for subjects. Furthermore, the verb in (39a) is third person singular, and thus does not show agreement with the NP denoting the experiencer of the cold (which is first person singular). Hence, no matter how hard we try, there is no subject in (39a). As illustrated in (38b) and (39b), English cannot do without a subject in such sentences.

The final criterion for subjecthood I want to discuss is a morphological one. In English there is a case distinction between subject and object. This means that depending on the function of a phrase in a sentence, this phrase will exhibit a certain form. Such forms that mark the grammatical function of noun phrases in a sentence or phrase are called **case** forms. The morphological distinction between subject case and object case in English is only visible with pronouns, as in (40), while full NPs always appear in the same form, as in (41):

(40) [He]$_{subject}$ took [her]$_{object}$ to a concert.
    [She]$_{subject}$ took [him]$_{object}$ to a concert.

(41) [My brother]$_{subject}$ took [my girl-friend]$_{object}$ to a concert.
    [My girl-friend]$_{subject}$ took [my brother]$_{object}$ to a concert.

(42) below gives the two sets of pronouns. As it becomes clear from this table, not all pronouns exhibit the said case distinction: the pronouns in bold do so, while the second person pronouns and the third person singular neuter pronoun are invariable:

(42)

subject case	object case	person	number	gender
I	me	1	singular	–
you	you	2	singular	–
he	him	3	singular	masculine
she	her	3	singular	feminine
it	it	3	singular	neuter
we	us	1	plural	–
you	you	2	plural	–
they	them	3	plural	–

In order to test now whether in a given sentence an NP is a subject, we can replace this NP by a personal pronoun and check its case form. If it is a pronoun in subject case (i.e. a subject pronoun), the noun phrase in question has the function of a subject. (43) illustrates this for the sentences in (35c) and (33), respectively:

(43) a. [**They**]/*[Them] were trained in computational linguistics. (Cf. (35c))
    b. [**He**]/*[Him] invited [**her**]/*[she] to his party. (Cf. (33))

The alleged subjects are well-behaved, they can only be replaced by the subject pronouns *they* and *he*, respectively, while the alleged object [*my sister*] must be pronominalised with an object pronoun, i.e. *her*. In sum, we arrived at four clear criteria for subjecthood: subject-verb agreement, position, obligatoriness and case marking.

Having clarified the notion of subject, we may now turn to the notion of object, for which similar criteria hold as for subjects. Thus, objects receive object case, as evidenced by pronominalisation facts just discussed. Objects do not show agreement with the verb, but instead are strongly restricted in their distribution. They must occur immediately after their verb, with other constituents not being allowed to intervene:

(44) a.   My brother often [invited]$_V$ [**her**]$_{object}$ to his parties.
     a'. *My brother [invited]$_V$ often [**her**]$_{object}$ to his parties.
     b.   My professor [wrote]$_V$ [**two textbooks**] last year.
     b'. *My professor [wrote]$_V$ last year [**two textbooks**].

In addition, objects are obligatory constituents, as can be easily seen if we erase the objects from the sentences in (44), as shown in (45). This leads to sentences of questionable acceptance. Note that I have erased also [*to his parties*] in (44a), although the status of this constituent as an object may be debatable. We will return to this issue below.

(45) a.   ?My brother often invited.
     b.   ?My professor wrote last year.

This means that there is a strong tendency for objects to be obligatorily present. Verbs that need an object are called **transitive verbs**, verbs that cannot take an object (e.g. *sleep, laugh*) are called **intransitive verbs**. However, there are sometimes sentences, in which even transitive verbs can do without an overtly expressed object. Consider (46):

(46) a.   John no longer eats regularly. He has lost a lot of weight.
     b.   They kissed and departed.
     c.   A: Did you receive the letter from your professor?
         B: Yes, he already wrote last year.

The objects of the verbs *eat* and *kiss*, respectively, are not surfacing in (46a) and (46b), although eating necessarily involves something to be eaten, and kissing involves someone or something to be kissed. Similar arguments hold for (46c). In such cases, we could say that the objects are only understood, or 'covert'. In general, it is not exactly clear under which circumstances which transitive verb can have a covert object. It should be obvious, however, that such cases are not the rule, but rather the exception, and that the admissibility of covert objects may have a lot to do with the specific discourse context in which such constructions occur.

Another criterion of objecthood is the behaviour of objects under passivisation. Sentences in the active voice can be passivised by making the object of the active sentence the subject of the passive sentence. This is illustrated in (47):

(47) a. She wrote [the novel]$_{object}$ at the end of the 19th century.
[The novel]$_{subject}$ was written at the end of the 19th century.
b. I prepared [breakfast]$_{object}$ for the whole family.
[Breakfast]$_{subject}$ was prepared for the whole family.
c. Next year the government will introduce [new tax laws]$_{object}$.
Next year [new tax laws]$_{subject}$ will be introduced.

In (47) the verbs *write*, *prepare*, and *introduce* have one object each, but there are also verbs that can take two objects, like *give*, or *show*. Such verbs are called **ditransitive**. In semantic terms, the two objects of ditransitive verbs play different roles in the event denoted by the verb. One of the objects denotes an entity that undergoes the action or process denoted by the verb. This object is commonly referred to as the **direct object**. The other object denotes the goal, the recipient or the beneficiary of the event denoted by the verb, and is known as the **indirect object**. Let's see how these objects behave under passivisation (we use subscript 'IO' to indicate indirect objects and 'DO' to indicate direct objects):

(48) a. Jill gave [him]$_{IO}$ [the book]$_{DO}$ yesterday.
[He]$_{subject}$ was given the book yesterday.
[The book]$_{subject}$ was given to him yesterday.
b. The director showed [me]$_{IO}$ [the new paintings]$_{DO}$ yesterday.
[I] was shown the new paintings yesterday.
[The new paintings] were shown to me yesterday.

(48a) and (48b) illustrate that both objects can be passivised, respectively, which means that we are indeed dealing with two objects. To summarise, we have found four criteria for objecthood: pronoun case morphology, sentential position, obligatoriness and passivisation.

As we will shortly see, the problem of obligatoriness raises another issue, namely that of the distinction between objects and adverbials. This brings us finally to the sentence function **adverbial** (or **adjunct**). Traditionally, adverbials are defined as constituents that provide information about the circumstances of the action denoted by the verb and its subject and object(s). Such circumstantial information may, for example, concern time, location, manner, cause or purpose. This is illustrated in (49), in which I have bracketed the constituents that convey temporal and locative information. Accordingly, they are classified as adverbials:

(49) a. We [often]$_{adverbial}$ go skiing [in the nearby mountains]$_{adverbial}$.
 b. They [never]$_{adverbial}$ came home [so late]$_{adverbial}$.
 c. My professor wrote two textbooks [last year]$_{adverbial}$.

Crucially, such circumstantial information is not obligatory and can be omitted without causing ungrammaticality:

(50) a. We ___ go skiing ___.
 b. They ___ came home ___.
 c. My professor wrote two textbooks ___.

Thus, apart from the type of information adverbials convey, non-obligatoriness is another defining property of this sentence function. Applying this criterion to the data is, however, often less than straightforward. Consider again sentence (44a), repeated here for convenience:

(51) My brother often [invited]$_V$ [**her**]$_{object}$ [**to his parties**]$_{?object/adverbial}$.

While it is clear that [*her*] must be an object, the status of [*to his parties*] is not so clear. Does it give the 'circumstances'? What exactly differentiates 'circumstances' from something that objects express, i.e. the affected participant in an event? Is a party to which one is invited a 'circumstance' or a 'participant' in an inviting event? Without a very good definition of 'circumstance' these questions are hard to answer. If we try out the obligatoriness criterion, it seems that the ungrammatical sentence (45a), in which both constituents were missing, only becomes significantly better if we add [*her*], but not if we add only [*to his parties*]:

(52) a. *My brother often [invited]$_V$.
 b. ✓My brother often [invited]$_V$ [**her**].
 c. ? My brother often [invited]$_V$ [**to his parties**].

This speaks against assigning object status to [*to his parties*], but confirms object status for [*her*]. Let us test this further with passivisation:

(53) a. She was often invited (by my brother) to his parties.
 b. *(To) his parties were often invited to (by my brother) (her).

The passivisation test also shows that [*to his parties*] or [*his parties*] does not act like an object should, since it cannot become the subject of a corresponding passive sentence, no matter how we twist and turn the sentence. Consequently, we are now in the position to say that [*to his parties*] behaves structurally like an adverbial, although it remains unclear in how far the criterion of 'circumstantial information' is really met.

To complicate matters further, there is often terminological confusion arising from the two terms 'adverbial' and 'adverb'. What is the difference between the two? In terms of their status as constituents the answer is clear: 'adverb' is the name of a word-class, while 'adverbial' is the name of a sentence function. The confusion arises, however, chiefly because the sentential function of 'adverbial' is often realised by an adverb, as illustrated in (49a) and (49b). In these two sentences, temporal circumstantial information is given by constituents that consist of only one word, namely an adverb (*often*, *never*), but this is not necessarily the case in other sentences. In fact, adverbials may not even contain a single adverb, but might formally be realised by PPs, as in (49a) ([*in the nearby mountains*]), or by NPs, as in (49c) ([*last year*]). These discrepancies bring us, finally, to the problem of the mapping of form and function, which we will discuss in the next section.

4.4. The mapping of form and function

We have already seen that the sentential function of adverbial can be fulfilled by different kinds of forms. This is schematically represented in (54):

(54)
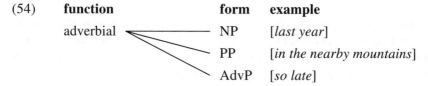

function	form	example
adverbial	NP	[*last year*]
	PP	[*in the nearby mountains*]
	AdvP	[*so late*]

We could add to the set of forms that can function as adverbials still other types of constituents, such as VPs and sentences, as shown in (55):

(55) a. Susan went to university [hoping for a successful career]$_{VP}$.
     b. Susan went to university [because she had hoped to make a successful career]$_S$.

Both adverbials in (55) give the reason why Susan went to university, and thus give circumstantial information in the above sense. Both constituents can be omitted from their respective sentences and thus meet all criteria for adverbials.

Turning to subjects and objects, the situation is very similar. Although there is a strong statistical tendency that subjects and objects are expressed by NPs, it is not hard to find other kinds of subjects and objects:

136 *The structure of sentences: syntax*

(56) a. [That you are lying]$_S$ is obvious.
     [That he is in love with his secretary]$_S$ will not improve his record.
   b. I know [that you are lying]$_S$.
     She said [Bob will buy a new car]$_S$.
   c. [Hoping for a career at university]$_{VP}$ was futile.
     He hated [going to his linguistics classes]$_{VP}$.
   d. She gave the book [to the librarian]$_{PP}$.
     They dedicated their book [to their parents]$_{PP}$.

As indicated by the subcripts, the bracketed constituents in (56a) and (56b) are sentences, and these sentences function as either subject (56a), or object (56b). In (56c) we find VPs in subject and object function, respectively, and (56d) shows PPs as objects. On the basis of our above data, we can enrich the mapping table from above as follows:

(57) **function**   **form**

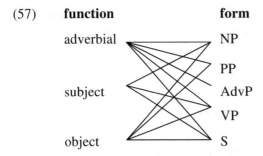

    adverbial   NP

          PP

    subject   AdvP

          VP

    object   S

(57) does not give all possible mappings of form and function that can be found in English sentences, but it suffices to show the crucial point: there is a complex mapping of form and function, to the effect that a given form may realise different functions, and a given function may be realised by a variety of forms.

4.5. Conclusion

In this chapter we have seen how one can investigate the structure of sentences. Syntactic constituency can be tested in different ways by observing the systematic structural and morphological behaviour of word strings. Using the systematic evidence obtained by pronominalisation, coordination, gapping, movement, passivisation, omission, or morphological operations, we can establish grammatical categories such as word-classes and phrases, which can then be used to account for the patterning of words in English sentences. Furthermore we have discussed in some detail the sentence functions subject, object, and adverbial and their mapping onto the formal categories established earlier in the chapter. It became clear that there are a number of criteria that can be used to distinguish these functions and describe their behaviour. Finally, we saw that each sentential function can be realised by a number of different formal categories and that a given formal category may perform different functions in a sentence.

Further reading

There is an abundance of introductions to syntax. A very nice one is Aarts (2008), which lays special emphasis on syntactic argumentation. A detailed discussion and justification of constituency can be found in Radford (1988). A theoretically oriented introduction is Radford (2004). Students of English should also make themselves familiar with the big reference grammars, such as Quirk et al. (1985) and Huddleston and Pullum (2002). Condensed (and better affordable) versions of these 1000-plus page grammars are also available: Greenbaum and Quirk (1990), and Huddleston and Pullum (2005). Another good grammar textbook, which is especially well suited for non-native speakers of English, is Downing and Locke (2006).

Exercises

Basic level

Exercise 4.1.: Constituency

Draw tree diagrams for the following sentences and provide tests for each of the constituents you postulate.

(58) a. The students must draw diagrams on the blackboard.
 b. Her obsession with tree diagrams was extremely disturbing.
 c. Flying planes can be dangerous.

Exercise 4.2.: Word-class

Some dictionaries give 'adverb' as the part-of-speech of the word *yesterday*. Check this categorisation with the help of the following data. What would you say is the part-of-speech of *yesterday*, given its behaviour in these sentences? Why do you think that some dictionaries classify it as an adverb?

(59) a. I met her yesterday and the day before.
   b. There is nothing so boring as yesterday's paper.
   c. Have you seen John's paper?
   d. The day before yesterday was Monday.
   e. I met Jill before John.

Exercise 4.3.: Object

In section 4.4. it is claimed that the bracketed constituents in (56d) above are objects. Apply the tests for objects and show that these constituents are indeed objects.

Exercise 4.4.: Mapping form and function

Determine the functions of the bracketed constituents in (60) and draw a schema similar to that in (57) that shows the mapping of form and function.

(60) [Yesterday] [Helen] worked [at the restaurant] [because she needs the money].

Advanced level

Exercise 4.5.: Constituency

Draw a tree diagram for the following sentence and provide tests for each of the constituents you postulate.

(61) We expected the teacher to give us good grades.

Exercise 4.6.: Constituency

Why is (62) ungrammatical? Go back to the coordination tests for constituency and apply the rationale behind these tests to sentence (62).

(62) *Could you turn off the fire and on the light?

Exercise 4.7.: Constituency

Give the internal structure of the NP [the chancellor of Germany]. There are the following three logical possibilities:

(63) a. NP → D N PP
   b. NP → D [N PP]
   c. NP → [D N] PP

Which of the three structures can account best for the language facts? Consider the following data and use them to give evidence for your analysis.

(64) a. The present [chancellor of Germany] is much more popular than the last *one*.
 b. *The [chancellor] of Germany cheated the *one* of Austria.
 c. She was the first [chancellor of Germany] and [chair of her party].
 d. She was elected [chancellor of Germany].
 e. A: What's her new job?
   B: [Chancellor of Germany]! I'm not kidding.

Devise similar arguments for the internal structure of the NPs [a student of linguistics] and [a student from Manchester].

Chapter 5
The meaning of words and sentences: semantics

5.1. Introduction

Semantics is the study of the structure of meaning. To us as speakers of a language, the idea that language is used to communicate meaning seems intuitively quite straightforward. However, we will see in this chapter that, if we look at how meaning is actually encoded in language, things are much more complex than they seem. First of all we may wonder what meaning is in the first place. This question will be discussed in section 5.2. Secondly, we may wonder which linguistic units are relevant for meaning, and we will look at this question in section 5.3. Section 5.4. will then be concerned in more detail with the ways in which meaning is organised in language. As an example, we will deal with the organisation of word meaning in the speaker's mind.

5.2. What does 'meaning' mean? Words, concepts, and referents

In contrast to maybe other linguistic structures, we are quite used to consciously dealing with semantic issues in everyday life. The linguistic unit with which we tend to associate meaning is the word. When we meet a word in a language that is unknown to us, we may consult a dictionary in order to find out about its meaning. Imagine, for example, you came across the word *box*, and you did not know what it meant. In (1) you find an extract from what the *Longman Dictionary of Contemporary English* will tell you about the meaning of *box*.

(1) *Longman Dictionary of Contemporary English*, s.v. *box*
a. A definition in English:
 'a container for putting things in, especially one with four stiff straight sides'

b. Six pictures:

(*Longman Dictionary of Contemporary English* (2003), printed with permission)

In how far can this definition and these pictures tell us something about what meaning is to speakers of a language? We can draw an analogy between the dictionary entry and the way in which language organises meaning.

The word *box* itself is a combination of four sounds: [b], [ɒ], [k], and [s]. This combination is arbitrary in the sense that there is nothing special about this sequence of sounds that would make them particularly suitable to be used to refer to box-like objects. For example, we may take three of those sounds, put them in a different order, and arrive at a completely different word that has absolutely nothing to do with boxes: *sock* ([s] + [ɒ] + [k]). As a further argument, consider words that are used for box-like objects in different languages:

(2) a. English: *box* [bɒks]
    b. German: *Kiste* [kɪstə]
    c. Spanish: *caja* [kaxa]
    d. Mandarin Chinese: *xiá* [çia], with a rising tone

Languages differ vastly in the way in which they combine sequences of sounds to refer to a given object. We conclude that the mapping of a sound sequence onto meaning in words is language-specific. Put differently, words are arbitrary symbols. They enable us to speak about objects, events, and situations.

As every dictionary user will undoubtedly confirm, the definition of *box* in (1a) provides a description of the meaning of the word *box*. So the meaning of *box* is the relation between the word form ([bɒks] or <box>) on the one hand and what the definition tries to convey on the other hand. But what does the definition try to convey? The definition provides the criteria which, if met, entitle a speaker to use the word *box* for a certain object, real or imaginary, that he or she wants to talk about. As a consequence, then, we can define meaning as in (3). Note that, as we will shortly see, this definition is only one of several possible definitions of meaning (and maybe not even the best one).

(3) Meaning, one possible definition:
Meaning is the relation between a linguistic expression and the entity for which it can be used.

The definition in (3) assumes a direct relationship between words like *box* and objects that speakers may talk about using the word *box*. It captures many speakers' intuitions that we use linguistic expressions to refer to things, and that the meaning of linguistic expressions corresponds to a description of the things we are talking about. There are, however, several problems with this approach to meaning. As a consequence, we need to assume that, apart from a linguistic expression and the thing we talk about, a third party is involved in the generation of meaning. This third party mediates between the linguistic expression, let's say the word, and the entity we talk about. In what follows we will review some of the evidence for this claim, again using our example word *box* for illustration.

First of all, the word *box* is not the only linguistic expression that can be used to talk about box-like objects. Consider the words and phrases in (4); given the appropriate context, all of them could be used to refer to a box.

(4) a. box
    b. container
    c. thingy
    d. the object in which she secretly kept all her love letters

If meaning was only concerned with the relation between linguistic expressions and objects, the four expressions in (4) could be identical in meaning in a given context. This assumption, however, is counterintuitive. First of all, it would mean that meaning was entirely dependent on situational context, without which speakers would not be able to tell whether or not the expressions in (4) are used for the same object. Secondly, even in a context in which (4a-d) can be used for the same object, we do not really want to say that (4a-d) have the same meaning. This becomes very clear if we embed them in a sentence which provides us with a situational context.

(5) a. As a token of her never-ending love, she gave him a **box**.
 b. As a token of her never-ending love, she gave him a **container**.
 c. As a token of her never-ending love, she gave him a **thingy**.
 d. As a token of her never-ending love, she gave him **the object in which she secretly kept all her love letters**.

Whereas we could accept sentences (5a) and (5d) as parts of a romantic tale, sentences (5b) and (5c) sound awkward. The reason why this is so is that there are aspects of the meanings of *container* and *thingy* that are not compatible with the romantic context. Crucially, these aspects are independent of the fact that *container* and *thingy* can be used for box-like objects. The meaning of *container* is mainly defined in terms of its technical function (holding something), and it is stylistically marked for occurring mainly in formal contexts. By contrast, the technical function is less important for the categorisation of something as a box. Apart from the function of being able to hold something, boxes are also defined in terms of their shape.

Similarly to the meaning of *container*, the meaning of *thingy* is also incompatible with our romantic context. This is due to the fact that it is part of the meaning of *thingy* that it provides information about how the speaker (or author) views the object for which (s)he uses the expression. The word *thingy* indicates that the speaker or author does not remember the 'proper' word for the object. This is not what we expect from the narrator of a romantic tale. We therefore see in these examples that meaning encompasses more than the mere relationship between words and objects in the real world. Meaning also involves criteria that are particularly important for classifying an object into a particular category (cf. *container* vs. *box*) as well as some information about the relationship between the speaker and the object in the outside world (cf. *thingy* vs. *box*). Neither of these two properties of meaning is captured by the definition in (3).

The second piece of evidence for the assumption that a third party is involved in the generation of meaning comes from the fact that not all objects for which we can use a particular word are equally good representatives of the kind of thing that the word can be used for. If, for example, you show the pictures of boxes provided by the *Longman Dictionary of Contemporary English* in (1b) to native speakers and ask them whether they would use the word *box* for any of these objects, they will probably immediately confirm that they would easily use the word *box* for all of these objects. By contrast, they may not be so sure about all of the exemplars in the following two sets of pictures:

(6) Boxes?

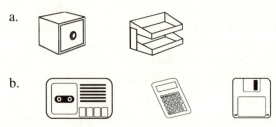

Although it may not be entirely incorrect to call the objects in (6) 'some sort of box', the objects differ in terms of how comfortable speakers are in calling them *boxes*. All the objects in (6) meet the dictionary definition of *box*: They are 'containers for putting things in', and they have 'four stiff sides'. Among the two pictures in (6a), speakers would probably be most comfortable with calling the safe in the left-hand picture a kind of *box*. In spite of the fact that it also has four stiff sides and serves as an object to put things into, speakers will probably be more likely to reject the word *box* for the filing tray. The three pictures in (6b) show that the 'things' that you can put into boxes may also be immaterial. However, again speakers will differ in their judgements of how 'box-like' the three objects are. Probably most speakers will accept the dictaphone as a kind of *box*, whereas they will be less sure about the calculator. Finally, I suspect that only very few people will be willing to call the floppy disk a *box*. Again this phenomenon is not captured by the definition of meaning in (3), which suggests that a particular word either can or cannot be used for a particular object.

What does the evidence show us about the nature of meaning? It shows that the decision of whether or not a word may be used for a particular object depends on speakers' **categorisation** of the object. Categorisation involves the classification of the object we want to talk about into categories. Where do categories come from? The most plausible explanation is that they are cognitive, mental categories. Categorisation is a phenomenon well-known in Cognitive Psychology, where of course it is not restricted to language. Mental categories are termed **concepts**. Thus, all objects that are represented in the pictures in the dictionary entry in (1b) as well as those represented in the not-so-clear cases in (6), may be classified as instantiations of the concept BOX. We will mark concepts through capital letters. Note, however, that concepts do not have to be linguistic in nature — in fact, it is very likely that they have nothing to do with language. As human beings we are in trouble here, because language is the only means we have at our disposal if we want to refer to or describe concepts. Thus, when we refer to a concept like BOX as 'BOX', we use an English word as a symbol of a nonlinguistic category. We face the same problem when we attempt to describe concepts — dictionaries like the *Longman Dictionary of Contemporary English* use language as an approximation to describe the criteria that have to be met for an object to be categorised into the concept BOX (1a). In this context it is interesting that the makers of the *Longman Dictionary* also decided to use a second means: pictures of representative exemplars of the category (1b).

We have thus found the third party that is involved in the generation of meaning: concepts. As in phonology, morphology, and syntax, also in semantics we need to assume the existence of abstract categories to explain what is going on. In semantics these abstract categories are mental concepts. We are now in a position to provide a definition of **meaning** that is more adequate than that in (3).

(7) Meaning, a more adequate definition:
Meaning is the relation between a linguistic expression (i.e. an arbitrary form, e.g. a word) and a mental category that is used to classify objects, i.e. a concept.

The evidence just presented also shows us something about the nature of concepts. First of all, concepts can be described in terms of properties which are important for classifying an object as an instantiation of that concept. This is what the dictionary definition of *box* in (1a) above is trying to do: It tells us that for some object to be classified as an instantiation of BOX, it is important that it has a specific function ('put things into it') and a specific shape ('four stiff sides'). Furthermore, the discussion of the objects in (6) has shown that many concepts have fuzzy boundaries. Among all objects that have the properties mentioned in the definition, there are objects for which the term *box* is undoubtedly the right term. This is what the picture from the dictionary entry in (1b) is trying to show us. But we have seen in our discussion of the objects in (6) that there are also many objects that straddle the boundaries of the concept BOX. When asked, speakers will typically describe them as 'some kind of box, but ...'.

Having established what meaning is, we finally need to discuss the role of the entity for which we use a linguistic expression. Although the relation between objects in the world and linguistic expressions plays a subordinate role in the discussion of meaning, this relation is nevertheless important. Why? Because, when using language, speakers do not only want to communicate meaning, but also information about real-world objects. In fact, they use the meaning of linguistic expressions with the intention of communicating information about real-world objects. As a consequence, it is often of paramount importance for hearers to be able to determine the object in the real world that the speaker tells us something about. We call the object for which a speaker uses a particular linguistic expression the **referent** of that linguistic expression. The relation between linguistic expressions and objects in the outside world is termed **reference**. But how is reference established? In (8) you find several linguistic expressions that involve the word *box*. What can you say about the referent of these expressions?

(8) a. **box**
 b. As a token of her never-ending love, she gave him **a box**.
 c. As a token of her never-ending love, she gave him **the box**.
 d. As a token of her never-ending love, she gave him **that box over there**.

The first thing that is obvious from (8) is that reference can only be established if a linguistic expression is used in a context. For (8a), where the word *box* is used without any contextual information, we cannot make out a concrete object as the referent. However, note that we can nevertheless say something about reference in this instance: On the basis of the meaning of the word *box*, we can describe the set of *potential* referents that the word *box* may be used to refer to. The set of potential referents of a word is called its **denotation**.

Unlike in (8a), the word *box* is embedded in a noun phrase (NP) in (8b-d). It is this NP that helps us establish a referent for the expression. The NPs in (8b) and (8c) differ in that in (8b) *box* is used with the indefinite article, *a*, whereas in (8c) it is used with the definite article, *the*. The two sentences allow us to observe how the two types of article function to manipulate the referential properties of the noun phrase. In *a box* (8b), the only thing that we as hearers know for sure about reference is that the expression has one particular referent — the speaker does not refer to an unspecific class of objects, but to one specific instance. However, we as hearers do not know which box in the world of box-like objects the speaker refers to. The expression is **indefinite**. By contrast, the phrase *the box* (8c) signals that we as hearers should be able to single out one particular box object as the referent of this expression. The expression is **definite**. The definite NP in (8c) may have struck us as awkward. The reason for this impression is that, contrary to what we know about the use of definite NPs in language, (8c) does not give us enough context to single out the referent of *the box*. The awkwardness of the expression disappears, however, if we embed the sentence in (8c) in more context. Consider, for example, the following context:

(9) For years she had fondly kept all the letters he had sent her in a small wooden box on her bedside table. Now, as a token of her never-ending love, she gave him **the box**.

Here the sentence preceding the sentence in (8c) contains a description of the referent, *a small wooden box on her bedside table*. Note the indefinite article in this phrase – the box object has not occurred in the story before, so it is just being introduced. The reader is not yet expected to know which box object is meant. After the introduction of the box object into the story with the help of the indefinite phrase (*a small wooden box on her bedside table*), however, this situation changes. In the following sentence the definite article in the phrase *the box* indicates that the reader is now expected to know which box is meant. Specifically, he or she is expected to use the information from the indefinite phrase in the previous sentence to determine the referent of *the box*. Note that the example also shows that referents may exist in an imaginary world. We therefore see that the things that we can talk about using linguistic expressions are not always real-world entities. Rather, we are talking about entities in worlds which are constructed as the context of linguistic expressions.

The sentence in (8d) shows us yet another possibility of how reference can be established. As in the case of (8c), the hearer should be able to single out the referent. But this time there is no definite article, but other expressions: the demonstrative determiner *that* and the pronominal phrase *over there* (cf. chapter 4.2.). Like *the* in (8c), the two expressions serve to establish a referent for the NP. Unlike *the*, however, the contextual information that is required to be able to establish the referent lies in the situational context in which the sentence is uttered. Without knowing where the speaker is, we cannot reconstruct the referent. The expressions *that* and *over there* are linguistic elements which signal to us that we have to use the situational context in which the sentence is uttered to determine the object referred to. Such expressions are called **deictic expressions**. The term is related to the classical Greek verb *deiknymi*, which means 'I show, I point'. Deictic expressions are linguistic 'pointing devices', which point to objects that are located in the situational context in which a sentence is uttered. In the example in (8d) the deictic expressions *that* and *over there* are used to point to a location, i.e. a place where the referent of an expression can be found. Deictic expressions can, however, also be used to point at other aspects of the context. Consider the following extreme example, found in Levinson (1983: 55). On a beach you find a bottle with a message. The message reads as follows (deictic expressions are underlined):

> MEET ME HERE a WEEK FROM NOW with a stick about THIS BIG.

To you as the person who has found this message in a bottle on the beach, the referents of as many as four expressions are totally unclear: Who is *me*? Where is *here* (given that the bottle has been floating in the water)? When is *now*? How much is *this* (given that you do not see the object or gesture which must have accompanied *this*)? The referents of *me*, *here*, *now*, and *this* are unclear because they are deictic expressions; readers must use the situational context in which the sentence was written in order to establish reference. However, given the circumstances under which you found the message (in a bottle on the beach), you do not know anything about the situational context in which this sentence was written. Furthermore, the expressions *me*, *here*, *now*, and *this* exemplify three types of situational context to which deictic expressions may point: Deictic expressions may point to people and objects (*me, this*), places (*here*), and time (*now*) in the situational context in which the expression was written or uttered.

To sum up our discussion of reference, we saw that reference is important if language is to be used for the purpose of communicating information about the world. We also saw that on its own, a word like *box* does not have a referent; it only has a meaning and a denotation. In order to determine concrete objects or classes of objects as referents of a linguistic expression, we need contextual information.

In this section we have likened the way in which language organises word meaning to a dictionary entry for a particular word. Meaning itself is a relation, i.e. a relation between an arbitrary form and a concept. A concept is like a dictionary definition in that it defines the relevant properties that make an object eligible to be classified as an instantiation of that concept. At the same time, we saw that concepts have fuzzy boundaries. Furthermore, if we want to explain how language can be used to communicate information about objects in the real world, we must establish the relation between linguistic expressions, concepts, and objects. The relation between linguistic expressions and objects is captured by reference. The sketch in (10) schematises the triangular relationship between word, concept, and referent for our example word *box*. For reasons of convenience, we will use a very abstract pictorial representation of the real-world object.

(10) *box*, BOX, and the real-world object

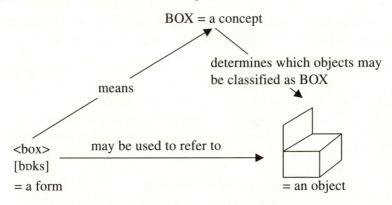

In what follows we will see that conceptual structure interacts with linguistic form in different ways to produce meaning. Crucially, like linguistic form, meaning can also be compositional in nature. In the same way in which we can formally combine morphemes into words, words into phrases, and phrases into sentences, we combine conceptual structures to produce new, compositional types of meanings. Meaning does not only exist on the (simplex) word level, but also on other levels of linguistic structure.

5.3. Compositional and non-compositional meaning

In the discussion in the previous section we have primarily focussed on words as units of meaning. Specifically, in our example *box* we have looked at one particular class of words only; *box* is a morphologically simplex noun. However, in our discussion of reference we already saw that also elements which are larger than a word can have different referential properties. For example, we compared the referential properties of the NP *the box* with those of the NPs *a box* and *that box over there*. If, however, units larger than a word can have referential properties, they should also be able to have meaning. The question that arises, then, is which different linguistic units can have a meaning. Furthermore, we may ask ourselves whether it is possible to classify meaning of different linguistic units into different types.

As a first start at this question, imagine you are caught in a traffic jam that winds itself along a huge construction site on the motorway. After hours of stop-and-go traffic, you finally reach the end of the construction site, where you see a road sign with a sentence on it. Read the sentence in (11) and, before reading on, write down a paraphrase of what it means.

(11) We would like to apologise for any inconvenience caused.

There are two basic aspects to the meaning of this sentence. Your paraphrase should approximately resemble one of the following two alternatives:

(12) a. 'An entity comprising the writer of this sentence and other people ('*we*')
       express their wish ('*would like*')
            to say that they are sorry ('*to apologise*')
                 in case something has become the cause of ('*for ... caused*')
                     problems which annoy someone ('*any inconvenience*').'
   b. 'The construction company, who have set up this road sign,
       want to apologise
            to me, the reader of this sentence,
                for the delay,
                     which they acknowledge to be their fault.'

The paraphrase in (12a) treats the meaning of the sentence as the sum of the meanings of its parts. The meanings of the parts of the sentence are expressed by paraphrases, and they are connected with each other in a meaningful way. Furthermore, we note that the parts of the sentence that are connected can be described in syntactic terms as syntactic elements (words and constituents). So, for example, the meaning of the noun phrase *any inconvenience* is closely connected with the meaning of the verb *caused*, because it expresses the situation that is caused. In a similar way, the noun phrase *any inconvenience caused* is connected with the verb *apologise for* by the fact that it expresses the situation to which the apology relates. Along very similar lines, the verb phrase *apologise for any inconvenience caused* is connected with *would like to*. Finally, the pronoun *we* is connected with the rest of the sentence, the verb phrase *would like to apologise for any inconvenience caused*, by way of the fact that *we* specifies the entity about which the information *apologise ... caused* is provided.

It is important to note that, apart from words discussed in the previous section, different parts of a sentence have a meaning; the same is true for the whole sentence. Furthermore, the parts of the sentence that we identified correspond to syntactic elements (words and constituents). Finally, we see that we can indeed describe the meaning of a sentence roughly as the sum of the meanings of its parts and the way these parts are combined. If, however, we compare our analysis of the meaning of the sentence in (12a) with what we said about the meaning of the word *box* in section 5.2, we note an important difference. Whereas the meaning of *box* can be captured with the help of a single concept BOX, we see now that this is not true for all types of meaning:

Sentences and phrases have a meaning, but their meaning is **compositional**, consisting of a combination of concepts.

Note at this point that we have somewhat simplified matters. Thus, we have suggested that the meaning of words is non-compositional. However, we will see below that this is only true for monomorphemic words. Secondly, we have suggested that phrase and sentence meanings are generally compositional. Whereas this is true for the overwhelming majority of possible phrases and sentences, this is not true for things like idiomatic expressions. A case in point is, for example, the phrase *kick the bucket*, meaning 'to die'. The meaning of this phrase is certainly not compositional in the above-defined sense.

Let us now turn to the paraphrase in (12b), which is very different from that in (12a). The main difference lies in the fact that (12b) contains elements which are not part of the actual meaning of the sentence. For example, there is nothing in the meaning of *we* that tells us that *we* refers to a construction company. Similarly, there is nothing in the phrase *any inconvenience caused* that tells us that it is the construction company that causes the inconvenience — it could in fact be anyone (e.g. the driver in the next car before us). Furthermore, there is nothing in the sentence that tells us that we as the readers of this road sign are the addressees of this sentence — the sign could be meant to address the construction workers who are forced to inhale the exhaust from our cars every day. Finally, and most importantly, there is nothing in the meaning of the sentence that tells us that the sentence is meant to be an apology. On the surface, the sentence merely states that the entity *we* has a wish ('would like'). We neither learn that they put their wish into practice, nor that they intend us to be the addressees.

So how come that (12b) is a possible paraphrase of the sentence in (11)? All the elements that we added to the sentence meaning have one thing in common. They all have their origin not in the meaning of the sentence, but in our general (and cultural) knowledge about what such road signs at major construction sites are usually like. In other words, we have used our knowledge of the situational context of the road sign. But why did we do that? We did that in order to 'make sense of the sentence', or, in more technical terms, in order to discover the communicative purpose of the sentence. The use of situational and world knowledge to discover the communicative purpose of a linguistic expression is called 'inferencing'. What made us start drawing inferences in the example is easy to see: If we only consider the meaning of the sentence (as paraphrased in (12a)), we do not have a chance to discover its purpose: Why should an unspecified entity *we* tell us something about what he or she would like to do?

Thus, the comparison of the two paraphrases in (12a) and (12b) shows that, looking at sentences, we need to distinguish between two fundamentally different categories of meaning: the meaning of the sentence itself (which is compositionally derived from the meaning of its parts and the way in which they are combined) and the communicative purpose of the sentence (which is determined with the help of our situational and world knowledge). Whereas in everyday language we tend to refer to both categories as 'meaning', only the former category is recognised as **semantic meaning** in a narrow sense. By contrast, communicative purpose is studied by the linguistic discipline of pragmatics (to be discussed in chapter 6), where it is often referred to as **pragmatic meaning**.

A good test for the distinction between semantic meaning and pragmatic meaning in our example sentence is to see what happens if we change the context. For example, consider the following context:

(13) The customer service department in our company is split into two fractions about how the company should react to the fact that, due to a computer problem, customers were unable to reach us for about ten hours on the weekend. **We would like to apologise for any inconvenience caused**, but other people say that this would make us vulnerable to a whole flood of law suits, so they'd rather keep quiet, hoping that nobody may have noticed.

Although the sentence that corresponds to our road sign in (11) contains the very same words, we do not interpret it as an apology anymore. The reason is that, whereas both sentences in (11) and (13) have the same sentence meaning, they differ in terms of their pragmatic meanings. The road sign expresses an apology to the reader, whereas the sentence in (13) informs the reader of the writer's wish to apologise to someone else.

In the remainder of this chapter we will limit our discussion to meaning as it is studied in semantics: semantic meaning. With respect to the question of which linguistic expressions may have meaning in language, there is, then, one level left to consider. Up until now we have looked at linguistic units larger than a word. Here we have found a new type of meaning, which we have called compositional. Equipped with our newly-gained knowledge about compositional meaning, then, we now need to take a fresh look at word meaning again. We have seen that the meaning of monomorphemic words like *box* is non-compositional. This is in line from what you have learned in the introduction to morphology in chapter 3, namely that morphemes, not words, are the smallest meaningful elements of language. So what about polymorphemic words? Is their meaning compositional or non-compositional? Consider the complex words in (14).

(14) a. inconvenience = {in-} + {convenient} + {-ce}
     b. to decompose = {de-} + {compose}
     c. dog house   = {dog} + {house}

All words in (14) are products of word-formation processes. Looking at their meaning, we now see that, similarly to meanings of sentences and phrases, word meaning may be compositional; this is the case in complex words. In (14a), the prefix *in-* has the meaning 'not X', whereas the meaning of the nominalising suffix *-ce* could maybe be described as 'a state of being X'. The meaning of *inconvenience* is, therefore, the 'state of being not convenient'. In a similar way, the meaning of *decompose* can be described as a combination of the meaning of *compose* and the meaning of *de-* ('to reverse the action of X-ing').

However, things are a bit different in (14c). In contrast to *inconvenience* and *decompose*, which are products of derivation, *dog house* is a compound. Like the meanings of the two derivatives, the meaning of *dog house* is clearly compositional. Unlike in the case of the two derivatives, however, the relation between the meanings of the two components of *dog house* is not entirely clear. All we can say about this is that a *dog house* is a type of house that is somehow connected with dogs, but not, for example, a type of dog that has something to do with houses (which would have to be a *house dog*, not a *dog house*). But what exactly does *dog* have to do with *house*? We are used to interpreting *dog house* as a small house that has been built for a dog to live in, but theoretically it could also be a normal house in which a lot of dogs live, a house that is shaped like a dog (maybe built by a crazy architect who furnished the house with ear- and tail-like structures), or a house that serves as a refuge for stray dogs. These are only some of all potential meanings of *dog house*. Further evidence to show that the relation between words that form a compound is not entirely specified comes from the fact that not all compounds which have *house* as a head involve the same meaning relation. What, for example, would a *cat house* be? Since we in our culture normally do not build small houses for cats to live in, the interpretation of the compound as 'a small house that has been built for a cat to live in' does not come as naturally to us as the analogous interpretation of *dog house*. Even more clearly, a *road house* is not a house which is meant to serve as a shelter for a road, because we do not build houses for roads. But if you think this is natural because we do not build houses for things, you may want to compare *road house* to one of the many meanings of *boat house*, where the house does serve to shelter a thing, namely a boat. We therefore see that the compositional meaning of compound words is somehow more difficult to capture than that of many derivatives, and certainly more difficult than that of many sentences. Compounds are inherently **ambiguous**, i.e. they have more than one meaning.

You may have wondered at this point why, looking at complex words, we have only considered products of word formation so far. Indeed, inflected words will be the last group of complex words that we will consider in this section. If we look at compositional meaning in inflected words, it is interesting to consider not only the word itself, but the syntactic constituent in which the word is embedded if used. Here are some examples:

(15) a. boxes
b. looked
c. The blue boxes looked terrific.

(15a) and (15b) show two inflected words in isolation: the plural form of the noun *box*, and the past tense form of the verb *look*. The meanings of both forms may be described as compositional: The meaning of *boxes* is the meaning of *box*, combined with the meaning of the plural suffix {PLURAL} ('more than one X'). The meaning of *looked* is the meaning of *look*, combined with the meaning of the past tense suffix {PAST} ('X happened in the past'). If, however, we use the inflected words in the sentence in (15c), there is something interesting to observe. What exactly is 'X' in the meanings of the inflectional suffixes, 'more than one X' and 'X happened in the past'? Although *boxes* is the plural form of *box*, we are inclined to say that in this sentence there is more than one exemplar of the entity *the blue box* and, crucially, not only of *box*. Similarly, although *looked* is the past tense form of *look*, the answer to the question of what happened in the past is *look terrific* and not just *look*. These two examples show that, although formally inflectional morphemes like {PLURAL} and {PAST} attach to nouns and verbs, their meaning extends beyond the base to which they attach. We call the extension of the semantics of a morpheme to one or more linguistic elements the **semantic scope** of that morpheme. We see in the example in (15c) that the semantic scope of the two inflectional morphemes can be described in terms of syntactic structure. The scope of {PLURAL} is the whole NP *the blue box*, the scope of {PAST} is the whole VP of the sentence, *look terrific*. It is typical of inflectional morphemes that their semantic scope may extend beyond the base to which they are formally attached.

In this section we have looked at which linguistic expressions other than simplex words like *box* can have meaning in English. We looked at sentences and different types of complex words. We found that we can assign to all of these structures a special type of meaning that can be characterised as compositional. Furthermore, looking at sentences, we found that it is important to distinguish between their semantic and their pragmatic meaning. Looking at complex words, we found that morphemes involved in inflection may differ in scope from morphemes involved in derivation and compounding. Furthermore, compounds differ from derivatives in terms of the extent to which they leave the meaning relation between morphological constituents unspecified.

In the following section we will return to simplex word meaning, exploring in more detail how word meaning is organised in English.

5.4. The network: organising word meaning

In our discussion of *box* in section 5.2. we have defined meaning as the relationship between a word form and a mental concept. Using the analogy of a dictionary entry, we have already discovered two basic properties of this relation. It can be described in terms of criteria that must be met in order for a word to be used to express a particular concept. Furthermore, we can distinguish between objects that are somehow typical of a particular category and those which are judged by speakers to be rather 'bad' representatives of a category. In this section we will look more closely at one aspect of meaning: the role which relations between words play in the definition of meaning.

5.4.1. Words and other words

Words are stored in the huge storage device known as the **mental lexicon**, which, similarly to a very large and complex dictionary, enables us as speakers of a language to use them in both speech production and comprehension. Entries in the mental lexicon are termed 'lexemes' — the term has already been introduced in chapter 3.6. Similarly to an entry in a (monolingual) dictionary, a lexeme comprises information about a word in terms of two aspects: its form (pronunciation, spelling, word class, inflectional class), and, crucially for the present discussion, its meaning (semantics). Lexemes in the mental lexicon are also similar to entries in a dictionary in that they do not form an unordered, chaotic jumble of entries. Instead of the alphabetic order that is characteristic of most print dictionaries, however, the order of entries in the mental lexicon can be characterised in terms of a multitude of links between lexemes, which make it comparable to a huge network. In morphology you have learned something about one aspect according to which lexemes are connected with each other: morphological relatedness. In this section we will look at a different aspect that structures the network of lexemes in the mental lexicon: meaning. Ties between words that are related in terms of meaning organise words into structures called **lexical fields**. In fact, meaning relations between different words have not only been shown to be relevant for the organisation of the mental lexicon; they are also generally assumed to be vital for the definition of what meaning is.

Let us start with the idea that relatedness in terms of meaning is relevant for the way in which the mental lexicon is structured. How do we know? We know from evidence that work in psycholinguistics has brought to light. Psycholinguistics is the field of linguistics that is concerned with the processing of language in the human mind. For a more detailed discussion of psycholinguistics, the interested reader is referred to chapter 7.4 of this book. For our present purposes, we will only look at one of the ways in which psycholinguists have investigated the relations between entries in the mental lexicon: association experiments. Speakers, the test subjects, are given a word and asked to name the first words that come to their mind when hearing the stimulus word. When conducting an association test, it is important that the words that speakers name really reflect their spontaneous reaction. Crucially, they must be prevented from starting conscious reasoning. The way this is usually accomplished is by giving the test subject the instruction to react as quickly as possible. Here is what native speakers of English have most frequently associated with the word *red* in an empirical study (Jenkins 1970). The data are sorted in terms of the frequency with which they occurred. I cite the list from Aitchison (2003: 86).

(16) The most common association responses triggered by *red*:

white   blue   black   green   colour   blood   communist   yellow   flag   bright

⟵───⟶

more   *less*
frequent   *frequent*

The ten words most frequently associated with *red* fall into three distinct groups in terms of their relation to the stimulus word: words that refer to other colours, the word *colour*, and words that are associated in some other way with *red*. We will discuss all three groups in turn.

The largest group comprises *white, blue, black, green,* and *yellow*. We already see in these five words how important meaning is in creating links between lexemes. What *red, white, blue, black, green,* and *yellow* have in common is one aspect of their meaning: They are all different colour terms. Indeed, *colour*, i.e. the term that covers *red, white, blue, black, green,* and *yellow*, is also among the list of frequent associations. The meaning relation between words like *colour* and *red* is termed **hyponymy**. Hyponymy relations are meaning relations that can be described using the paraphrase 'is a ...' (e.g. 'Red is a colour'). The word *red* is a **hyponym** of the word *colour*; conversely, the word *colour* is a **hyperonym** of the word *red*. Like *red*, also *white, blue, black, green,* and *yellow* are colours. They are thus hyponyms of *colour*. If we want to describe the relation between our associated words *white, blue, black, green,* and *yellow* and the stimulus word (*red*), we need to say that they all have a common hyperonym (i.e. *colour*). Using the correct terminology, we say that they are **co-hyponyms** of *red*. The schema in (17) summarises the hyponymy relations found in our association test for *red*.

(17) Hyponymy relations among associations for *red*:

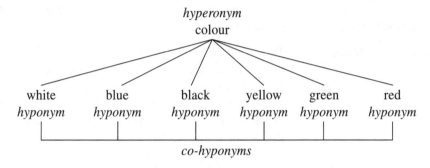

Hyponymy relations are among the most frequent relations to be found in word association tests. However, this is not the only context in which we find hyponymy to play an important role. Thus, hyperonyms are very frequently employed in definitions of word meaning. How, for example, would you explain the meaning of the word *lion* to someone who does not know the word? Probably one of the first sentences in your definition would be something like: *A lion is an animal.* Only then would you go on to be more specific about what lions look like, where they live, what they eat, etc. What is interesting for us is that, by saying that a lion is an animal, you begin your definition by explaining what the hyperonym of *lion* is. Note that we found the very same kind of procedure in the dictionary definition of the word *box* that we discussed at the beginning of this chapter. Similarly to our definition of *lion* above, the definition of *box* in the *Longman Dictionary of Contemporary English* starts with an explanation of what the hyperonym of box is: *A box is a container* ....

All this shows that the hyponymy relation is a very important relation between words in the mental lexicon. Apparently, it is important for the organisation of meaning that words are grouped according to whether or not they can be classified into a common higher-level category, i.e. whether or not they have a common hyperonym. In association experiments we find that co-hyponyms form the most frequent class of words mentioned by test subjects. In definitions of unknown words by speakers or in dictionaries we find that the hyperonym of the target word plays a predominant role. Hyponyms and their hyperonyms are related in terms of their meaning. Specifically, they share a crucial aspect of their meaning. For example, 'being a colour' is a crucial ingredient of the meaning of the hyponym *red* as well as of the meaning of the hyperonym *colour*. Semantic relations between words that share crucial aspects of their meaning are termed **sense relations**.

Having defined sense relations, we can now come back to our discussion of the words commonly associated with the word *red* in English. There is only one group of words left that we have not discussed so far: *blood, communist, flag, bright*. But how do they relate to *red*? (18) constitutes an attempt to describe this relation in paraphrases:

(18) a. *blood*:   The colour of blood is red.
                        Red is often used as a colour symbol of blood.
     b. *communist*:   The colour symbol used for communists is red.
     c. *flag*:   The colour of a flag may be red.
                        There are many red flags (esp: communist flags).
     d. *bright*:   Red is one of the bright colours.
                        or: There is a type of red that is bright
                        (as opposed to dark red).

The first thing we see is that the relation of *bright* and *red* is not entirely clear. For this reason, I will omit *bright* from the following discussion.

With respect to *blood, communist*, and *flag*, we note that their relation to *red* somehow differs from the relation that we found to exist between *red* and its co-hyponyms or its hyperonym in the previous discussion. There is nothing in the meaning of *red* itself that relates the meaning of *red* to the meaning of *blood, communist*, or *flag*. Therefore, the relation between *red* and *blood, communist*, and *flag* cannot be considered a sense relation. It is interesting to note, however, that this relation can only be determined within a particular cultural context. We have to know that *red* is used as a symbol of *blood* and *communism*. Especially in the associations *communism* and *flag*, you see the context-dependent nature of this relationship very clearly. Maybe you were surprised to see in (16) that *red* is so closely associated with communism that the words *communism* and *flag* show up among the 'top 10' associations for the word *red*. If you have followed our suggestion above and conducted your own association test for *red*, you may, contrary to the associations in (16), even have got only very few words (or none at all) that are related to communism as associations for the stimulus *red*. But remember that the study from which the associations in (16) have been cited has been published in 1970 (Jenkins 1970). Furthermore, the data used in this study go back as far as the 1950s. At that time communism was a big issue, and this is reflected in the associations that you get for the word that refers to a colour that is highly symbolic of communism. We thus see that words in the mental lexicon are not only connected with each other according to sense relations. Apart from sense relations, also other principles are at work. The principle that creates the relation between *red* and *blood, communism,* and *flag* is dependent on speakers' world knowledge about contextual factors like symbols used by political movements or, in the case of *blood*, other types of cultural symbolism. Associations that come with a particular word, but are related to the word through world knowledge rather than through true sense relations, are referred to as **connotations**. Note that connotation is not a relation between words; rather, it refers to the association of a word with particular concepts via our world knowledge. So in the 1950s, *red* apparently had the connotation of being strongly associated with communism. It is an open empirical question of whether this has changed nowadays. I suspect it may have.

Up until now we have only dealt with one sense relation, hyponymy. However, there is another type of sense relation which also creates very strong links between words in the mental lexicon. This type of sense relation can be brought to light empirically if you conduct association tests with words like the following three: *female, big,* and *teacher*. In association tests with these three words, we can be very certain to find the words in (19) among the most frequent associations.

(19) a. female: male
     b. big: small
     c. teacher: student

Without doubt, all associated words in (19) are related to their stimulus words in terms of their meaning; their relation to the stimulus words is, therefore, a sense relation. The term for this sense relation is also quite straightforward: The words associated are **opposites** of the stimulus words. *Male* is the opposite of *female, big* is the opposite of *small*, and *teacher* is the opposite of *student*. Oppositeness of meaning is, alongside hyponymy, the second important sense relation that exists between words in the mental lexicon. We can recognise opposites by testing them with a paraphrase. For all pairs of opposites, which we may label word 1 and word 2, we must be able to say that 'word 1 is: not word 2'. That we can do this with the examples in (19), is shown in the paraphrases in (20).

(20) a. 'female is: not male'
b. 'big is: not small'
c. 'a teacher is: not a student'

You may wonder at this point what distinguishes oppositeness from hyponymy, because you can, for example, use the same paraphrase to describe the relation between the co-hyponyms of *red* that we discussed above: 'red is: not yellow', etc. The difference resides in the fact that oppositeness is always concerned with a pair of two terms, not with more than two.

Apart from the fact that they are opposites, you may have noticed that the word pairs in (19) also exhibit subtle differences in terms of the meaning relations between them. Indeed, opposites do not form a homogeneous group; instead, we need to distinguish between three subclasses. Each subclass is represented by one pair of words in (19). You may intuitively have grasped the difference between the pair *female — male* and *big — small*. Animate entities must in our world be either female or male. Thus, if you are not female, you must be male, and vice versa. By contrast, this is not true for the pair *big — small*. An entity that is not big is not automatically small. Instead, it could be something in-between, i.e. neither big nor small (i.e. medium-sized). So in contrast to the pair *male — female*, which refers to a dichotomous distinction where speakers are forced to make an either-or choice, the terms *big* and *small* refer to the two extreme points on a scale, where there is also an in-between. Pairs like *male — female*, where there is no in-between are called **complementaries**. Pairs like *big — small*, where there is a scale, are termed **antonyms**. Examples of complementaries and antonyms are provided in (21).

(21) a. **complementaries**
temporary   permanent
animate   inanimate
dead   alive
voter   non-voter
b. **antonyms**
old   young
hot   cold
high   low
love   hate

It is characteristic of antonyms that they are gradable. Structurally, this is reflected in the fact that pairs of antonyms which are adjectives usually have comparative and superlative forms, whereas pairs of complementaries which are adjectives do not. Furthermore, pairs of antonyms which are adjectives can be modified by adverbials like *very* or *extremely*; again, pairs of adjectival complementaries normally cannot. The structural differences between adjectival complementaries and antonyms are illustrated in (22):

(22) a. **complementaries**

temporary	permanent	*more temporary	*very temporary
		*more permanent	*very permanent
animate	inanimate	*more animate	*very animate
		*more inanimate	*very inanimate
dead	alive	*deader	*very dead
		*more alive	*very alive

b. **antonyms**

old	young	older	very old
		younger	very young
hot	cold	hotter	very hot
		colder	very cold
high	low	higher	very high
		lower	very low

If we now turn to the third pair of opposites from (19) above, *teacher — student*, and compare the relation between the two words to complementaries and antonyms, we see that the relation is similar to what we said about complementaries: If you are an entity that is actively involved in an educational institution (e.g. a school), you must be either a teacher or a student; there is no in-between, and it is not possible that you are neither a teacher nor a student. However, there is more to the relationship between *teacher* and *student* than that. The pair *teacher — student* looks at two entities that are involved in one and the same event, teaching, in two different roles. One is the entity who teaches (*teacher*) and one is the entity who is being taught (*student*). This type of opposite sense relations is called **converse relation**; pairs of words which are in a converse relation are termed **converses**.

Linguistically, converse relations are characterised by the fact that we may use either of the two members of a pair of converses to express the same situation. The data in (23) provide further examples of converses.

(23) buy — sell   above — below
     mother — daughter   lend — borrow

Both verbs *buy* and *sell* describe an event which involves the transaction of goods in exchange of money from different perspectives. Likewise, pairs of kinship terms like *mother* and *daughter* describe one single family relation from different perspectives. The two prepositions *above* and *below* refer to the location of something with respect to something else — again, they describe the same locative relation from different angles. Similarly, the two verbs *lend* and *borrow* both describe an event in which some property of one person or entity is given to another person or entity, with both parties mutually agreeing that the property will be returned to its owner. What is interesting about converses is that we can express the same situation in a sentence using either of the two members of a pair of converses. If we substitute one member of a converse pair by the other one, the syntactic functions of the elements in the sentence will be swapped accordingly. This is demonstrated in (24).

(24) Pairs of converses in sentences:
    a. Mary buys a book from John.
    a.' John sells a book to Mary.
    b. Mary is Joan's mother.
    b.' Joan is Mary's daughter.
    c. The first floor is above the ground floor.
    c.' The ground floor is below the first floor.
    d. Mary lends the book to John.
    d.' John borrows the book from Mary.

All pairs of sentences in (24) describe the same situation. They differ in that they use a different member from a pair of converses. They also differ in terms of the syntactic functions of the linguistic expressions that refer to the entities involved in the situation (*John* and *Mary*, *the ground floor* and *the first floor*).

To sum up, we have seen that semantic relations between words play a very important role in the organisation of words in the mental lexicon. We have looked at one experimental method that can be used to investigate relations between words in the mental lexicon: association tests. Words that are semantically related to the stimulus word form a large group among words brought to light in association tests. We furthermore distinguished in this section between sense relations between words in the mental lexicon and other relations. There are two basic types of sense relations, which play an important role not only in word association experiments, but also in the definition of word meaning: hyponymy and oppositeness of meaning. Among opposites, we further distinguished between complementaries, antonyms, and converses. Hyponymy and oppositeness of meaning are assumed to organise lexemes in the mental lexicon into lexical fields.

5.4.2. Same or different?

Apart from sense relations and connotations, there is yet a third type of meaning-related property of lexemes. Whereas sense relations and connotations reflect the fact that lexemes are interconnected in a network-like structure, this third property has to do with the problem of determining whether some linguistic form should count as one or two (or more) different lexemes. Consider, for example, the pairs of words in bold print in (25). Would you assign them to one single lexeme or to two different lexemes?

(25) a. The **university** will introduce study fees.
     a.' They built this **university** in the 1970s.
     b. Sam was tall, dark, and **handsome**.
     b.' He made a **handsome** profit.
     c. I did a pretty good **job**.
     c.' I'm looking for a new **job**.

You will probably intuitively assign each of the three pairs of cases in (25) to one single lexeme (*university*, *handsome*, and *job*, respectively), and indeed this intuition corresponds to the view standardly held in semantics. However, if you look closely, you will notice that the words in (25a), (25b), and (25c) differ in meaning from the words in (25a'), (25b'), and (25c'). Thus, in (25a) the meaning of the word *university* is 'a high-level educational institution'. The word *university* in (25a'), by contrast, means 'a building which houses high-level educational institution'. In (25b) the word *handsome* means 'good-looking', but in (25b') the meaning of the word *handsome* can be paraphrased as 'an impressive amount of'. Finally, in (25c) the word *job* means 'task', whereas in (25c') it means 'professional employment'.

In spite of the differences in meaning, however, the two members of the word pairs in (25) are felt to belong to the same lexeme. This is so because the meanings of the two members of the pairs are very closely related. The building which houses the institution university (25a') is a part of the institution itself (25a). A handsome profit (25b') is a profit that looks good (25b) in a metaphorical sense. A professional employment (*job* in (25c')) is a very specific type of task (*job* in (25c)). We conclude, then, that lexemes may have more than one meaning. As we have seen in the examples in (25), these meanings are related. Lexemes which have more than one meaning are called **polysemous** lexemes. The phenomenon that a given lexeme has multiple related meanings is termed **polysemy**.

The importance of the idea that different meanings of a single lexeme must be interrelated becomes even clearer if we look at cases in which meanings are not interrelated. Intuitively, we would not assign them to the same lexeme. Examples are provided in (26). Again, the relevant words are embedded in sentences.

(26) a. I quickly **swallow** the rest of my coffee.
 a.' A **swallow** can fly thousands of miles.
 b. He switched on the **light**.
 b.' The parcel is as **light** as a feather.
 c. We've got all our savings in the **bank**.
 c.' They walked home along the **bank** of the river.

Like the cases in (25), the pairs of words in (26) are identical in form (*swallow, light, bank*). Unlike in (25), however, their meanings are entirely unrelated. You can test this by trying to explain the meaning of one member of a pair in (26) with the help of the second member. Whereas this works beautifully for the cases in (25), this does not work for the cases in (26). For example, you can describe the meaning of *university* in (25a') by saying that it is 'a building which houses a university'. By contrast, there is no way in which you can describe the meaning of *swallow* in (26a) with the help of the meaning of *swallow* in (26a'), or vice versa. Swallows cannot be characterised as birds which are particularly well-known for swallowing anything. Nor is the act of swallowing something that resembles or is in any way associated with what a swallow does or looks like. An analogous argument can be made for the two other pairs of words in (26). We conclude, then, that the formal (phonological and orthographic) identity of *swallow*, *light*, and *bank* in (26a), (26b), and (26c) with *swallow*, *light*, and *bank* in (26a'), (26b'), and (26c') is accidental; the two members of each pair belong to different lexemes. Two lexemes which are identical in form (phonological and orthographic), but have unrelated meanings are termed **homonyms**. The phenomenon that there exist linguistic expressions which have the same orthographic and phonological form, but different, unrelated meanings is called **homonymy** (or 'homophony', if restricted to the same phonological form).

Having looked at homonymous words, which are identical in form but different in meaning, you may wonder whether there are also cases which differ in form, but are identical in meaning. This phenomenon does indeed exist; it is called **synonymy**. Like homonymous words, **synonyms** are to be considered different lexemes. Examples of synonymous words are provided in the sentences in (27).

(27) a. You look **beautiful** in that dress.
   a.' You look **lovely** in that dress.
   b. His **job**? — He is a teacher.
   b.' His **occupation**? — He is a teacher.
   c. He **tried** to escape.
   c.' He **attempted** to escape.

The sentences in (27a'), (27b'), and (27c') differ from the sentences in (27a), (27b), and (27c) in only one word. This difference does, however, not result in a difference in meaning. This is so because the word pairs *beautiful — lovely, job — occupation*, and *try — attempt* are synonyms.

Having gone through educational institutions like secondary school and university, you probably already have some experience in actively working with synonyms. For example, it is common practice in composition-writing or essay-writing to consult a thesaurus if you are lost for words. Specifically, a thesaurus will be helpful if you are looking for a word that is similar to a word that you have in mind, but that you want to avoid for some reason (e.g. to avoid repetition). In other words, you consult a thesaurus if you are looking for a synonym. Apart from the awareness of the existence of synonyms, your work in composition-writing will also have shown you that things are not as easy as the examples in (27) may have suggested. Imagine, for example, that you are writing an essay, and you are looking for a word with the same meaning as the adjective *beautiful*. Here is what the thesaurus in *Webster's New Encyclopedic Dictionary* will tell you:

(28) The thesaurus in *Webster's New Encyclopedic Dictionary*, s.v. *beautiful*:

> **beautiful, lovely, handsome, pretty, comely, fair** mean exciting sensuous or aesthetic pleasure. **Beautiful** applies to whatever excites the keenest of pleasure to the senses and stirs emotion through the senses (*beautiful* mountain scenery). **Lovely** is close to beautiful but applies to a narrower range of emotional excitation in suggesting the graceful, delicate or exquisite (a *lovely* melody). [...]

The first sentence of the thesaurus entry gives you six synonyms of the word *beautiful* – including the term *lovely*. From this sentence in the thesaurus we may infer that *beautiful, lovely, handsome, pretty, comely*, and *fair* all have the same meaning, and that we as language users are, thus, free to use all six words interchangeably in any context in which we need a word with that meaning. This is, however, not true. The rest of the thesaurus entry is devoted to a description of the differences between the words listed as synonyms. These differences are usually subtle, but important. In our example, we can use *beautiful* and *lovely* interchangeably in contexts in which we talk, for example, about a dress (*a beautiful/lovely dress*) or about the weather (*beautiful/lovely weather*). In the following contexts, however, only one of the two words can be used. Awkward sentences are marked with a question mark.

(29) a. She is more **beautiful** than ever.
 a.' ?She is more **lovely** than ever.
 b. Big is **beautiful**.
 b.' ?Big is **lovely**.
 c. ?Richard is a **beautiful** person.
 c.' Richard is a **lovely** person.
 d. ?That was a **beautiful** cup of tea.
 d.' That was a **lovely** cup of tea.

From these data we may hypothesise that *lovely* cannot be used to describe purely visual attractiveness (as in (29a') and (29b')), whereas *beautiful* cannot be used to describe a person's character (as in (29c)) or an experience that has given us pleasure (as in (29d)). The thesaurus entry in (28) tries to capture this difference by saying that *lovely* 'applies to a narrower range of emotional excitation in suggesting the graceful, delicate or exquisite'. Note that, if our hypothesis about the data in (29) is correct, the description in the thesaurus does not tell the whole story. It suggests that there are restrictions on the use of *lovely*, but not on the use of *beautiful*.

So what does the discussion of the thesaurus entry for *beautiful* tell us about the nature of synonymy? It provides us with a showpiece example of how difficult it is to find true synonymy in a language. Indeed, most words that we would assume to be synonymous at first sight turn out to exhibit semantic differences upon closer inspection. This has led some linguists to believe that there is no such thing as true synonymy. In the case of *beautiful* and *lovely*, we have seen that the two words exhibit subtle differences in meaning which make it, for example, impossible to describe a nice person as *beautiful* (29c). We have also seen that a thesaurus is a tool which tries to represent the complexities of synonymy in language for the purpose of practical language tasks.

The way in which dictionary (or thesaurus) makers proceed to determine subtle meaning differences between near-synonyms closely resembles what we did in (29), but on a much larger scale. What we need to have in order to determine differences in meaning between words is very large amounts of data, showing us the use of the relevant words in context (such as our four sentences in (29a-d)). These data can then be used to determine in which types of contexts a word may be used, which in turn allows us to infer their semantic properties – the factors which make them eligible to be used in a given context. Data about the use of words in context nowadays mostly comes from large electronic **corpora**. A corpus is a compilation of machine-readable texts, both written and spoken, from a language. The corpora used by dictionary makers are compiled in such a way that they are as representative as possible of the language as it is spoken and written today. For British English, the largest and most well-known corpus is the **British National Corpus (BNC)**. It contains about 100 million words from samples of both written and spoken British English, and it is standardly used by dictionary makers and linguists alike (dictionary publishers have a large share in the BNC Consortium, which owns and manages the corpus). For North American English, the corresponding corpus is the **American National Corpus (ANC**, website: http://americannationalcorpus.org). Another major corpus of American English, which is freely available on the internet, is the Corpus of Contemporary American English (COCA, at http://www.americancorpus.org/). The BNC can be explored using the internet (at http://www.natcorp.ox.ac.uk/), which you are very welcome to try out. It provides a restricted, but nevertheless quite comprehensive search function free of charge, which allows you to explore the kinds of things that can be done with a corpus. For example, if you type our example word *beautiful* into the search box, the search engine will show you that the corpus contains 8,394 occurrences of the word *beautiful*. Additionally, it will provide you with a random sample of 50 examples in which the word *beautiful* is used in the texts in the BNC. This you could use, for example, to check whether *beautiful* is used to describe a person's character; according to our hypothesis from above, it should not.

As a final point in our discussion of the problems involved in synonymy, I would like to come back to our examples in (27). Our detailed discussion of *beautiful* vs. *lovely* has served as an example to show that the concept of synonymy is in many cases problematic because synonyms may exhibit subtle meaning differences. The two other examples in (27), *try* vs. *attempt* and *job* vs. *occupation*, illustrate yet two more reasons for why it is problematic to assume that two words have the same meaning, i.e. are synonyms. Like *lovely* and *beautiful*, the two pairs *job* and *occupation*, and *try* and *attempt* can be used interchangeably in the sentences in (27); they are synonyms. Again, however, they are not interchangeable in any context. Consider the following sentences as examples:

(30) a. I did a good **job**.
 a.' *I did a good **occupation**.
 b. I **tried** sushi today.
 b.' *I **attempted** sushi today.

We know already from our discussion of polysemy at the beginning of this section that the word *job* is polysemous (cf. 25c). What we see illustrated in (30a/a'), then, is that the polysemy of *job* is not reflected in the synonym candidate, *occupation*. Whereas *job* can also mean 'task', *occupation* cannot. Of course, also *occupation* is polysemous, but the meanings of *occupation* are not the same as the meanings of *job*; the overlap of meanings between *job* and *occupation* is restricted to only one meaning ('professional employment'). An analogous argument can be made for the word pair in (30b/b'), *try* and *attempt*. Like *job*, *try* is polysemous: For example, it can mean 'to attempt to do something' as well as 'to do or use something for a short while to discover if it is suitable, successful, enjoyable etc.' (both definitions of meaning are taken from the *Longman Dictionary of Contemporary English*). The word *attempt* only shares the former of these two meanings, but not the latter.

Even if we ignore polysemy, there are further problems with synonymy. This becomes particularly obvious if we look again at the word pair *job* and *occupation*. In (31) you find two sentences from the BNC which contain either *job* or *occupation*. In (32) you see what happens if we exchange the two words in the sentences.

(31) a. Anne wondered if Ella knew just how queer they were but only said, `;I think it would be better all round if Cormac tried to get a **job**. (BNC G16 502)
 b. The certificate also includes details of the name, sex, final **occupation** and place of residence of the deceased person. (BNC ECE 452)

(32) a. ?Anne wondered if Ella knew just how queer they were but only said, `;I think it would be better all round if Cormac tried to get an **occupation**.
 b. ?The certificate also includes details of the name, sex, final **job** and place of residence of the deceased person.

In all sentences in (31) and (32) the words *job* and *occupation* mean 'professional employment'. However, whereas the sentences in (31) are acceptable, the sentences in (32) sound awkward, and the interesting question is, of course, why this is so. If we look more closely at the original BNC sentences in (31), we notice that they differ in terms of the level of formality of the context in which they are uttered. Whereas the sentence in (31a) is obviously part of a casual, informal conversation among friends, the sentence in (31b) is part of a formal, written text. We say that the sentences in (31a) and (31b) belong to different **registers** of English. The term register is used in linguistics to capture the fact that language varies in a systematic way according to the situation in which it is used. Important parameters that determine this situation-dependent variation are the level of formality (formal vs. informal, colloquial language), the medium (spoken vs. written language), and the social or personal relationship between interlocutors (e.g. talk among close friends vs. talk between teachers and their young pupils). The sentences in (31a) and (31b) thus differ in terms of all three of these parameters: (31a) belongs to an informal and spoken type of register, whereas (31b) belongs to a formal, written register. Furthermore, in (31a) the interactants are friends or at least people who know each other quite well, whereas in (31b) the author of the sentence will probably not be personally known to the reader.

What the differences between the sentences in (31) and (32) show us is that, although both *job* and *occupation* may mean 'professional employment', they differ in terms of the register in which they may be used. *Occupation* is inappropriate in informal, oral registers, whereas *job* is less likely to be used in highly formal, written registers. Note that this does not mean that the registers in which *job* and *occupation* can be used may not overlap. We already saw in (27) that in some contexts, *job* and *occupation* may indeed be used interchangeably.

In this section we have been concerned with the problem of how we can differentiate between different lexemes in the mental lexicon. We have seen that there are three different aspects to this problem: First of all, there are polysemous lexemes, i.e. lexemes which have more than one meaning. Polysemy is widespread among lexemes in English. Secondly, there are homonymous lexemes, which resemble each other in terms of form, but which differ in meaning. In contrast to the meanings of a polysemous lexeme, the meanings of homonyms are completely unrelated. Finally, lexemes may also differ in form, but resemble each other in terms of meaning. These are synonyms. The three cases are illustrated in figure 5.1.:

170   *The meaning of words and sentences: semantics*

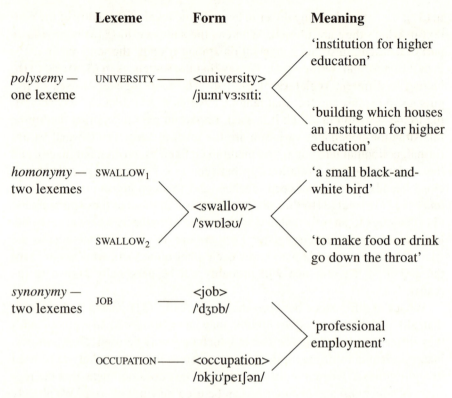

Figure 5.1. Polysemy, homonymy, and synonymy

In our discussion of synonymy we have then seen that this is a difficult concept. Many linguists assume that true synonymy does not exist; word pairs which we may consider to be candidates for synonymy turn out to be only near-synonyms upon closer inspection. Using some examples, we saw that near-synonyms indeed exhibit subtle meaning differences, and that meaning equivalences between lexemes usually do not include all meanings of polysemous lexemes. Finally, near-synonyms often differ in terms of the registers in which they may be used.

5.5. Conclusion

In this chapter we have looked at the linguistic discipline which is concerned with the meaning of linguistic expressions: semantics. We saw that meaning is a relational property which describes the relation between the form of a linguistic expression and a mental concept. This relation needs to be distinguished from the relation which links linguistic expressions and mental concepts to the objects (or events or situations) that we talk about, which is described in linguistics in terms of reference and denotation.

Concerning the question of which kinds of linguistic expressions can have meaning, we saw that meaning arises on different levels. Depending on whether the meaning of a linguistic expression involves the combination of the meanings of parts of that expression, we distinguish between compositional and non-compositional types of meaning. Non-compositional meaning can be found in morphologically simplex words and in morphemes. Compositional meaning can be found in morphologically complex words as well as in larger syntactic constituents such as phrases and sentences. The compositional meaning of a linguistic expression can be decomposed into the meanings of the parts of that expression. Interestingly, we saw that in such complex expressions the semantic scope of some elements (e.g. inflectional suffixes) may pertain to the whole expression. Furthermore, we saw that it is necessary to distinguish compositional semantic meaning from pragmatic meaning.

In the third section of this chapter we looked at the organisation of word meaning in the mental lexicon. The mental lexicon can be compared to a huge network — lexemes are not isolated entries, but entertain a multitude of links to other lexemes. Some of the main categories that create links in the mental lexicon are semantic in nature. Lexemes are organised into lexical fields, whose members are linked through sense relations such as hyponymy and oppositeness. Sense relations are different in nature from connotation, a phenomenon which also plays an important role in creating links in the mental lexicon. Finally, we looked at meaning-related properties of single lexemes. Here we saw that polysemy is a widespread property of lexemes. Polysemy needs to be distinguished from homonymy. A third type of meaning-related property of lexemes is that they may have nearly the same meaning as other lexemes. True synonyms are very rare; most pertinent words may be considered near-synonyms because they may be used interchangeably in some contexts, but not in others.

In what follows we will add a wider perspective to the study of meaning of linguistic expressions. From the analysis of semantic meaning we will move on to pragmatic meaning.

Further Reading

There are many good textbook-length treatments of semantics on the market; I recommend in particular Löbner (2002), Portner (2005), Saeed (2000), and Kreidler (1998) — the latter deals explicitly with English semantics, but Löbner, Portner, and Saeed also have a focus on English. If you want to know more about English word semantics, you may want to have a look at Lipka's (2002) textbook on English Lexicology. In addition to word semantics, Lipka (2002) covers phenomena like idioms and collocation, and provides a useful, up-to-date overview of basic resources for the study of English word meaning: dictionaries and corpora. Finally, if you are interested in the mental lexicon, the reading of your choice will most likely be Aitchison's (2003) book *Words in the Mind*. It provides quite a thorough introduction to research into the mental lexicon that covers both psycholinguistic methodology and its major results. On top of that the book is written in such a way that it is fun reading even for absolute beginners in linguistics.

Exercises

Basic level

Exercise 5.1.: Meaning and reference

Explain the difference between meaning and reference, using the pairs of expressions that are in bold print in the following sentences as examples.

(33) a. **The President of the United States** visited Germany in 2005.
 a.' **George W. Bush** visited Germany in 2005.
 b. Someone **stole** my wallet.
 b.' Someone **nicked** my wallet.
 c. Peter went to **London**.
 c.' Peter went **there**.

Exercise 5.2.: Sense relations

Determine the sense relations between the words in the following sets.

(34) a. animal, bird, robin
 b. arrogant, humble
 c. wipe, sweep, polish, scrub, vaccuum
 d. possible, impossible
 e. give, take
 f. guest, host

Exercise 5.3.: Word associations and semantics

Here is a selection of words frequently associated with the word *butterfly* (from Jenkins (1970), quoted by Aitchison (2003: 86)). Analyse the words in terms of their semantic relation with the stimulus word. Which of them are sense relations? Which of them are connotations?

(35)
moth   insect   bird   fly   yellow   net   pretty   flower(s)   bug

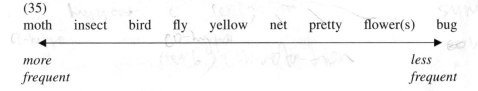

more frequent   *less frequent*

Advanced level

Exercise 5.4.: Lexical fields in English and German

a. Here are four of the most important hyponyms of the German word *Straße* ('road', [ʃtʁaːsə]). They are classified in the schema according to the criteria which are most relevant for subclassifying roads in German. Explain the semantic differences between the four co-hyponyms.

(36)

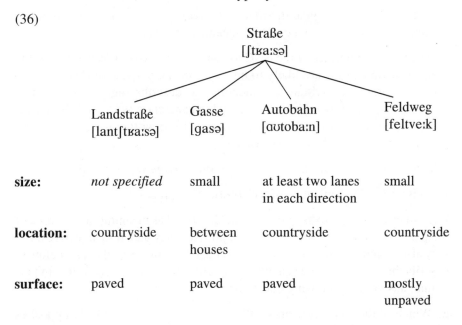

b. Use a good monolingual dictionary to determine the meaning differences between the co-hyponyms of English *road* that are given below. Use the same categories that were given for the German data in (36).

(37)

```
                        road
         ┌────────┬──────┼──────┬──────────┐
      street   alley  motorway  lane   country road
```

c. Set up a schema for English that is analogous to the one for German in (36).

d. Discuss the similarities and differences between the ways English and German organise hyponyms of *road / Straße*.

Exercise 5.5.: Synonymy

Investigate the similarities and differences in meaning in the two word pairs given below. Discuss whether we can call the members of the pairs synonyms. How do they differ in meaning? Proceed as follows:

a. Use a good monolingual dictionary to investigate whether the two words are polysemous and, if so, how their meanings overlap.

b. Use the web interface of the BNC to compare the two words in terms of the register in which they are likely to be used; for the purpose of this exercise, use only 'oral' vs. 'written' as categories to describe register in terms of meaning. Type each word into the search box, and classify the 50 hits you get according to whether they come from oral or from written texts. Then compare your results for the two words.

(38) a. *intrude* vs. *butt in*   b. *change* vs. *alter*

Exercise 5.6.: The semantics of word formation processes

English has many prefixes which can be described as meaning 'not'. Three of them are *un-*, *non-*, and *anti-*. All three prefixes may attach to adjectives; *un-* may also attach to verbs, *anti-* may also attach to nouns. Use the data below to describe in more detail the semantic properties of *un-*, *non-*, and *anti-*. In particular, answer the following questions:

a. Which of the complex words with *un-*, *non-*, and *anti-* are truly opposites of their bases and which are not?

b. How many different types of opposites do you find in the data?

c. Would you consider *un-*, *non-*, and *anti-* polysemous? Give reasons.

(39) **un- + adjective**　　　　　　　　　　　　**un- + verb**
　　　unhappy　　　　　< happy　　　　　unwind　　　< wind
　　　unwise　　　　　 < wise　　　　　　uncover　　 < cover
　　　uncomfortable　　< comfortable　　 unwrap　　　< wrap

　　　non- + adjective
　　　non-scientific　　< scientific
　　　non-commercial　< commercial
　　　non-biological　　< biological

　　　anti- + adjective　　　　　　　　　***anti- + noun***
　　　anti-capitalistic　< capitalistic　　　anti-hero　　< hero
　　　anti-social　　　　< social　　　　　　anti-climax　< climax
　　　anti-clockwise　　< clockwise　　　　anti-matter　< matter

Chapter 6
Studying language in use: pragmatics

6.1. Introduction

In the previous chapters many interesting facts about how a language is structured have been introduced. There is, however, one question we have not raised so far and which might strike you at first sight as being rather simple: What do speakers use language for, and how do they use it? The answer is by no means simple as we will come to realise in this chapter. But for you to get a rough idea for a start, consider the examples below. Before reading on, try to decide for each example what intentions the speakers have when uttering these sentences.

(1)   a.   a mother to her son: Take some more vegetables!
      b.   a teacher to schoolchildren: Lions have gold-coloured fur.
      c.   a friend to a friend: I'll phone you tomorrow.
      d.   a priest to a child: I baptise thee Alexander Frederic.

You might guess that in (1a) the speaker uses this sentence in order to make her son do something, namely eat more vegetables. In (1b) the speaker wants to state a fact and to inform schoolchildren of this fact. (1c) is a typical example of somebody indicating a promise. Finally, the speaker in (1d) has yet a different intention: to baptise a child.

What do we learn from this brief analysis? We can say that when people use language, they apparently do not do this just for the sake of using it. Usually, speakers have a certain intention, such as stating, promising, declaring, requesting, making somebody do something, and many other things. But what about the listeners, you might be tempted to ask. Think of your own experience as listeners. Supposedly, in most cases you listen to somebody in order to figure out these intentions.

What we also learn from the examples above is that being able to pronounce words, to combine morphemes and words, and to understand the semantic meaning of sentences is only one part of the linguistic knowledge speakers carry with them. Besides having this knowledge, which linguists often call 'grammatical competence', users of a language are also able to employ it to state certain communicative intentions. Therefore, in addition to studying the phonological, morphological, syntactic, and semantic aspects of a language (and this is what we did in the previous chapters) we can also analyse how speakers use language to express their **communicative intentions**, and how hearers decode and understand these intentions. And the insight that humans use a language to state certain intentions raises many other, more specific questions: How do speakers express their intentions? What different kinds of intentions are there? How do listeners extract these intentions from what is being said? Are there any rules or principles speakers and listeners observe in order to use language effectively and successfully? The area of linguistics that deals with all these questions is called **pragmatics**.

Yet another important observation is due here. If I asked you to carry out phonological, morphological or syntactic analyses of the sentences in (1), you would primarily deal with the pertinent linguistic units of analysis, such as phonemes, morphemes, words, sentences, etc., and investigate what they look like and how they are structured, i.e. you would mainly deal with the form of these linguistic units. In a pragmatic investigation, the primary concern is what the speakers use language for, i.e. its function in discourse. Pragmatic studies deal with the question of what speakers want to achieve by using language and look at which linguistic forms speakers employ for this purpose.

In this chapter we will first clarify what exactly is meant by the fact that intentions can be expressed through language. We will then explore different kinds of intentions which speakers pursue when communicating. This will lead us to the question of how speakers convey these intentions linguistically and what knowledge hearers need in order to figure out the speakers' intentions. Finally, we will see what principles language users observe to make communication successful.

6.2. Expressing intentions through language

6.2.1. Using language to act: speech acts

When I asked you above what people use language for, we saw that they do so to express certain communicative intentions. Interestingly, if I asked you what you use a mixer or a spade or your eyes for, you would most likely answer that you do so to perform certain actions, such as mixing, digging, or seeing. Now, can we also say that expressing communicative intentions is a kind of action, similar to mixing, digging, or seeing? To answer this question, let us go back to our examples from the previous section, repeated below for convenience. Think about whether we can say that the speakers perform a certain action in each of the examples.

(2) a. a mother to her son: Take some more vegetables!
    b. a teacher to schoolchildren: Lions have gold-coloured fur.
    c. a friend to a friend: I'll phone you tomorrow.
    d. a priest to a child: I baptise thee Alexander Frederic.

The mother in (2a) does not just express the intention of making her son eat more vegetables. In fact, what she does is commanding her son to do so. Similarly, the schoolteacher in (2b) also does something: She states a fact. And by uttering *"I'll phone you tomorrow"*, the speaker in (2c) performs the action of promising. Finally, the priest in (2d) is involved in the action of baptising.

So we can say that when rendering their intentions through language, the speakers in (2) actually perform different actions, such as commanding, stating, promising, and baptising. Thus, in the same way in which we use a mixer to perform the action of mixing, or our eyes to see, we use language to perform different actions. Speakers act through language.

This insight was formulated by the philosopher John L. Austin (1962), who developed it into a fully-fledged theory. Austin called the linguistic actions performed by speakers in a certain context with a certain communicative intention **speech acts**, and his theory came to be known as **Speech Act Theory**. So, in Austin's terms the speaker saying *"I'll phone you tomorrow"* performs the speech act of promising, and the speaker baptising a child the speech act of baptising, etc. Now you might ask whether everything speakers say can be regarded as performing a certain action. To answer this question, let us take a look at the example in (3) and decide whether it can be regarded as a speech act.

(3) Well, I mean there was a ...

The example in (3) is an incomplete sentence, which leaves its intention unclear to us. Therefore, we can hardly say that an action is performed through it. In general, however, it seems that the notion of speech act can cover a considerable number of instances in speakers' linguistic behaviour. We should therefore conclude that speakers perform certain acts by using language and that in cases where we cannot recognise such acts we should possibly seek for other explanations, outside Speech Act Theory. In the next section we will take a closer look at how acting through language actually works.

6.2.2. Speech acts: a closer look

In the present section we will deal with the question of how performing a certain speech act works in detail. To do so, we will use the following example. Imagine your aunt, a champion cake-baker and tea-time-organiser, invites you and your younger sister to have a cup of tea with her one nice afternoon. You really enjoy your aunt's apple pie and want to pay her a compliment. What you say is:

(4) What a delicious pie!

What aspects are conveyed in this speech act? One crucial thing conveyed in (4) is a certain semantic meaning. We have discussed this type of meaning in chapter 5 already. You have seen that semantic meaning can be derived compositionally from the semantic meanings of separate words a given sentence consists of. So the semantic meaning of the example in (4) can be expressed as follows: 'The sweet fruit cake is tasty'. Besides the semantic meaning, the sentence in (4) also has a certain syntactic structure. It is an 'exclamatory sentence', i.e. a sentence beginning with *what* or *how* which function as modifiers within a noun phrase or an adjectival phrase. Quite often, exclamatory sentences do not contain any verb. They are typically used to signal speakers' emotions. Another crucial aspect conveyed in (4) is the speaker's communicative intention. Evidently, the intention the speaker wants to express through (4) is to pay a compliment.

Quite often, the performance of a certain act does not end with uttering a sentence. Consider what might happen after you have uttered the sentence in (4). Your aunt, whom we assume to be a polite person, would most likely react to it by, for example, saying something like *"Oh, thank you."* or by offering you some more of her apple pie. Another possibility is that she just says nothing because she might not be listening to you but to your younger sister right at the moment. This means, then, that in addition to the linguistic form and the communicative intention there is one more aspect of speech acts that is of interest to us: what reaction, if any, they cause in the hearers.

The three aspects of speech acts we have just explored are an intrinsic part of Speech Act Theory, and each of them is given a special term. The term **locution** is used to refer to the linguistic form of a speech act. The communicative intention rendered by the speaker, such as promising, commanding, making complements, etc. is called **illocution** or 'illocutionary force'. Finally, the effect produced on the hearer is termed **perlocution**. Note that the term 'speech act' is also used by some linguists to refer solely to the illocution since the illocution is the most crucial part of a speech act.

You might have noticed that there are many different terms used to refer to speakers' intentions: communicative intention, communicative purpose, intended meaning, implied meaning, illocution, illocutionary force. In chapter 5 you have also encountered another important term used to refer to a speaker's intention, pragmatic meaning, and you have seen that in contrast to semantic meaning, this type of meaning cannot be extracted from the meanings of the individual words. In our example, for instance, the pragmatic meaning is 'I complement you on baking such a delicious pie'. There are some differences in the use of different terms referring to communicative intentions by different linguists which are sometimes motivated by the adherence to different theoretical positions. We will, however, use these terms interchangeably throughout this chapter since these differences are not significant in the present context.

Our observations above also lead us to another important terminological remark. Until now we have referred to our examples as 'sentences'. This term is suitable for syntactic or semantic analyses, since it refers to an important structural entity. For pragmatic analysis, however, the term 'sentence' is not satisfactory since it does not allow us to draw the distinction between the structural, formal level of analysis and the pragmatic one. Hence, in pragmatics, a distinction is made between 'sentence' and 'utterance'. Whereas the term 'sentence' refers to a formal, structural unit, the term **utterance** refers to a realisation of a speaker's communicative intention: what the speaker says at a given point in time at a given location with a given intention. This distinction is important because utterances quite often do not equal sentences formally. On the one hand, there are utterances which consist of less than a sentence. For instance, if somebody asks you: *"Where is your dad?"* you might answer *"At home."*, which is formally a phrase (a PP), and not a sentence, but pragmatically it is an utterance. On the other hand, there are utterances that comprise more than a sentence. For example, if somebody asks you about a new educational programme, and your answer is *"This programme is simply awful. It's absolutely frustrating."*, this answer should be regarded as one utterance whose purpose is to show the speaker's feelings. Formally, however, this one utterance consists of two sentences. You might have noticed that most of the time we have marked utterances by double quotation marks in this chapter so far and we will continue to use this notational convention in the sections to follow.

The insight that speakers act through language and communicate certain intentions when performing these acts raises the question of which different intentions can be expressed through language. Is there a system that allows us to describe and perhaps classify them? The next section will deal with this problem.

6.2.3. Classifying speech acts

You might have noticed above that speakers may have rather diverse intentions, such as promising, commanding, complimenting, etc. Thus, there must be a great variety of speech acts performed by speakers. To get a slightly better idea of how diverse communicative intentions really are, consider the following examples and try to identify the intention behind each utterance:

(5) I christen you Marie Claire.
My hypothesis is that compound stress is variable.
I apologise for this awful mess.
You are under arrest.
Shall I get you some water?
I claim that this theory needs revision.
Congratulations on your appointment.
Our team has won the competition.
Thank you for taking care of my daughter.
Good job, Claire!
You are fired.
Be quiet, Jaye.
I name this ship 'Fortune'.
Do this again, and I'll tell your parents.
Do come and visit us tomorrow.
I am sorry that I could not come to your birthday party.
I'll bring you a map of London.
I hereby pronounce you husband and wife.
I refuse to answer this question.
Could you please show me the way?

You might have come up with a similar identification as is provided in (6):

(6)
utterances	intentions
I christen you Marie Claire.	baptising a child
My hypothesis is that compound stress is variable.	stating a hypothesis
I apologise for this awful mess.	apologising to somebody
You are under arrest.	arresting a person
Shall I get you some water?	offering something to somebody
I claim that this theory needs revision.	stating a claim
Congratulations on your appointment.	expressing a congratulation

(6) **utterances** **intentions**

utterances	intentions
Our team has won the competition.	stating a fact
Thank you for taking care of my daughter.	expressing gratitude to somebody
Good job, Claire!	expressing a praise
You are fired.	firing a person
Be quiet, Jaye.	making somebody do something
I name this ship 'Fortune'.	naming a ship
Do this again, and I'll tell your parents.	threatening somebody
Do come and visit us tomorrow.	inviting somebody
I am sorry that I could not come to your birthday party.	expressing a regret about something
I'll bring you a map of London.	promising something to somebody
I hereby pronounce you husband and wife.	marrying a couple
I refuse to answer this question.	refusing to do something
Could you please show me the way?	asking somebody to do something

We can conclude so far that there is a great diversity of different intentions, and thus of different speech acts. Our finding about this diversity raises two questions. First, how many different kinds of speech acts are there to be recognised? Five, fifty or five hundred? This seems to be a question to which pragmaticists do not have a ready-made answer. As Mey (2001: 105) reports, some linguists suggest that there are between five hundred and six hundred speech act types, others name only five or so. This leads us to our second question: Although it is undeniable that there are many kinds of speech acts, are there certain similarities between them that allow us to group them into certain classes?

To answer this question, we may try to find such similarities using the data above. Since any classification must be based on a more or less well-defined set of criteria, we will need such criteria for our purpose as well. We have seen that illocutions are the most crucial aspects of speech acts, and we might try to base our classification on these. More precisely, we take a look at whether some of the utterances we identified above can be regarded as similar to each other in what the speakers want to achieve by uttering them and whether we can make any generalisations about this aspect. Taking these similarities into account, one way of classifying the data could result in the five groups in (7a–e):

Expressing intentions through language 183

(7)	**utterances**	**intentions**
a.	I christen you Marie Claire.	baptising a child
	I hereby pronounce you husband and wife.	marrying a couple
	I name this ship 'Fortune'.	naming a ship
	You are under arrest.	arresting a person
	You are fired.	firing a person
b.	I claim that this theory needs revision.	stating a claim
	My hypothesis is that compound stress is variable.	stating a hypothesis
	Our team has won the competition.	stating a fact
c.	Thank you for taking care of my daughter.	expressing gratitude to somebody
	Good job, Claire!	expressing a praise
	I am sorry that I could not come to your birthday party.	expressing a regret about something
	I apologise for this awful mess.	expressing an apology for something
	Congratulations on your appointment.	expressing a congratulation
d.	Be quiet, Jaye.	making somebody do something
	Could you please show me the way?	asking somebody to do something
	Do come and visit us tomorrow.	inviting somebody to do something
e.	Shall I get you some water?	offering something to somebody
	I'll bring you a map of London.	promising something to somebody
	Do this again, and I'll tell your parents.	threatening somebody
	I refuse to answer this question.	refusing to do something

Now let us discuss in detail where the similarities in the intentions within each group in (7) lie. We will start with the utterances in (7a). By uttering *"I now pronounce you husband and wife."* the speaker wants to change an unmarried couple into a married one, and the utterance *"You are under arrest."* makes a free person a prisoner. If you consider the descriptions of the intentions indicated by the other utterances in (7a), such as marrying, arresting, naming, etc., you notice that all these actions change an existing state of affairs. An interesting fact about the utterances in (7a) is that we can make them more explicit by using *"I now declare"*: *"I now declare you husband and wife."*, *"I now declare that you are under arrest."*, and so on. The utterances in (7a) change an existing state of affairs by declaring something, and we can thus identify a first class of speech acts: **declarations**.

Let us now turn to the utterances in (7b). You might have noticed that some of them contain verbs such as *claim* or *name*. What do we use such words for? Usually, if we say *"I claim that this theory needs revision."* we describe what we believe to be true, or what we view as the existing state of affairs. Remarkably, even if no such verb is used, as in *"Our team has won the competition."*, it is clear that the speaker again describes something that she believes to be the actual state of affairs. In fact, you might imply verbs such as *claim* or *state* when using this utterance: *"(I claim/state that) our team has won the competition."*. Thus, all the utterances in (7b) can again be regarded as similar in their purpose of representing or asserting a state of affairs as it is viewed by the speaker. They can be put into a class of their own and can be termed **representatives** or **assertives**.

An interesting fact about the utterances in (7c) is that they contain words such as *sorry, apologise, thank*. What might speakers indicate by using these words? *Sorry* usually expresses the feeling of regret, *thank you* the feeling of gratitude, etc. Even if no such overt marker of feeling is used, as in *"Good job!"* we can say that what the speaker tries to convey here is a feeling of admiration or satisfaction. You might have noticed that some of these utterances have the form of exclamatory sentences, which often signal an emotional state of the speaker. Note, however, that exclamatory sentences represent only one of many possible forms through which emotions can be expressed. All in all we can conclude that the utterances in (7c) are similar in that they express feelings and speakers' inner states, and consequently we can single out yet another class: **expressives**.

And what is the similarity in the intentions behind the utterances in (7d)? When we say *"Be quiet, Jaye!"* we want to make Jaye perform a certain action, and if we ask *"Could you please show me the way?"* we usually want to make somebody show us the way. The same is achieved if our intention is to invite somebody: By saying *"Come to visit us tomorrow."* we want to make somebody visit us the next day. To sum up, utterances such as in (7d) direct hearers to perform some action and therefore form a class of their own, called **directives**.

Finally, let us take a look at the similarities between the utterances in (7e). By uttering *"Shall I get you some water?"* the speaker commits herself to bringing somebody some water in the future. By saying *"I refuse to answer this question."* the speaker commits herself to not answering this question in the future. In similar ways, when speakers promise something to somebody or threaten somebody, they commit themselves to doing something in the future. Note also that some of the utterances in (7e) contain expressions such as *I'll* which indicate the speaker's intention or willingness to perform some action in the future. So we can conclude that the intentions behind the utterances in (7e) are similar to each other, i.e. in that they commit speakers to certain actions. Therefore, such utterances can be regarded as a separate class: **commissives**.

Summarising, we can say that a great diversity of different speech acts can be classified into a set of only five classes, with each class comprising a number of intentions. The classification we discussed above and the terms for the different classes of speech acts were developed by the philosopher John R. Searle (1969). Still you might be tempted to ask whether Searle's classification really covers all the existing types. Can any utterance be fitted into this classification? To answer these questions, let us consider the following utterances and see how they can be classified according to Searle's categories.

(8) a. Did you manage to do the shopping?
 b. One more step, and I'll call the police.
 c. The salad tastes awful.

You might have some problems with clearly categorising these utterances, for different reasons. Thus, (8a) is difficult to categorise because in it, the speaker's intention is to ask a question and it is unclear whether asking questions should be regarded as a directive, a representative, or something else. Since asking a question usually makes the hearer answer this question, we could suggest to classify utterances like in (8a) as directives, or more specifically, requests for information.

The utterance in (8b) presents another problem in terms of speech act classification. You might agree that the intention behind this utterance is to threaten the interlocutor. We have dealt with threats in (7e) above and we classified them as commissives. Indeed, at first glance, the threat in (8b) can be classified as a commissive since by uttering it, the speaker commits herself to calling the police in case the hearer makes one more step. However, a closer look at such utterances as in (8b) reveals that committing herself to a future action is not the only intention the speaker has. In addition to this intention, the speaker also has the intention to make the hearer do something, namely, she wants to make the hearer stop moving any further. So what we have in the case of such a threat is not just one speech act, a commissive, but a combination of two speech acts, a commissive and a directive. For Searle's classification, this means that some speech acts cannot be assigned to one particular type, but seem to be combinations of two different types.

Straightforward classification in terms of speech act type is also problematic for the utterance in (8c) because we do not really know whether its intention is to state a fact, to complain, or something else, and thus we do not know what type of speech act it should be assigned to. Consider if embedding this utterance into the following situations, all taking place at a restaurant, makes the classification easier:

(9) a. Jane: I will meet Mr. Stevenson tomorrow. By the way, **the salad tastes awful**.
Robert: I don't find it tasty either.
b. Jane: **The salad tastes awful!**
Waiter: I am sorry.
c. Jane: **The salad tastes awful**, but I am too hungry and too tired to go somewhere else.
Robert: Shall I get you something else?

Now you will be able to say that in the first example the utterance is intended to inform the listener of the fact that the salad tastes awful, and can therefore be classified as a representative. In the second dialogue it expresses a complaint about the bad quality of the salad. So it should be an expressive. In (9c), it makes the hearer get something else and is therefore a request, i.e. a directive. As we can see, the utterance *"The salad tastes awful"* can be assigned to three different speech act classes depending on the context it is embedded in.

We gain two crucial insights from the discussion of the examples in (9) above. First, different illocutions can be expressed through one and the same linguistic form, i.e. one locution. Second, to identify the illocutionary force, and thus the type of speech act, it is important to take not only the linguistic form of an utterance into account, but also some additional information. As the examples in (9) above show, what we need on the one hand is information about what has been said before and after this utterance, i.e. the linguistic setting of this utterance, which is called its **linguistic context**. On the other hand, we need clues about who said something when, where, and to whom, and what the relation between the interlocutors is (e.g. whether they are friends, strangers, customer-waiter, etc.). In other words, we need information about the physical and/or social setting of the utterance. This is called the **non-linguistic context**.

To summarise, there is a great diversity of speech acts and of different contexts for a certain locution, which makes an all-embracing classification a difficult task. Indeed, Searle's classification is only one of several possible ways of grouping speech acts into larger classes. Although we should bear in mind that there are certain problems with Searle's classification, we can also say that it provides a good basis for dealing with the diversity of speech acts in an ordered way.

6.2.4. Realisations of speech acts: direct and indirect speech acts

We have seen above that one and the same locution can have different illocutions. We can now ask whether the same illocution can be expressed in different ways. Or, in more general terms, how are speech acts realised linguistically? To find an answer to this question, think of at least two alternative ways of advising somebody to see a doctor. You might come up with something like the following:

(10) a. I strongly advise you to see a doctor.
    b. Why don't you see a doctor?

This example illustrates that one and the same type of speech act can be realised in different ways. But what is the difference between these alternatives?

Let us first investigate how the illocutionary force is signalled in (10a). We can say that by using the verb *advise* the speaker directly indicates what speech act is being performed. Interestingly, the semantic meaning of this utterance is the same as its pragmatic meaning: 'I strongly advise you to see a doctor'. We can generalise that one way of conveying the illocutionary force is to signal it directly, for instance, by using a verb that explicitly indicates this force. Such verbs are known as **performative verbs**. Some examples of such verbs are listed below for illustration (the performative verbs are in bold):

(11) a. I **promise** to be there on time.
    b. I **claim** that this is my car.
    c. I **warn** you not to open this box.
    d. I **apologise** for my son's behaviour.

In contrast to the utterance in (10a), the utterance in (10b) does not contain any direct indications of advice. In fact, at the formal level, (10b) is an 'interrogative sentence', i.e. a sentence which is used to ask a question and has an inverted order of constituents where the subject is preceded by an auxiliary verb. However, at the functional level, (10b) is a piece of advice. So we can say that there is a mismatch between the form of this utterance (an interrogative sentence) and its function (to render advice). Note also that in contrast to (10a), the semantic meaning of the utterance in (10b) is 'What is the reason of the addressee's not going to a doctor?', and it differs from its pragmatic meaning which is 'I advise you to see a doctor.' We can generalise then that in (10b) advice is expressed indirectly through a request for information. In fact, (10b) is quite a common way of conveying advice in English. We can draw the conclusion that there are speech acts in which the illocution is conveyed indirectly.

To summarise our observations, we can say that the same illocution can be realised in different ways and these ways can differ in terms of directness. On the one hand, there are speech acts in which the relation between the linguistic form (i.e. locution) and the linguistic function (illocution) is straightforward. The speaker's communicative intention is therefore rendered directly. On the other hand, there are speech acts where there is a mismatch between linguistic form and linguistic function. Searle, who introduced this classification, termed the first type **direct speech acts** and the second type **indirect speech acts**.

Given the two patterns of realising speech acts, the question arises which of them is more common. Consider the following utterances. Identify their function and their form, and analyse them in terms of directness:

(12) a. Please share your course-book with me.
 b. Could you share your course-book with me?
 c. Oh goodness, I have left my course-book at home!

You might have recognised that the three examples have the same function: they are requests to share a course-book with the interlocutor. But in terms of form, there are interesting differences between the three. In the first example, the request is formally expressed through an 'imperative sentence', i.e. a sentence that has no overt subject and is usually used to convey an order. The imperative form and the use of the politeness marker *please* indicate the illocutionary force of the utterance in (12a) directly, there is a straightforward relation between the form and the function of this utterance. The semantic meaning of the utterance in (12a) is 'I want you to share your course-book with me', and it is the same as its pragmatic meaning. Hence, the utterance in (12a) is a direct request.

In the second example, the request is formally expressed by an interrogative sentence whose semantic meaning is 'Are you physically or otherwise able to provide me with this course-book?' In terms of form, we can classify (12b) as a question about the hearer's physical ability to perform a certain action. We can thus say that the request is expressed here indirectly through a question about the hearer's physical ability to perform a certain action. The form of this utterance and its function do not match. Hence, (12b) can be regarded as an indirect request.

Finally, in the third example, the request is formally realised by a 'declarative sentence', i.e. a sentence that has a subject-verb order of constituents and is usually used to state something. The semantic meaning of the utterance in (12c) is 'I forgot to bring my course-book with me', and it is not the same as its pragmatic meaning. Thus, the request in (12c) is expressed indirectly through stating a fact. Again, there is no one-to-one relation between the form and the function of this utterance. Therefore, similarly to (12b), it is an indirect request.

If you now consider how often you ask people to do something by using the indirect type of request, as in (12b) or (12c), you will realise that indirect speech acts are possibly more frequently used than direct ones. They are often used in cases when politeness comes into play, as we will see in the last section of this chapter.

To conclude, we have seen that the same illocution can be realised in a number of ways that differ in the degree of their directness. This insight raises a rather interesting question: If there are different ways of rendering the same intention, are there some that are more effective than others? In other words, what is necessary to make a speech act successful? The next section is devoted to this question.

6.2.5. Performing speech acts successfully: felicity conditions

When a certain speech act is performed, the speaker normally wants it to count as this certain speech act. This presupposes that the illocution is properly conveyed by the speaker and properly recognised by the hearer. For instance, when we perform the speech act of requesting, we want it to count as a request. In other words, speakers want the speech acts they perform to be successful. But what makes a certain utterance a successful or unsuccessful speech act? To answer this question, consider the utterances in (13). Try to figure out what type of speech act we are dealing with here, and whether there are any problems with these acts. Pay special attention to the context provided for each example.

(13) a. If you move, I'll call the police. (addressed to somebody who does not understand English)
   b. If you don't pay me, I resigned. (addressed to your boss)
   c. If you spill the milk all over you, I will buy you an ice-cream. (a mother to her child who really likes ice-cream)
   d. If you leave the bathroom in this awful state again, I will kill you. (a wife to her husband)

In all the utterances above the speakers state that they will do something unpleasant under certain circumstances. We are therefore dealing with threats. By uttering a threat, speakers commit themselves to a certain action in the future, in case hearers do, or do not do, something the speakers want them to do, or not to do. Given this fact, each of the threats in (13) is problematic in its own way and we will discuss why.

In the first example the problem is that since the hearer does not understand English, she does not understand the threat at all. The natural consequence of this is that she is unable to recognise the intention behind this speech act and does not feel threatened by it. Thus, this speech act does not count as a threat, and is therefore not successful. What does this tell us about the conditions under which a given speech act can be successful? The example in (13a) shows that one condition for a successful speech act is that the hearer must be able to understand the locution, i.e. the utterance with its phonological properties, syntactic structure, semantic meaning, etc. This condition is termed 'general condition', and it holds for any utterance, be it a request, a congratulation, a greeting or a declaration.

But what is wrong about (13b), you might wonder. Indeed, the general condition is met for (13b) since there is no indication that the hearer does not understand English. Take a close look at the second part of the utterance in (13b). What should strike you is that it is in the simple past, a tense form which indicates an action that took place in the past. And we definitely cannot threaten somebody with a past action. We can say then that successful threats must refer to future actions. So if we formulate the utterance in (13b) differently, as in *"If you do not pay me, I will resign"*, it would count as a threat and would thus be a successful speech act. The problem with the speech act in (13b) allows us to formulate another type of condition which should be met for a speech act to be successful: A speech act should clearly and properly render its content. This condition is called 'propositional content condition' and it also holds for all different types of speech acts. 'Proposition' is the term used in semantics and pragmatics to indicate the semantic content of a sentence.

The threat in (13c) is another puzzling case. Since the hearer understands English, and the threat is about a future act, and this is properly conveyed by the use of *will*, the general and the propositional content conditions are met. However, given the fact that the child likes ice-cream, this threat is ridiculous, since you cannot threaten somebody with something pleasant. So for a threat to be successful, a certain prerequisite must be fulfilled, namely that the future action expressed in the threat be unpleasant for the hearer. Since eating ice-cream is in the child's interest, this prerequisite is not fulfilled in the case at hand.

What are the prerequisites for other types of speech act? Let us investigate the case of requests, for instance *"Please lift this table"*. Surely one would not ask a three-year-old child or a sick-looking skinny person to lift a heavy table. Why not? Because we usually impose requests only upon those people we can assume to be able to fulfill what is requested. So, one of the prerequisites for a successful request is that the listener is able to carry it out. In more general terms this means that, for a given speech act to be successful, certain prerequisites must be fulfilled before it takes place. These prerequisites prepare the ground for a successful speech act, and therefore this condition is termed 'preparatory condition'. We can assume that there should be preparatory conditions for each type of speech act, but the nature of these conditions is different for different speech acts, as we have seen in the cases of threats and requests.

Turning now to the threat in (13d), you might have noticed that it cannot be successful because no mentally sane person can earnestly intend to kill somebody for such a trifle as leaving a bathroom in an awful state. And you might imagine that the husband does not really feel threatened by it. So what makes the threat in (13d) not successful is the presumed insincerity of the wife. She would normally not intend to carry out the threat. Sincerity plays a role in other speech acts as well. Requests or promises, offers or invitations are normally successful when speakers really intend to ask, promise, offer, or invite. Imagine a friend of yours addresses you with the words *"You are under arrest!"* at a party. This would not count as a declaration since first, your friend is not a recognised authority in charge of arresting people. Second, declarations change the state of affairs, and since your friend is joking and not really intending to arrest you, this declaration does not change anything. So we can conclude that for a speech act to be successful, yet another condition should be fulfilled. The speaker should earnestly and sincerely intend to carry out the act. The term used to refer to this condition is self-explaining, it is the 'sincerity condition'.

In addition to the conditions just discussed, there is yet another condition which is necessary for a speech act to be successful. For instance, for a threat to be successful, the speaker must really regard it as a threat, and the hearer should interpret it as a threat, and not as something else. For instance, in the case of the utterance *"If you do not do your job properly, I will complain to the boss."* the speaker should believe that he or she really threatens somebody by uttering it, and the hearer should recognise it as a threat. Similarly, the compliment *"You've done a wonderful job!"* is a successful compliment only if the speaker believes it to be a compliment and the hearer recognises it as a compliment, and not, for instance, as a joke or as a complaint. In general, we can conclude that for a speech act to be successful, it should count for both the speaker and the hearer as the realisation of this act. Since this condition must hold in any case it is called 'essential condition'.

To sum up, we have seen that for speakers to perform speech acts successfully, certain types of conditions should usually be met. We have mainly used threats here as an example for illustrating these conditions, but such conditions can be elaborated for each type of speech act. The collective technical term for such conditions as introduced by Searle is **felicity conditions**, since they make an utterance a felicitous, i.e. successful, speech act. We have seen in our discussion of the examples in (13) that in order to determine whether a speech act is felicitous, contextual information should be taken into account. In general, we can say that felicity conditions are like hidden rules for speech acts. When a speech act is performed, both the speaker and the hearer usually believe that the conditions are met. Misunderstandings between the speaker and the hearer thus often arise because some felicity condition is not met, although the speaker or the hearer believe it is.

6.3. Understanding utterance meaning

We have seen above that there are different ways of expressing communicative intentions. Given this diversity and complexity, we might wonder how hearers manage to understand utterances. Indeed, processing utterances proceeds so fast that we normally do not reflect on what we do in order to understand them. In this section we will explore some of the technical details of understanding utterances and discuss which factors enable hearers to decode speakers' intentions.

Let us start with the following situation. Imagine your friend and you enter a coffee shop and want to choose a piece of cake from a variety of cakes displayed. It is the first time that you enter this shop, whereas your friend has been there before and knows what kinds of cakes are available. You are allergic to nuts, and your friend knows about this allergy. After some contemplation of the cakes, your friend addresses you with the following utterance:

(14) That cake over there contains nuts.

How would you proceed to understand the utterance in (14)? Since normally the process of understanding utterances takes place in milliseconds, it might seem strange to you that we are speaking of a procedure. But what we will try to do here is to reconstruct a slow-motion version of how hearers arrive at utterance meaning.

To understand the utterance in (14), you as a hearer would most likely first try to figure out the semantic meaning, and then deal with the question of what your friend intends by uttering it, i.e. what its pragmatic meaning is. In general, the process of discovering the pragmatic meaning of utterances is called **inferencing** and the results of these inferencing procedures are called **inferences**. You have already seen in chapter 5 that semantic meaning is usually construed compositionally from the meaning of the individual words or phrases. In our case, you might arrive at something like 'The sweet baked food a short distance away from you has dry brown hard-shelled fruits inside.' The next step is to sort out what the speaker means by this utterance. To do so, you need to know a variety of different things which we will discuss below.

First, you need to know which cake is meant by *that cake over there*. Here, the linguistic entities *that* and *over there* provide the necessary clue. As we have seen in chapter 5, *that* and *over there* are deictic expressions, i.e. linguistic 'pointing devices' which help the hearer to locate and identify objects in a given situation. The deictic expression *that* usually refers to a more distant object available in a particular situation, and *over there* localises the object in question a short distance away from the speaker, with potentially other objects in between. However, in order to understand which cake is actually meant you need to know where 'that' and 'over there' are located exactly in this particular situation. You can figure this out only if you are part of the situation in which this utterance is spoken, and if you are aware of all the pertinent physical objects, as well as the gestures, the mimic, posture, etc. of the participants that are part of this situation. In other words, you share with the speaker the knowledge of the **situational context** of this utterance, also called **situational knowledge**. Hence we can state that understanding utterance meaning requires the knowledge of the situational context in which this utterance is made.

Now you know what is meant by *that cake over there*, but you still have to figure out what your friend intends to say by stating the fact that this cake contains nuts. To do so, you can ask yourself why it might be important that your friend mentions this fact. You might recollect that your friend knows that you are allergic to nuts. So this is knowledge that the two of you share, presumably because friends talk about such things. This type of knowledge is therefore termed **interpersonal knowledge**.

However, the fact that your friend knows about your allergy does not help you to completely understand what she means. In fact, you are able to understand what your friend means if you know that eating something you are allergic to is dangerous. And where do you have this knowledge from? On the one hand, you know it from your own experience since you might have already been in a serious health danger after eating nuts. On the other hand, you might also have gained it by reading about allergies, or by watching a programme about it on TV, or by being informed about it by a doctor. The knowledge you gained in the latter way is similar to your knowledge about many other things around you in the world, such as that dogs are four-legged animals or that rivers flow in valleys and not on mountain tops. It is a part of your **world knowledge**.

You might have noticed that the last two types of knowledge differ from situational knowledge in one respect. Facts such as which cake is meant and which gestures are made can be inferred by the interlocutors in a particular situation. By contrast, other facts such as the knowledge about the interlocutor's allergy, or about the fact that allergies are dangerous are stored in the interlocutors' minds and can be used in any situation. Interpersonal and world knowledge together are therefore called **background knowledge**.

Let us summarise our observations. You now know what is meant by *that cake over there*, and that your friend knows about your allergy, and knows that eating nuts is dangerous to those who are allergic to them. Knowing all this, and given the fact that you can assume that your friend does not wish you any harm, you can draw the inference 'My friend warns me not to eat this cake'. To draw this inference you used different types of contextual knowledge, such as situational, interpersonal, and world knowledge.

You might object to our analysis above by saying that this is only one possible pragmatic meaning of this utterance. And you are right. Let us imagine a different situation. Suppose you are not allergic to nuts, quite on the contrary, you love them! In this case you know that your friend is aware of the fact that cakes with nuts are your favourites. Again, the situational clues remain the same, but the interpersonal knowledge changes. You will therefore draw a rather different inference, namely, that your friend wants to do you a favour by recommending this cake to you. What we learn from this analysis is that first, different types of context lead to different inferences and that drawing proper inferences largely relies on the context.

There is yet another type of context that might be crucial for understanding utterances. To understand what is meant, we will modify the situation discussed above. As in the previous situation, your friend knows that you are allergic to nuts, and she has been to this coffee shop several times already. In our newly modified situation a brief dialogue takes place between your friend and you. After some contemplation of the cakes, you decide to choose one piece of a tasty-looking cake and you say the following to your friend pointing to the cake you want to choose:

(15) I would like to have that cake over there.

Your friend reacts to your utterance in the following way:

(16) But it contains nuts.

Let us now discuss what knowledge is necessary to understand the utterance in (16). To understand that this is a warning, we again need interpersonal and world knowledge. However, we also need to understand what is meant by *it*. To find this out, it is necessary to identify what *it* refers to. We can establish the reference of the pronoun *it* if we take into account what has been said in the conversation before. By doing so, we can state that the pronoun *it* refers to the cake mentioned in the preceding utterance as *that cake over there*. This means that in order to understand the utterance in (16), we need yet a different type of knowledge: the knowledge of what the interlocutors have said before, i.e. the knowledge of the context of the surrounding text, sometimes called 'co-text' (note that 'text' is used here in a modality-neutral sense, encompassing the spoken and the written modality). This type of context is therefore called 'co-textual'.

In general, we can say that context plays a crucial role in understanding utterance meaning and that speakers employ different kinds of knowledge, both linguistic (co-textual) and non-linguistic (situational, interpersonal, and world knowledge), in order to be able to draw pragmatic inferences. In the next section we will deal with other factors that contribute to drawing proper inferences.

6.4. Exploring pragmatic principles

6.4.1. The Cooperative Principle

As shown previously, to attain a proper understanding of utterances, and thus to arrive at proper inferences, interlocutors have to possess different types of knowledge. The question that arises now is what actually initiates inferencing. In other words, how do hearers know that speakers want to convey a certain pragmatic meaning? And how do hearers know that they should draw inferences? Below, we will explore factors that initiate inferencing and thus contribute to the success and efficiency of human communication.

For a start, consider the following dialogue between two colleagues who meet at their work-place one morning. Think of what is unusual about the conversation between them.

(17) A: Hello, how are you?
B: Oh, my legs are aching and I have a pain in my arm, and actually, on top of all this, my cat ran away in the morning, and my neighbour played the guitar till late in the evening. Besides, my sister fell ill and wants me to drive her to the doctor.
A: Do you know at what time the meeting starts?
B: What a wonderful day we have!
A: Hhm, dear, what did you do yesterday?
B: Oh, I went to bed, then danced a lot, first I had supper and visited my friend.
A: Well, then, did you manage to get enough sleep?
B (lying): Absolutely.

In one respect this dialogue looks like a normal conversation between two people: One person asks questions, the other one provides answers. However, it seems that speaker A can hardly draw proper inferences on the basis of B's utterances. In general, the communication between the two colleagues cannot be viewed as successful. Note that they are participants in the same situation, and, since they are colleagues, they should share at least some interpersonal knowledge. So what is the problem then?

There is no problem with the utterances of speaker A. She makes her communicative intention clear in every case. However, the answers provided by B are unexpected and unusual, they do not help A to gain the information she asks for and to draw proper inferences. In fact, we can say that speaker B is difficult to understand and acts in a strange way. But what is it exactly that makes us think her replies are unexpected and unusual?

To answer this question, let us take a closer look at each question—answer sequence of the conversation in (17). We begin by asking ourselves how the first question—answer pair could be changed to look more appropriate and more usual. One common possibility would be the following:

(18) A: Hello, how are you?
B: Fine, thanks, how are you?

The problem with B's answer in (17) becomes evident by comparison. The answer is too long, it provides much more information than is expected and required by the communicative conventions established in our culture. In general, we would say that we normally expect our interlocutors to provide as much information as necessary and not too much or too little.

Let us now look at what is unexpected in the second sequence of the dialogue in (17), repeated here for convenience:

(19) A: Do you know at what time the meeting starts?
    B: What a wonderful day we have!

In (19) the reply does not answer the question since it has no obvious relevance to it. Based on this example we can say that interlocutors expect that the information provided should be relevant in a particular context and not be completely unconnected to it. The next sequence presents yet another problem:

(20) A: Hhm, dear, what did you do yesterday?
    B: Oh, I went to bed, then danced a lot, first I had supper and visited my friend.

The information given by B is not quite clear. Did she have supper alone or with her friend, and what actually came first, the supper, the dancing, going to bed or the visit? Since we normally expect our interlocutors to retell something in a chronological order, we might be rather puzzled by this utterance which seems to jump from event to event in a haphazard fashion. We can conclude, therefore, that expressing one's ideas and intentions clearly and in an ordered way is one of the prerequisites for smooth communication. Finally, let us take a look at the last part:

(21) A: Well, then, did you manage to get enough sleep?
    B (lying): Absolutely.

In (21) B deliberately provides information which is false, and this is usually not expected or desirable in a normal interaction.

We can conclude that for initiating appropriate inferences, and thus for a communication to work properly, the mere knowledge of the different types of context is not sufficient. Evidently, interlocutors have to stick to certain conventions, such as being relevant, as informative as necessary, clear, and orderly, and not providing information which they know is false. By sticking to these conventions speakers allow the hearer to draw proper inferences and thus show a behaviour which is rational and contributes to mutual understanding. The general idea that communication is a rational and cooperative activity was first worked out by Grice (1975), who called it the **Cooperative Principle**. The different conventions we were talking about can thus be regarded as sub-principles of this rather general and abstract pragmatic principle since they show in a more specific way what contributes to the cooperative behaviour of the interactants. These sub-principles are known as the **maxims of the Cooperative Principle**, or as 'conversational maxims'. The convention to provide as much information as required for the purposes of the conversation, and not to make it more informative or less informative than required was called by Grice the 'maxim of quantity'. The convention to be relevant was termed the 'maxim of relevance'. In making their contributions in a clear, brief, and orderly manner speakers follow the 'maxim of manner'. Finally, the expectation that speakers should not say what they believe to be false or for what they lack adequate evidence is known as the 'maxim of quality'.

We can now explain our intuitive analysis of the strange conversation from above using Grice's terminology. We can say that most of the time speaker B is not cooperative in the conversation in (17) since she does not stick to the maxims and thus does not allow speaker A to draw proper inferences. In this case we say that the maxims are 'violated', and this is the reason why the dialogue in (17) seems strange to us. Normally the maxims are not violated. We usually expect our interlocutors to be cooperative, and this expectation initiates inferencing, so that we can make sense of their utterances.

But what would the conversation in (17) look like if the maxims were not violated, you may ask. One possibility is given in (22):

(22) A: Hello, how are you?
    B: Fine, thanks, how are you?
    A: I'm fine, too. Do you know at what time the meeting starts?
    B: It's at eight.
    A: Thank you. Hhm, dear, what did you do yesterday?
    B: Oh, I visited my friend who turned forty, and we had a wonderful supper together, and I danced a lot.
    A: Sounds good. But did you manage to get enough sleep then?
    B: Absolutely. We went home before eleven.

In (22) both speakers make their contributions as required, at a proper stage, with a proper purpose, and the contributions are sufficiently informative, relevant, clear, orderly, and not false. Such a behaviour initiates inferencing. In this case we say that the speakers observe the maxims, they are cooperating and the communication proceeds smoothly and successfully.

Given the fact that observing the maxims leads to efficient communication, whereas not observing them might create problems, can we say that interlocutors have only two choices, either to observe or to violate the maxims? In other words, can we say that the speakers can be either clear, relevant, informative, etc., or quite the opposite? To answer this question, take a look at the following short dialogue and think about whether the maxims are observed or violated:

(23) A: Do you know what time it is, I have left my watch at home, and we are going to have this meeting at eight thirty.
B: The church bells are ringing.
A: Great, half an hour left.

At first sight it might seem that speaker B gives an answer which is irrelevant to the question asked by A and that she therefore violates the maxim of relevance. Strangely, however, speaker A does not seem surprised, irritated or puzzled by this answer, a behaviour we might often expect when the maxims are violated. In contrast, she even thanks speaker B. So what is happening here?

Evidently, speaker A is able to draw a proper inference from what is uttered by speaker B. The inference she draws is 'It is eight o'clock'. Why is she able to do so? Because in fact, speaker B is not saying something completely nonsensical and irrelevant. She just renders the implied meaning 'It's eight' indirectly by saying 'The church bells are ringing.' Fine, you may say, but how does speaker A know that speaker B wants to render a certain meaning and is not just violating the maxims? And how does she know what this meaning exactly is, i.e. how does she know that speaker B wants to say 'It's eight' and not something else?

Crucially, interlocutors assume that their conversational partners are cooperative and follow the maxims. If you communicate with somebody, you would hardly expect that your interlocutor tells something irrelevant or lies. On the contrary, we initially assume that what we hear is somehow meaningful and connected to what has been said previously. As hearers we normally try to find meaning in every bit of interaction we are part of. Therefore, when speaker A receives the answer *"The church bells are ringing."* she would not think that speaker B violates the maxims. Speaker A would rather assume that speaker B is cooperative, and A would therefore start to reflect on what the speaker might have meant and to draw inferences. Speaker A would try to figure out the implied meaning using the different kinds of linguistic and non-linguistic knowledge we discussed in the previous section. In our case speaker A knows that the church bells in that town usually ring, for instance, at eight o'clock in the morning and at six o'clock in the evening. And since the conversation takes place in the morning, she will draw the inference that it is eight, and not six o'clock.

Overall, speaker A would draw inferences from speaker B's answer on the basis of, first, the assumption that interlocutors usually conform to the Cooperative Principle and thus observe the maxims, and second, the background or situational knowledge she possesses. An inference drawn in this way is called **conversational implicature** because it holds only in the context of a particular conversation. The conversational implicature in our case is 'It's eight o'clock'.

Let us now come back to our original question: Does speaker B observe or violate the maxim of relevance? Since she provides a seemingly irrelevant answer, we cannot say she observes it. Does she violate this maxim, then? As we have mentioned above, violations usually do not lead to efficient communication. Here, however, speaker A is able to uncover the implicature which leads to a successful interaction between the two. So speaker B does not violate the maxim of relevance. Speaker B assumes that the listener knows that the utterance should not be understood literally and thus expects the listener to be able to understand the implied, indirect meaning. In such cases we say that a speaker 'flouts' rather than violates the maxim of relevance. Flouting is a rather frequent phenomenon in everyday interactions. Consider the following short dialogues and think about which maxims are flouted by the speakers and what conversational implicatures can be drawn.

(24) a. A: Are you all right, dear?
B: I am boiling!
b. A: Do you like my new sofa?
B: Well, its colour is lovely.
c. A: What did you do yesterday?
B: Oh, I went to one of these large houses which sell different nice things and bought a round leather object used in a special game.
A: Really? I bought the same thing!

In (24a) speaker B provides an answer which is not true, if taken literally, since human beings usually do not boil in the literal sense. However, speaker A (and actually anybody who knows English) would know that the expression *I am boiling* is an exaggerating expression, or 'hyperbole'. Speaker A would therefore be able to draw the conversational implicature 'Speaker B feels very hot'. So we can conclude that speaker B flouts the maxim of quality.

In (24b) speaker B is clear, relevant, and provides information which is not false. Nevertheless, since the question of speaker A refers to the sofa, and not only to its colour, B does not give as much information as required and is not as relevant as is normally required by A's question. However, you can imagine that what B implies is that she does not particularly like the sofa and that speaker A would be able to understand this implicit meaning. Instead of directly saying 'I do not like your sofa' she flouts the maxims of quantity and relevance.

Finally, in the last example speaker B gives a seemingly strange answer. She uses the expressions 'round leather object used in a special game' and 'large houses that sell different nice things' so that her answer seems unclear and ambiguous at first sight. However, imagine that A is a friend of B's, and B is a mother who has just bought a Christmas present for her little son. Since her son, who is also present in this situation, should not know about the present and what it looks like, speaker B explains what she did in this rather vague fashion. However, her friend understands the message, as becomes clear through her reaction. We can therefore argue that speaker B flouts the maxim of manner.

Flouting makes the hearer's task more complex in that he or she has to look for the implied meaning. But why then would speakers flout the maxims and not just observe them? In (24a), for instance, speaker B has no particular reason not to say *"I feel very hot."* apart from probably wanting to appear very informal. Flouting the maxim of quantity in (24b) is a somewhat different case. Why should speaker B not simply say *"I don't like your sofa."* instead of saying something about the colour of the sofa? I can imagine that if you were the owner of the sofa, it would feel unpleasant if somebody told you they did not like it. Moreover, if you were in speaker B's position, you would feel embarrassed to say straightforwardly that you do not like the sofa. So the reason for flouting the maxims of quantity and relevance in (24b) is the desire not to upset or insult the addressee of your utterance, i.e. the desire to stay on good terms with your interlocutor. Finally, flouting the maxim of manner in (24c) is due to another reason. The speaker who flouts it does not want the third party to understand the message and conveys it in an indirect way which she expects to be comprehensible to the hearer, but not to the third party. To summarise, speakers often flout the maxims, and flouting may be due to rather different motives, one of them being the management of our personal relationships, as in the cases of the sofa and the round leather object above.

We have seen that interlocutors are usually cooperative and follow certain communicative principles when interacting with each other. As you might have noticed from our discussion above, we did not call the maxims of the Cooperative Principle 'rules', but we called them 'principles'. Now what is the difference between rules and principles, you may ask. Normally rules are more or less unbreakable regulations that show how a certain phenomenon works. Principles such as the Cooperative Principle and its maxims, as we have learned above, are by no means unbreakable. Nor are they prescriptive, i.e. they do not dictate a certain kind of behaviour. Rather, they are expectations that interlocutors have in verbal exchanges. Besides, they are by no means universal, i.e. they do not hold for every society or culture. Thus, whereas in some cultures being talkative is not necessarily a virtue, in other cultures providing only as much information as necessary could be regarded as socially improper.

Is the Cooperative Principle the only principle underlying and determining human communicative behaviour? To answer this question, consider the following situation. Speaker A has invited her colleague, speaker B, to a supper which speaker A has prepared herself. Speaker B finds the meal awful. However, when speaker A asks about the meal, the following dialogue takes place:

(25) A: How do you like the sauce?
 B: Oh, it's delicious.

Evidently, speaker B is lying. She therefore violates the maxim of quality, and displays a behaviour which is not cooperative. However, we can argue that she has a reason for not being cooperative since she does not want the hearer to feel unpleasant. We might think that she presumably follows a different principle or principles which seem to be in some contradiction to the maxim of quality. Apparently, besides the maxims of the Cooperative Principle, there must be some other pragmatic principles at work. One of them is politeness, to which we turn in the next section.

6.4.2. Politeness

As mentioned above, politeness is another principle underlying human interactions. But what is politeness? All of you surely have a more or less clear idea of what being 'polite' or 'impolite' means. Presumably you would agree that shouting at somebody in public is impolite, whereas giving way to an elderly person is polite. However, the concept of politeness developed in pragmatics differs in some respects from this intuitive idea. In this section, we will see what it means to be polite in linguistic terms.

We approach this question by investigating in which situations there is a need to be polite and why. First we use our intuitive knowledge of what is polite or impolite before we come to discuss how we can describe politeness linguistically. Imagine your friend has just obtained her driver's license and, full of pride and self-esteem, wants to take you for a drive. Afterwards she asks how you liked her way of driving. You did not like it since you felt unsafe. Below you will find two possibilities of how you might react in such a situation. Which of them would you choose and why?

(26) a. You are a danger to everybody.
 b. When I started driving after I got my driver's license, I was much more nervous.

You would probably choose the one in (26b), and not the one in (26a). The first utterance implies something rather negative about your friend: She is a miserable driver. In contrast, the second one states something positive by signalling that she is less nervous than you were during your first driving time. So why would you choose being positive rather than expressing criticism openly? Surely, you would agree that normally we as speakers do not want other people to feel confused or unpleasant because of what we say. And as hearers we know that we do not want others to think of us negatively. What we want to hear in our daily interactions is rather praise and admiration of our achievements and our abilities, since this raises our social and personal image whereas criticism damages it.

Several insights emerge from this discussion. First of all, all of us have a certain social self-image. The idea of people having such a self-image was first articulated by the sociologist Goffman (1967) and was later taken up in the linguistic work on politeness by Brown and Levinson (1987). Goffman called this self-image **face**. The second insight is that the desire to be admired, loved, and accepted by others is a crucial part of this self-image. Brown and Levinson (1987) called this part of the self-image the speaker's **positive face**. If a speaker endangers the hearer's positive face, we say that she 'threatens' it or performs a **face-threatening act**. In (26a), for example, the criticism is expressed directly and thus threatens your friend's positive face. In (26b) there is no direct criticism. In fact, what the speaker says is not the answer to the question, i.e. the question about the quality of driving. So the speaker is irrelevant on the surface, thus flouting the relevance maxim. However, there is a clear inference the hearer can draw from this utterance: 'You are not that good at driving yet, but I was much worse'. By flouting the maxim, the speaker avoids direct criticism and thus minimises the threat to the speaker's positive face. Besides, she talks about her own similar experience and thus indicates solidarity with the hearer. And knowing that you are not worse than others may be reassuring. By flouting the maxim of relevance and showing solidarity the speaker indicates that she is aware of the hearer's positive face and does not want to damage it. And this is one way of being polite. In cases such as this one, where the polite behaviour is directed towards the positive face of the interlocutor, we speak of **positive politeness**.

Let us consider a different situation. Imagine you have a hard time studying for a linguistics exam, and your car has to be brought to the garage since it urgently needs repair. You decide to ask your friend to do this for you because you need the time to prepare for the exam. Below you find two possible ways of doing so. Which one would you prefer and why?

(27) a. Bring my car to the garage.
b. Could you possibly bring my car to the garage?

Your choice would probably be (27b), but why? If we say *"Bring my car to the garage."*, we at first sight do not do anything really bad. We neither criticise somebody nor damage their self-image. But what do we do then? Evidently, we want somebody to do something. And in doing so, we urge the hearer to lose their private time, we restrict their freedom, interfere with their plans and intrude into their affairs. But people usually do not want anybody to intrude into their affairs. They want to think of themselves as personalities who are free in their choices as to what to do, and when, and how. This desire of not being disturbed can be regarded as another part of the speakers' self-image, and was termed **negative face** by Brown and Levinson. Negative face does not mean 'bad face', but 'not desiring to be disturbed in privacy'. This means then, that if a speaker wants the hearer to do something, the speaker threatens the hearer's negative face.

Now back to our examples in (27). We now know that asking somebody to bring the car to the garage is a face-threatening act and that there are at least two different ways of dealing with this act. Why should a speaker prefer to say *"Could you possibly bring my car to the garage?"* instead of *"Bring my car to the garage."*? The matter is that the utterance *"Bring my car to the garage."* has the form of an imperative which is a rather straightforward way of confronting an interlocutor with the perspective of intruding into her life. It leaves the interlocutor little possibility to say 'no'. Therefore, by performing the face-threatening act in such a way, we might make our interlocutor feel uncomfortable. By contrast, the utterance *"Could you possibly bring my car to the garage?"* has the form of an interrogative, which is on the surface a question about the ability (physical or other) of the hearer to perform some action. It is an indirect request and leaves the interlocutor a possibility of escape. After all, it is easier to say 'no' if you are asked *"Could you ... "*, because you can then directly refer to the things that may restrict your ability to follow the request. Besides, the use of *possibly* brings in an element of doubt and suggestion. By using it the speaker implies that she is aware of the fact that the action she wants the hearer to perform may or may not take place. So the use of such an element minimises the face-threat and is therefore a so-called 'mitigating device'. All in all, by using an indirect speech act and mitigating devices, the speaker indicates that she is aware of the hearer's desire not to be imposed on, i.e. of her negative face, and shows respect towards it. Again, as in the example of positive politeness, the speaker uses her linguistic knowledge in such a way as to signal face-awareness, and thus to be polite.

However, in this case, the speaker is oriented towards the negative and not towards the positive face of the hearer. This type of being polite is therefore called **negative politeness**.

When speakers feel that they threaten somebody's face, positive or negative, they try to use language in a way that somehow signals to the hearer their awareness of this threat and their desire to minimise it. This is called **politeness**. We have seen that there are different ways of using language in a polite way, such as using indirect speech acts, mitigating devices, or expressing solidarity. But are these different ways always polite to the same extent? Intuitively, it seems that some way of speaking is more polite than a different one. For illustration, imagine you ask your fellow-student to help you with some writing assignments you have to submit in a pragmatics course. By doing so you definitely intrude into her life and you are aware of the fact that you are performing a face-threatening act. Below I have listed several possibilities of what you might say in such a situation. Think about how they differ in their degree of politeness.

(28) a. Please, help me with this assignment.
 b. Jenny, I know you are so knowledgeable in pragmatics, help me please.
 c. Could you help me with this assignment? If your time permits, of course.
 d. I have absolutely no idea what I should write in this assignment!

The first utterance has the form of an imperative sentence and sounds like a command. However, the speaker shows her awareness of the hearer's negative face by using *please*, which mitigates the threat. This type of asking for help is rather direct through its imperative form and does not leave the hearer much choice. The second utterance also has the imperative form which makes the illocution explicit. It is therefore also a direct speech act. However, here the speaker addresses the hearer by her first name, Jenny, thus showing closeness. Besides, by mentioning the hearer's good knowledge of pragmatics the speaker articulates praise and thus makes the hearer feel good. These devices indicate that the speaker appeals to the hearer's positive face and uses positive politeness in this utterance. Although this type of asking is direct, this directness is somewhat disguised by applying positive politeness. The third utterance states the request indirectly by asking a question about the hearer's ability to do something and is oriented towards the hearer's negative face. It leaves the speaker the freedom of choice. The final utterance does not even mention the point of the request. It simply states the fact that the speaker has problems with the assignment. It is again an indirect speech act. It is even more indirect than the one in (28c). Upon hearing it, the hearer might not feel directly addressed by it, or might feel no obligation to follow the request, if the utterance is recognised as a request at all.

We can conclude so far that evidently, strategies of politeness can differ in their degree of directness. Often, more polite utterances are expressed more indirectly. Now, taken the variety of strategies and the differences in the degree of politeness, how do we make our choices as to what strategy to use in a particular situation? You can imagine that if you ask your friend to pass you the salt, it would be quite appropriate to say *"Pass me the salt please"*. However, if you ask her to bring your car to the garage as in one of the examples above, you would most likely use an indirect strategy. Why is this so? Quite naturally, passing the salt is an action which is a trifle in terms of imposing on the hearer's privacy. Asking to bring a car to the garage is a much more serious imposition on the hearer's freedom. We can conclude therefore that the greater the degree of imposition, the more indirect and thus the more polite the speaker should be.

Consider yet a different case. How would you ask somebody at a restaurant whom you don't know to pass the salt? And what about your boss who is dining with you? Again, you would rather say *"Could you please pass me the salt?"*, but why? Presumably, we tend to be more polite to those people who we do not have a close relationship with, or to those who are in a superior position in terms of the social hierarchy. So, apart from the degree of imposition, the degree of politeness is also influenced by the power distance and closeness of the relationship between the interlocutors.

In the present section we have seen that politeness is another pragmatic principle governing human interactions. It has been shown that when communicating with each other, interlocutors usually try to avoid threatening each other's face, i.e. their social self-image. To do so, they employ politeness, i.e. they use language in a way that signals their awareness of this threat and their desire to minimise it.

6.5. Conclusion

In the present chapter we have discovered another area of linguistic investigation, pragmatics, which is concerned with how speakers use language to convey certain communicative intentions, such as promising, requesting, regretting, warning, and many more. We have argued that using language to express such intentions can be regarded as performing certain linguistic acts called speech acts. We then found out that performing a certain speech act usually involves three components: the locution, which is the linguistic form (phonological, semantic, syntactic, etc.) of an utterance, the illocution, which is the communicative intention the speaker expresses through the utterance, and the perlocution, the effect on the hearer produced by the utterance. Another crucial insight was that the great variety of different speech acts can be classified into five larger classes: declaratives, representatives, commissives, directives, and expressives. Furthermore it became clear that there are different ways of expressing intentions and thus of realising the same subclass of speech acts. These can be grouped into two major categories depending on the degree of linguistic explicitness of their illocutionary force: direct and indirect speech acts, the latter being a rather common choice in many interactions. We then saw that rendering intentions successfully requires that certain felicity conditions are met. Another aspect we discovered was that understanding an utterance is a complex task that requires different types of knowledge on the part of the hearer: situational, background, and co-textual. Finally, we have learned that interlocutors usually follow certain principles when using language, such as being cooperative and polite.

Further reading

There is a variety of introductions to pragmatics. I recommend Cutting (2008), Grundy (2008) and Peccei (1999) for an overview of major pragmatic notions and problems. LoCastro (2003) is especially useful for those who intend to become language teachers. A more detailed account of pragmatic concepts can be found in Mey (2001). Students of English should also consult *A Communicative Grammar of English* by Leech and Svartvik (2002), which deals with how English can be employed for achieving different communicative intentions.

Exercises

Basic level

Exercise 6.1.: Speech acts

a. Identify the locution, the illocution, and the perlocution in the following utterances. Specify the type of speech act performed. What is the role of context in your analysis?

b. Which of the utterances in which context can be regarded as indirect speech acts? Explain in detail what is indirect about them.

(29) a. I was stuck in an enormous traffic jam.
  b. When will this bicycle be removed from the garden path?
  c. Do you know whose car this is?
  d. I nominate Peter Sweet for an award for producing the best film of the year.
  e. Come in, won't you?
  f. I hate this music.
  g. I won't remind you of this deadline again, mind.
  h. Your car stands in a no-parking area.
  i. Oh, dear, the sun is shining outside!
  g. Happy New Year!
  k. I forbid you to smoke in here.
  l. It's rather windy outside.

Exercise 6.2.: Felicity conditions

The utterance below is an apology. Discuss when this apology would be infelicitous. On the basis of this discussion formulate felicity conditions for a felicitous apology. If you encounter any problems, try to identify their source and think about whether they can be solved within Speech Act Theory.

(30) I apologise for losing my temper.

Exercise 6.3.: Understanding utterances and context

Discuss which types of knowledge interlocutors need to share to understand each other in the following conversations. Give arguments for your position by using the linguistic notions you have learned in the present chapter.

(31) a. girl 1: Did you enjoy yourself last night?
    girl 2: Oh, Jamie was not there, and this awful girl-friend of Mike's, isn't she terrible?
    girl 1: Yeah, acting so stupid ...
    girl 2: Oh yeah, but Steve was making funny jokes all the time. Like at the party two weeks ago, remember?
  b. Mike: Oh, damn, I left my passport at home!
    David: Now, this is the end of our journey.
  c. Mother: What is this?
    Son: Oh, I have forgotten to put it into the laundry basket. Could you put it there?
    Mother: No, I want *you* to put it there. And do it immediately.

Advanced level

Exercise 6.4.: The maxims of the Cooperative Principle

Discuss whether the maxims of the Cooperative Principle are observed, flouted or violated in the examples below and provide arguments for your position. In those cases where the maxims are flouted, explain what conversational implicature can be drawn by the hearers. If you encounter any problems, discuss them.

(32) a. A: Did you read the whole chapter?
        B: I read the first ten pages.
    b. A: How was your presentation?
        B: I have no idea.
    c. A: How was the concert?
        B: Better than it was last year, but worse than three years ago.
    d. A: Can you fix my car by tomorrow morning?
        B: Oh, many of our workers are on sick-leave.
    e. A: When does the course 'Introduction to Linguistics' start?
        B: Next Friday.

Exercise 6.5.: Politeness

a. Consider the utterance below. Discuss in how far the speaker performs a face-threatening act by uttering it.

(33) Have some more tea.

b. Think of alternative ways of expressing the offer in (33) and group them according to their degree of indirectness. Discuss how the speaker shows face-awareness and what type of politeness is employed in each case.

Chapter 7
Extensions and applications: historical linguistics, sociolinguistics and psycholinguistics

7.1. Introduction

In the preceding chapters you have encountered a host of language phenomena from various domains (phonetics, phonology, morphology, syntax, semantics, pragmatics), and you have learned how these phenomena can be investigated in order to find out more about the structure and use of language. Apart from these areas of linguistic research, scholars (and laypersons) are interested in many more questions concerning language and languages. In this chapter we will deal with three of such sets of questions. First, there are historical questions. How do languages develop and where do individual languages come from? What is the historical relationship between languages, e.g. between English and German? Why and how do languages change? Another set of questions concerns the social significance of language. Why is it that after listening to only a few words a speaker has uttered, we seem to know a lot about this speaker's social background, for example her education, her social status, in which region she probably grew up, etc.? What exactly is it that is so telling? Third, many people are curious about how humans store and process language, and what language can reveal about our cognitive capacities in general.

We will deal with each set of questions in turn, looking at important studies in these fields in an exemplary fashion. As you will notice, trying to meaningfully answer such questions necessitates a general understanding about how language 'works', i.e. what kinds of structural entities language consists of and how these entities interact with each other to create that highly complex system we call language. Having worked through the preceding chapters, you are now equipped with this kind of understanding.

7.2. Historical linguistics: how languages develop

In the late 18th century, William Jones made a discovery that was seminal for the study of the historical development of languages, i.e. for the academic field that later came to be known as **historical linguistics**. Studying the ancient Indian language Sanskrit he found that

[t]he Sanskrit language, whatever be its antiquity, is of a wonderful structure; more perfect than the Greek, more copious than the Latin, and more exquisitely refined than either, yet bearing to both of them *a stronger affinity*, both in the roots of verbs and in the form of grammar, *than could possibly have been produced by accident*; so strongly indeed, that no philologer could examine them all three, without believing them *to have sprung from some common source which, perhaps, no longer exists*: there is a reason, though not quite so forcible, for supposing that both the Gothic and the Celtic, though blended with a very different idiom, had the same origin as the Sanskrit; and the Old Persian might be added to the same family. (Jones 1786, emphasis added)

At the time little was known about the 'common source' of the languages mentioned, and Jones was mostly speculating. However, his hypothesis was so strong and attractive that many people started investigating the alleged 'affinity' in a systematic fashion. Let us follow in their footsteps by looking at data from English and German, two languages which also show a remarkable affinity that does not look accidental. In (1) I have listed a number of word forms from English and German that show some potentially non-accidental correspondences in both meanings and sounds. Before reading on, try to figure out all correspondences between English and German sound, concentrating on the consonants (you may find it useful to differentiate between word-initial, word-medial, and word-final positions). For the benefit of the reader I also give the phonemic transcription of the German words (or roots, where pertinent).

(1) Some similar English and German words

English	**German**		**meaning of German word**
pan	Pfanne	/pfanə/	'pan'
pole	Pfahl	/pfaːl/	'pole'
path	Pfad	/pfaːd/	'path'
plough	Pflug	/pfluːg/	'plough'
plant	Pflanze	/pflantsə/	'plant'
pipe	Pfeife	/pfaɪfə/	'pipe'
town	Zaun	/tsaʊn/	'fence'
toll	Zoll	/tsɔl/	'customs (duty)'
tame	zahm	/tsaːm/	'tame'
foot	Fuß	/fuːs/	'foot'
hate	Hass	/has/	'hate'
bite	beiß(en)	/baɪs-/	'bite'

heart	Herz	/hɛrts/	'heart'
book	Buch	/buːx/	'book'
grip	Griff	/grɪf/	'grip'
make	mach(en)	/max-/	'make'
dream	Traum	/traʊm/	'dream'
shape	schaff(en)	/ʃaf-/	'create'
break	brech(en)	/brɛx-/	'break'
reckon	rechn(en)	/rɛxn-/	'calculate'
open	offen	/ɔfn/	'open'
ship	Schiff	/ʃɪf/	'ship'

Although the corresponding words do not all mean exactly the same thing in both languages, the meanings are sufficiently close so that the similarities in both meaning and sound cannot be accidental. Let us look at the sound correspondences of these words more systematically. In (2) I have listed the correspondences of consonants evidenced by the data in (1):

(2) Systematic sound correspondences

	English	German	Example
a.	/b/	/b/	break — brechen
	/f/	/f/	foot — Fuß
	/n/	/n/	pan — Pfanne
	/l/	/l/	plant — Pflanze
	/ʃ/	/ʃ/	shape — schaff(en)
	/r/	/r/	dream — Traum
	/h/	/h/	hate — Hass
b.	/p/	/pf/ or /f/	pipe — Pfeife, grip — Griff
	/t/	/ts/ or /s/	town — Zaun, hate — Hass
	/k/	/x/	book — Buch

The correpondences in (2a) might look rather boring since the corresponding consonants in the two languages are the same. However, such a close correspondence of so many sounds may be taken as a strong indication of a close historical relationship. In (2b) things look more intricate, since each English sound systematically corresponds to a different, but phonetically very similar, sound in German. A closer look at this set reveals an interesting generalisation: what is a voiceless plosive in English corresponds systematically to a fricative or an affricate in German. Fine, you might be tempted to say, but what do such systematic correspondences tell us about language history?

To answer that question we must return to the very basic idea that words are essentially arbitrary pairings of sound and meaning (cf. chapter 3). This is the reason why the same form can mean entirely different things in two languages, and why two languages can have two entirely different forms to designate the same thing. For example, the string of sounds [ti] means 'not' in the West African language Yemba (spoken in Cameroon), but 'a hot brown drink made by pouring boiling water onto the dried leaves from a particular Asian bush' (*Longman Dictionary of Contemporary English*, s.v. *tea*) in English. In contrast, the numeral '2' is [tuː] in English, but [mɛmbɪja] in Yemba. In other words, if two languages happen to have very similar sound sequences to represent the same concepts it is highly unlikely that this is due to chance, since there is such a huge number of possible combinations for the sounds available in a language. Excluding chance, two possibilities remain, borrowing or common ancestry. 'Borrowing' means that either one language took over the words from the other, or both languages took them from a third. Common ancestry means that both languages developed from a common ancestor language, preserving the words in question, with minor changes in form or meaning in one or the other language.

Now, how do we know whether the words in (1) are a case of borrowing? We cannot be 100 percent sure, but we know from many studies of language contact that everyday vocabulary items such as the ones in (1) are not easily borrowed from one language into another. We have therefore good reason to assume that both English and German developed from a common ancestral language. Which language could that be and how did that language look like? In order to answer that question, we would have to check many more languages which may be potential offspring candidates from that ancestral language. If you have learned any Dutch or Frisian, it may have occurred to you that these languages have many words that are very similar to German or English words. If you have ever learned some Finnish, Japanese, or Thai, your feeling might be quite the opposite. Finnish, Japanese, or Thai words hardly ever seem to be even remotely similar to English or German words (unless they have been borrowed from one of these languages). Given this intuitive feeling of similarity, we would rather start looking for a historical relationship between English, German, Dutch, and Frisian than for a relationship between English, German, Finnish, Japanese and Thai. And indeed, the data do suggest a systematic relationship between English, Dutch, and Frisian on the one hand, and German on the other. Thus, Dutch and Frisian, like English, often have voiceless plosives, such as /p/, where German has affricates or fricatives (such as /pf/ or /f/) in corresponding words (cf. English *path*, Frisian *paad*, Dutch *pad*, German *Pfad*). To account for such facts, it seems most likely that there was one ancestral language from which all four languages developed. Either one of the languages, i.e. German, underwent some systematic sound change, or the other three together underwent some change, and German preserved the old sounds. The two possibilities are given in (3), using /p/ as an example:

(3) a. Hypothesis A

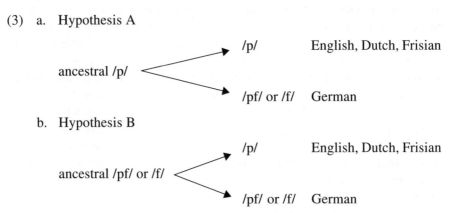

b. Hypothesis B

The obvious question is, which hypothesis is more likely? Two arguments can be used. First, it may seem more likely that one language undergoes a sound change, as in (3a), than that three languages undergo the same sound change independently, as in (3b). This favours (3a). We have to be cautious, however. It could also be the case that the split resulted in only two languages, let us call them 'Germanic 1' and 'Germanic 2', and only later 'Germanic 2' split up into the three languages English, Dutch, and Frisian, while 'Germanic 1' became German. Under this assumption, the scenarios in (3) would involve only two daughter languages and our first argument against hypothesis B would be less compelling.

The second argument is that the development of plosives into affricates (or fricatives) is a very common change that is very well motivated by articulatory considerations. Thus, the strong aspiration of a plosive is articulatorily very similar to the fricative part of an affricate. You may try this out by producing, for example, an aspirated [tʰ] very slowly, which makes the [tʰ] rather sound like a [ts]. Over time, strong aspiration may thus turn phonetically into frication, which turns the plosive into an affricate. A good example of this is Italian, in which the Latin [k] has turned into [tʃ] in certain environments (through some intermediate stages that also affected the place of articulation), as in pa[tʃ]e 'peace' or [tʃ]ento 'hundred'. As a second step in the development from plosive to fricative, the first element of an affricate may be weakened, which eventually may lead to a fricative (e.g. [pʰ] > [pf] > [f]). These facts strongly favour hypothesis A. At the same time, it is highly unlikely that an existing affricate and an existing fricative would develop into a plosive.

In sum, we have an argument against hypothesis B, and two arguments for hypothesis A. Hence we can posit that an ancestral sound /p/ developed into an affricate or fricative in German, and remained a /p/ in the other languages.

What we have just done is apply one of the oldest and still well-respected methods in linguistics, **comparative reconstruction**. Following this method, the systematic comparison of corresponding words (so-called **cognates**) in very many languages can be used to establish genetic relationships between these languages. In the case at hand, we have reconstructed a sound of a common ancestral language of English, Frisian, Dutch, and German. Such ancestral languages are called **proto-languages**, and the common ancestral language of our four languages (but also of Icelandic, Gothic, Danish, Norwegian and Swedish) is called 'Proto-Germanic'. Of course one would need a lot more data and many more potentially related languages to figure out the detailed genetic relationships among them, but our little investigation above should have shown how this could be done. Genetic relationships are usually represented in the form of tree diagrams, just like family trees. The proto-language and its descendents together are called a **language family**. Branches of a larger language family can be referred to as subfamilies.

Below you find the family tree for the Germanic languages. As you will see, the genetic relationship between our four Germanic languages is much more complex than our simple example might have suggested.

The Germanic languages in turn belong to the larger family of Indo-European, of which I only give the main branches in figure 7.1. below:

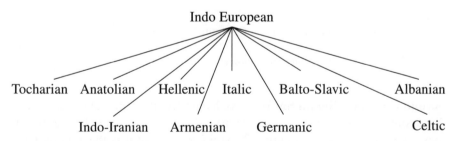

Figure 7.1. The Indo-European language family

Let us now return to our data in (2). Apart from having reconstructed a genetic relationship between some languages (i.e. English and German), we have also found a systematic sound change German has undergone, namely the development of voiceless plosives into affricates and fricatives, as illustrated by the correspondences in (2b). This change, which probably started between the 3rd and the 5th centuries AD and ended in the 9th century, is known as the

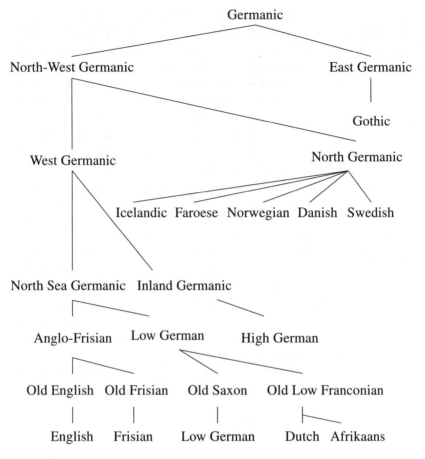

Figure 7.2. The Germanic language family

Second Germanic Sound Shift. As we have seen, the other languages under discussion (English, Frisian, and Dutch) did not undergo that change. If you now take a look again at figure 7.2., you can see that it is the Second Germanic Sound Shift that resulted in the split between what is called 'North Sea Germanic' and 'Inland Germanic' in the tree. Out of these two proto-languages the modern languages developed: English, Dutch, and Frisian on the one hand, and German on the other.

Note that, curiously, German still has voiceless plosives, which should be impossible if the Second Germanic Sound Shift had turned them all into affricates or fricatives. The answer to this apparent puzzle is that the German voiceless plosives in today's language are either those that survived the sound shift (because the shift in fact did not uniformly affect all voiceless plosives in all positions in all words), or they were re-introduced with words that were borrowed into the language after the shift was completed.

The term 'Second Germanic Sound Shift' suggests the existence of another such shift, the **First Germanic Sound Shift**, and indeed, there is such a thing. Historical linguists have provided overwhelming evidence that Proto-Germanic underwent a change in its consonant system that separates this branch from all other branches of Indo-European. The shift presumably happened around 1000 BC and is quite complex, so that the details need not concern us here. The major developments of the First Sound Shift are schematised in (4). The shift is also known as **Grimm's Law**, since it was the German scholar Jakob Grimm who first formulated the generalisations in this way in 1822:

(4) Grimm's Law (partial representation, in phonemic transcription)

Proto-Indo-European	Proto-Germanic	Generalisation
b^h	> b	
d^h	> d	aspirated voiced plosives > voiced plosives
g^h	> g	
b	> p	
d	> t	voiced plosives > voiceless plosives
g	> k	
p	> f	
t	> θ	voiceless plosives > voiceless fricatives
k	> x	

Apart from reconstructing genetic relationships between languages, historical linguists are of course also interested in the development of individual languages. Given the lack of speakers or tape recordings from a few centuries back, they try to find as many texts from earlier stages of the language as possible, such as medieval manuscripts, or, in the case of older Germanic languages, runic inscriptions on stone crosses, bones, or gravestones. From such historical attestations, the development of lexicon, pronunciation, and grammar of these languages can be reconstructed.

Let us take a brief look at the history of English, which began in 449 AD with the invasion of Britain by the Saxons, Angles, and Jutes. The invaders spoke various Germanic dialects, and out of this set of dialects grew the language that we know as English today. In the course of its history, English came under heavy influence of various other languages, such as (in chronological order) Celtic, Scandinavian, French, and Latin. Scholars usually distinguish four major periods in the history of English: Old English (440–1100), Middle English (1100–1500), Early Modern English (1500–1700), and Modern English (1700 until today). To get an idea about how English looked like at earlier stages, consider the Bible verses 21 and 22 from three different English versions of the Parable of the Lost Son, straddling about a millennium:

Old English version (Anglo-Saxon, 10th century)
²¹Dā cwæð his sunu, "Fæder, ic syngode on heofon and beforan ðē. Nū ic ne eom wyrþe þæt ic þīn sunu bēo genemned." ²²Da cwæð se fæder tō his þēodum, ...

Middle English version (Wyclif Bible, ca. 1380)
²¹And the sone saide to him, "Fadir, Y haue synned in to heuene and bifor thee; and now Y am not worthi to be clepid thi sone." ²²And the fadir saide to hise seruauntis, ...

Modern English version (New International Version, 1978)
²¹And the son said to him, "Father, I have sinned against heaven and in your sight, and am no longer worthy to be called your son." ²²But the father said to his servants, ...

As can be easily seen, changes have taken place on all levels of the language and its written representation. I will mention only very few here to give you a taste of what kinds of phenomena could be further investigated. Perhaps most striking upon your first encounter with Old English is the fact that on the way to Modern English, the writing system has changed. Some letters were lost altogether (e.g. <ð>, <Þ>, or macrons above vowel letters, as in <ō>), and some letters had a different function (<u> was used to represent also what is now <v>, as in *seruauntis* 'servants'). Furthermore, the pronunciation has changed (e.g. the plosive /d/ in *fæder* is now a dental fricative /ð/, or some final vowels are lost, as in *sone > son*). On the lexical level, some words have fallen out of usage (e.g. *þēod* 'people', or *cwæð* 'said', but compare archaic *quoth*, which we still read occasionally in 19th century literature). Other words have changed their meaning. Thus, in Old English *heofon* still meant both 'heaven' and 'sky', while at later stages its meaning became narrowed down to 'heaven'. With regard to morphology, we can see that some inflectional affixes are now obsolete (e.g. the past participle prefix *ge-* in Old English *genemned*, or the dative plural suffix *-um* in Old English *þēodum*). The word order has also changed, as illustrated by Old English object-verb order in *þīn sunu bēo genemned* 'your son be called' becoming verb-object *be clepid thi sone* 'be called your son' in Middle English. In sum, it is rather obvious that English has undergone massive changes in the course of its history.

Seeing all these changes attested in documents of earlier times, and having gained some insight into even earlier developments by comparative reconstruction, the question arises why language should change at all. And, more interestingly perhaps, why do certain changes occur in one language, but not in others? And can we predict the types of changes a language will undergo? Obviously, these questions are much too complex to be dealt with in this rather brief section on historical linguistics and language change. But some of the mechanisms at work in language change can be understood much better if we relate them to the set of questions concerning the social significance of language. To these questions we now turn.

7.3. Sociolinguistics: the social significance of language

As mentioned already in section 7.1., the way we speak reveals quite a lot about our social background, for example how educated we are, where we come from, etc. In the 1960s linguists began to systematically investigate the relationship between language and society by looking at the variable use of certain linguistic features by different groups of speakers. This branch of linguistic research is called **sociolinguistics**. Take, for example, the familiar variability of how speakers of English pronounce the final sound in the following words: *surfing, walking, sleeping*. They either use the velar nasal [ŋ] or the alveolar nasal [n]. This is illustrated in (5):

(5) surfing [sɜːfɪŋ] [sɜːfɪn]
    walking [wɔːkɪŋ] [wɔːkɪn]
    sleeping [sliːpɪŋ] [sliːpɪn]

Is this possible with any word ending in <ing>? Let us see:

(6) thing [θɪŋ] *[θɪn]
    sing [sɪŋ] *[sɪn]
    Beijing [beɪdʒɪŋ] *[beɪdʒɪn]

As the data in (5) and (6) show, the variation is restricted to the verbal suffix *-ing*. We can therefore say that the verbal suffix *-ing* has two variants: [ɪŋ] and [ɪn]. For that reason, the suffix *-ing* can be seen as a 'variable', i.e. a linguistic entity which varies in its manifestations in speech. The concept of variable should remind you of the concept of allomorphy, where we also found an abstract linguistic entity (i.e. the morpheme) to have differing manifestations in speech. While morphologists study which linguistic factors determine the distribution of the different variants, sociolinguists are interested in the social factors that may be responsible for the choice between different possible variants. In such cases we then speak of a **sociolinguistic variable**. Sociolinguistic variables are notationally given in normal orthography, but in parentheses, e.g. (ing). In the case of our suffix *-ing* the morphologist would find that there are two allomorphs [ɪŋ] and [ɪn], whose distribution cannot be explained by linguistic factors. Speakers can use both variants with any given verb. The obvious question now is: if there are two variants and no strictly linguistic rules that determine their usage, what makes a speaker choose between one or the other variant in a given situation? Is this entirely arbitrary or at least to some extent systematic? We could venture, for example, the hypothesis that the variable (ing) is distributed in such a way that one variant, [ɪŋ], is the variant used in the standard language, while [ɪn] rather occurs in non-standard, colloquial English. By 'standard' we mean a variety of English which is used in formal settings (such as educational institutions, business, and the media) and which enjoys the highest social prestige.

A word is in order here on the notion of standard and correctness. Speakers of the standard variety often tend to regard non-standard varieties, including regional dialects, as incorrect or sloppy forms of English. From a scientific point of view this does not make sense. The speakers of a regional dialect are native speakers of their dialect and their dialectal speech involves the correct application of the grammar (i.e. the system of rules) of their dialect. That these rules differ from the rules of the standard variety is obvious, because otherwise we could not make the distinction between that dialect and the standard. The difference between dialect and standard is thus a difference between two different linguistic systems, just like the difference between English and German is a difference between two different linguistic systems. Of course, a regional dialect of English is more similar to standard English than German is, but the dialect still constitutes its own system with its own words, rules of pronunciation, morphology, and syntax. In view of these facts it is nonsensical to say that a given regional dialect is 'incorrect (standard) English' (we would also not say that German is incorrect English). We are simply dealing with two different varieties of English. The crucial point is, however, that the two varieties are socially not equal. While the standard provides the norm for a whole country and is socially highly prestigeous, the regional dialect is restricted to its local setting and is not supposed to be used in official or formal social contexts. So if a dialect speaker uses her dialect in a formal situation, it is not the case that her grammar is 'incorrect', or she is too sloppy to apply the rules of English grammar. It is simply that her choice of language variety is inappropriate.

Returning to the problem of [ɪŋ] and [ɪn] and its potential social significance, we can now take a look at a classic study of the variable (ing) in the English town Norwich, in which Trudgill (1974) discovered that the distribution of this variable is indeed determined by social factors. He collected data from various speakers from different social classes and counted the occurrences of the two variants. **Social class** is a construct borrowed from sociology, according to which the members of a society can be categorised. The basis for this categorisation is usually income, occupation, and education, but other parameters (e.g. occupation of parents, neighborhood in which a person lives, social status, etc.) are also sometimes taken into consideration. In his study, Trudgill distinguished between five different classes: lower working class (LWC), middle working class (MWC), upper working class (UWC), lower middle class (LMC), and middle middle class (MMC). He also distinguished between four different speaking styles, ranging from the reading out of a word list, over the reading out of a passage of prose text, to formal speech, and finally casual speech. The assumption here was that reading out a word list is the most formal and most standard-like type of speech, while casual conversations represent the least formal type of speech. Here are his results:

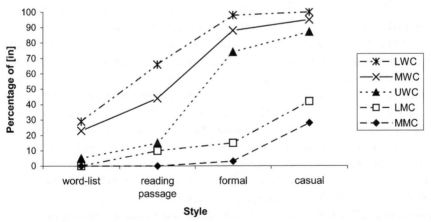

Figure 7.3. The variable (ing) in Norwich (adapted from Trudgill 1974)

On the y-axis we find the percentage of the variant [ɪn], and on the x-axis we find the four different styles, ranging from the most formal on the left to the least formal on the right. The graph shows that there are indeed important differences in the distribution of the two variants between the different styles and between the different classes. Thus there is a general trend that we find fewer [ɪn]'s (and hence more [ɪŋ]'s) in more formal styles. The second trend is that, in general, the lower the class of a speaker, the more often does the speaker use [ɪn] and the less often does he or she use [ɪŋ]. In other words, we now have firm evidence for our above hypothesis that [ɪŋ] is the more formal, standard variant and tends to occur more often towards the upper end of the social ladder, whereas [ɪn] is non-standard and indicative of the speech of people from the lower end of the social ladder.

Such results are quite common in investigations of the distribution of standard and non-standard variants and have led to the conclusion that language is a marker of class membership and social identity (similar to clothing, hair style, leisure activities, etc.). In a nutshell, by speaking in a certain way we express who we are and where we belong (socially and geographically). The marking of social identity can be found on all levels of linguistic description, such as lexicon, phonology, morphology, and syntax. For instance, people vary in socially significant ways in their use of different words for the same thing (e.g. *prof* vs. *professor*), or of different morphological or syntactic constructions (cf. *She don't want no coffee* vs. *She doesn't want any coffee*).

How can this behaviour of people from different social classes be explained? How come that speakers from different classes differ in their usage of the different variants? Or, to put it more bluntly, why don't we all speak alike? To understand this phenomenon, it is instructive to look at a classic sociological study that showed that the social class system restricts communication (Bogart 1950–1). The author investigated how the news about a particular event that was important for the community disseminated in a small rural American prairie town. A local girl won an invitation to visit the New York Philharmonic Orchestra and was interviewed on the national radio during the intermission of the concert. This news was an important event for the whole town and was very much talked about in all kinds of social contexts. Three weeks after the event in question, the researchers conducted 268 interviews and found out that the knowledge of the event had spread unevenly across town. Age, sex and neighbourhood of the interviewees did not make a difference as to their knowledge of the event, i.e. the knowledge of the event had spread equally through all age groups, across both sexes and through all neighbourhoods. However, social class made a difference. Among the lower classes, only 27 percent knew of the event, while it was 77 percent among the highest social group. As all other factors could be ruled out, the only explanation for this difference was that the social classes were not in constant or close contact. In general, we can thus say that members of a given social class may have — on average — less contact with speakers of other classes than with speakers of their own class. As a consequence, different social groups may come up with differences in their speech, which may first go unnoticed, but which may later be reinterpreted as markers of social identity.

Let us look at another interesting study that will substantiate the point that language can serve as a marker of social identity. Labov (1972) investigated the speech of the people living on Martha's Vineyard, a very popular summer vacation island off the coast of Massachusetts. Labov found that the local pronunciation of certain diphthongs differed remarkably from that of the standard language. For example, on the island one could hear islanders pronounce /aʊ/ as [ʌʊ] and /aɪ/ as [ʌɪ]. In technical-phonetic terms, islanders 'centralised' their diphthongs: [ʌʊ] and [ʌɪ] have more central initial vowels than their standard counterparts [aʊ] and [aɪ] (cf. the vowel and diphthong charts in chapter 1.4.2. for illustration). Labov found, however, that islanders showed a considerable amount of variation in their use of the local variants [ʌʊ] and [ʌɪ]. Upon closer inspection of the two variables (ai) and (au) it turned out that the attitude towards the island and life on the island determined the degree to which a given speaker centralised the diphthongs. Consider the following figure (adapted from Labov 1972):

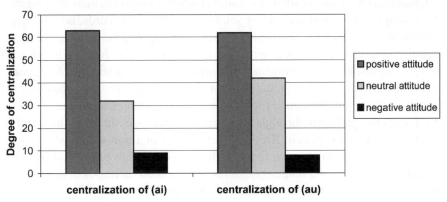

Figure 7.4. The centralisation of diphthongs on Martha's Vineyard

The height of the bars indicates how much and how often the speakers centralised, and for each diphthong the graph gives us three bars, with each bar representing one group of speakers with an either positive, neutral, or negative attitude towards the island, respectively. The graph clearly shows that a more positive attitude correlates with a higher degree of centralisation. The local, centralised variant was favoured by those islanders who wanted to distance themselves from the incoming tourists and felt a high allegiance to their island and to traditional island life, while the standard pronunciation was favoured by people who did not feel strongly connected with the traditional life style of Vineyarders. In other words, islanders favouring the local pronunciation wanted to stress their identity as native Vineyarders (as opposed to the incoming tourists, who use mostly standard diphthongs).

Again, this example shows how language (or rather: the way we use the options the language offers us) can serve as a badge of identity. In the examples above, we only looked at variability in pronunciation, but this is by no means the only area where language use may vary. People differ according to which words they choose in a given social context, or which syntactic constructions they prefer. Wherever possible, we tend to use those linguistic variants that — apart from conveying the right message — are felt to express certain pertinent and important non-linguistic concepts, such as attitude, group identity, or level of formality.

7.4. Psycholinguistics: how do we store and process language?

The field of study which investigates how human beings store and process language in the brain is called **psycholinguistics**. Psycholinguists investigate, for example, how we discriminate sounds, how we store words, how we produce sentences, how we segment sentences into meaningful units, or how we acquire language. In the following we will focus on one field of inquiry of psycholinguistics, the organisation of words in the mental lexicon. As already mentioned in chapter 5, 'mental lexicon' is a metaphor for the repository of words in our mind. Evidence for its structure and configuration can not only be indirectly gathered through experiments, but also through the careful analysis of deviant speech. 'Deviant' refers here in a non-technical sense to everyday speech errors, or to the speech of patients with brain damage who suffer from speech and language disorders (so-called 'aphasics'). In this section we will concentrate on experiments and speech errors.

In chapter 5 you already saw a kind of experiment which showed that the words in the mental lexicon are stored in a systematic way. Association tests demonstrate that semantically related words are more strongly linked to each other than to words that are semantically unrelated.

Another standard experiment to tap the organisation of words in the mind is the so-called 'lexical decision task'. In such an experiment the subjects see a word on a computer screen (or hear the word over headphones, or both) and must press a button as quickly as they can, deciding whether the word that they see or hear is a word of their language. If we then measure their reaction times (so-called 'latencies') we find a strong negative correlation between frequency and reaction time. The more frequent the word, the shorter the reaction times. In other words, the more often we read, hear, or use a given word, the easier it is to retrieve that word from our mental lexicon. That this effect also holds for second language speakers is familiar to most learners of foreign languages, who generally have a much harder time to memorise rare words (e.g. *purchase*) than words that they come across or use more frequently (e.g. *buy*). Psycholinguists have created the metaphor of 'resting activation' to account for this phenomenon. The idea is that words are sitting in the lexicon, waiting to be called up, or 'activated', when the speaker wants to use them in speech production or perception. If a word is retrieved at relatively short intervals, it is thought that its activation never completely drops down to zero in between. The remaining activation is called 'resting activation', and this resting activation becomes higher the more often the word is retrieved. As mentioned above, it can be observed that more frequent words are more easily activated by speakers. Such words are therefore said to have a higher resting activation, while less frequent words have a lower resting activation.

Getting deeper into the nature of the frequency effect, scholars have recently detected another factor influencing response latencies, the 'morphological family'. The morphological family of a word is a set of derived words or compounds that contain the same root. For example, *derivation, derivational, trans-derivational, non-derivation, derivative, zero-derivation,* and *cross-derivation* all belong to the morphological family of the root *derive*. Baayen and Schreuder (1997) have shown that simplex words (such as *derive*) which occur as constituents in many complex words (such as *derivation, derivative,* etc.) are processed faster than words with only a few morphological family members. No matter how we would account for that effect, we have to admit that the morphological family must have some psychological reality, and that, therefore, morphological relatedness and morphological structure must somehow play a role in lexical organisation.

When speakers search for a word in their mental lexicon, not only the target word is activated but also phonologically, morphologically, semantically, and syntactically similar words. One experimental paradigm used to test such effects is 'priming', which works as follows. Subjects hear or see a certain word, the so-called 'prime', before they read out, or make a lexical decision on, a different word, the so-called 'target'. If the prime is orthographically, phonologically, morphologically, semantically, or syntactically similar to the target, subjects tend to be faster in their reading out or their decision on the target word. Thus, a prime that rhymes with a target word (e.g. *mask — task* vs. non-rhyming *mask — beach*) will facilitate access to the target. The same effect occurs with words that have the same onset in their first syllable (cf. related *train — try* vs. unrelated *train — fly*). Facilitation of access can also be expected for pairs such as *train — car*, in which the semantically related prime facilitates access to the target, while this is not the case with semantically unrelated primes, as in *tree — car*.

Based on such evidence we can conclude that the structure of the lexicon can be conceptualised quite adequately in the form of a highly complex network (with many sub-networks) in which similar bits of information are linked to each other. Along the same lines, lexical search (i.e. the search for words when we want to speak) can be modeled as activation spreading through networks of related words. Usually only the target item is (successfully) retrieved from memory when we speak, which means that the activation of the target must have been strongest. Sometimes, however, things go wrong when we try to retrieve words from our memory and of two or more competing words or structures, the wrong one is picked and uttered. Given that we produce speech at an enormous speed (at a regular rate of about six words per second), the occurrence of such mistakes seems rather expectable. In cases where something goes unintentionally wrong in our speech production, we speak of 'speech errors'. Such speech errors can be an important kind of data for psycholinguists. Let us look at some of them and see what they can tell us about the representation and processing of linguistic structure in the brain. On the left hand side I give the intended utterance, on the right side the one that came out of the speaker's mouth:

(7) **intended** **produced**
    a. instantaneous/momentary → momentaneous
    b. [k]lear [b]lue sky → [g]lear [p]lue sky
    c. Are my tires touching the curb? → Are my legs touching the curb?

In (7a) the two words *instantaneous* and *momentary* are blended into one erroneous word **momentaneous*. What does this tell us about the mental lexicon? First of all, the two words must have been simultaneously activated in order to become blended. A major reason for their being activated simultaneously is of course their close semantic relationship (both refer to time concepts and both involve short periods of time) and their being both adjectives. Second, we see that the morphological structure must have played a role, since the suffix of one word, *-aneous*, has been attached to the stem of the other word, *moment*. This can be taken as evidence for the fact that the words *momentary* and *instantaneous* are not only stored as whole words, but that they also have very strong links to their constituent morphemes. Third, morphological blending can be interpreted as evidence for the psychological reality of theoretical constructs such as the stem or the morpheme. In sum, the example shows relatedness effects on the level of meaning, syntax (i.e. word class), and morphology.

The data in (7b) are more subtle. What we see here is the exchange of a phonological feature between two sounds in adjacent words. The voiceless [k] in *clear* becomes voiced in [g]*lear*, while the voiced [b] in *blue* becomes voiceless in [p]*lue*. This shows that the pronunciation information, i.e. the phonological representation of the word is broken down to the level of phonological features, in this case voicing. Only if the speaker has access to these features can he or she confuse them and insert them erroneously into the adjacent word's phonological information.

The final example (7c) again shows semantic and syntactic relatedness. The two competing words are both nouns. In fact, most errors where entire words are exchanged concern words of the same word-class. Furthermore, *tire* and *leg* share important semantic features. They both refer to the lower parts of an object and both are of crucial importance to transportation. Metaphorically, one could even say that the tires are a car's legs.

To summarise, we have seen that different kinds of evidence can be adduced to investigate how humans store and process language, and words in particular. The mental lexicon is a very complex place of storage in which many different kinds of information are linked with each other in a network-like structure. We have to be aware, however, that terms such as 'mental lexicon' and 'network' are metaphors that help us to make sense of what we have not yet fully understood. Much more work needs to be done in order for us to be able to explain in depth how human beings can produce and comprehend language.

7.5. Conclusion

In this chapter we have taken very brief tours into three very different fields of linguistics, namely historical linguistics, sociolinguistics, and psycholinguistics. We have seen that these areas offer fascinating research questions that are tackled using very different methodologies ranging from comparative reconstruction to psycholinguistic experiments. What all three branches of linguistics have in common is that they all involve the application of the fundamental notions of the discipline, such as phonological features, phoneme, morpheme, suffix, word, etc. Reading this book should have enabled you to further probe into these areas and to ask interesting questions about this everyday thing that is so close to us, and at the same time so hard to investigate: language.

Further reading

Good introductions to historical linguistics are Trask (1997) and Campbell (1998). Pyles and Algeo (1993) is an accessible introductory textbook to the history of English. Another one is van Gelderen (2006), which has a great companion website (http://www.historyofenglish.net/). Hogg and Denison (2006) present a concise and authoritative handbook on that topic. For sociolinguistics, you may start with any of the textbooks by Chambers (2003), Holmes (2001), or Meyerhoff (2006). More advanced handbook articles can be found in Chambers (2002). Field (2003) is a text for students with no prior knowledge in the field of psycholinguistics, and Aitchison (2003) provides a nice introduction to the mental lexicon.

Exercises

Basic level

Exercise 7.1.: Comparative reconstruction

Consider the data in (8) and explain the systematic correspondences of the initial consonant between the English words on the one hand, and the Latin and Greek words on the other. Do these correspondences show that English is a daughter language of Latin and Greek?

(8)

English	**Latin**	**Greek**
thin	tenuis	tanu-
thou	tū	tu
three	trēs	treis
foot	pēs	pous
for	per	peri
flat	planus	platos

Exercise 7.2.: Language change

English has several native Germanic words that refer to domestic animals. When these animals end up on our plates as food, they are no longer referred to by these names, but by other names. Consider the data in (9):

(9) pig   pork   deer   venison
    calf   veal   sheep   mutton
    cow   beef

Check the etymologies of the words in the right columns in the *Oxford English Dictionary*, and find out what they have in common. Can you think of an explanation for this state of affairs, given your knowledge of the history of England?

Advanced level

Exercise 7.3.: African-American English

In the U.S., many African-Americans speak a variety of English, so-called African-American English, that is quite distinct from the standard. Consider the following table with figures from a study by Ash/Myhill (1986), who investigated the use of a number of non-standard African-American English forms in the speech of whites and of African-Americans in Philadelphia. These non-standard structures involved the absence of third person singular present tense *-s* (as in *she like it*), the absence of a form of BE in certain constructions where it would be required in the standard (such as *he a teacher*), the marking of possession by simple juxtaposition of the NPs denoting the possessor and the possessed (as in *John book*), and the use of the auxiliary *ain't* where the standard has *didn't* (as in *I ain't do it*).

Table 7.1. Percentage of non-standard forms in African-American and white speech in Philadelphia (from Ash/Myhill 1986, 'AfrAm' stands for 'African-American')

	3sg	BE	possessive	auxiliary
examples	*she like it*	*he a teacher*	*John book*	*I ain't do it*
AfrAm's with low contact with whites	73	52	79	43
AfrAm's with high contact with whites	16	4	15	8
Whites with high contact with AfrAm's	12	8	2	20
Whites with low contact with AfrAm's	0	0	0	0

What correlations can be found between linguistic behaviour and group membership? Describe the patterning of the data and relate these findings to the basic insights of sociolinguistic research described above.

Exercise 7.4.: Speech errors

Consider the following speech errors and discuss their possible origin. What do they say about the storage and processing of words in the mental lexicon, or about the processing of syntactic structure? As above, the intended utterance is given on the left of the arrow, the actual utterance on the line below it.

(10) a. I'm not really sure / I don't really know →
         I'm not really know
     b. As the individual grows older →
         As the individual grows more older
     c. I want to thank all the speakers →
         I want to spank all the thinkers
     d. This is the grid on the floor where the rat dug →
         This is the grid on the floor where the rat digged

Glossary

The glossary provides only short and crisp definitions. For further explanations and exemplification the reader should consult the pertinent chapters. All terms can be accessed via the index.

abbreviation Word-formation process used to create words by means of combining the initial letters of multi-word combinations. There are two types of abbreviations: initialisms and acronyms (e.g. *UN* and *NATO*, respectively).
acronym Word created by abbreviation and pronounced by applying regular reading rules (e.g. NATO [neɪtəʊ]).
adjectival compound Compound that has an adjective in the head position (e.g. *knee-deep*).
adjective A word-class of English. Adjectives head adjective phrases, can be premodified by adverbs and can typically occur in comparative and superlative forms.
adjective phrase Syntactic phrase that has an adjective as its head (e.g. [*extremely fond of basketball*]).
adjunct See the synonymous term 'adverbial'.
adverbial A type of sentence function. Adverbials are not obligatory and give circumstantial information (e.g. on time, manner, reason, etc.).
affix Bound morpheme that is attached to a root or a base.
affricate Manner of articulation of complex sounds consisting of two articulations: a stop followed by a prolonged release with audible friction.
agentive affix Affix used to create words denoting persons.
allomorphs Different morphs representing the same morpheme; different concrete physical realisations of a morpheme. For example, [s], [z] and [əz] are allomorphs of the English noun plural morpheme.
allophones Different phones representing the same phoneme. For example, in English [pʰ], [p], and [p̚] are allophones of the phoneme /p/.
alveolar Place of articulation of sounds that are produced at the ridge behind and above the upper teeth, i.e. at the alveolar ridge.
ambiguous Having more than one meaning.
American National Corpus (ANC) Text collection of some 100 million words from both written and spoken North American English. Website: http://americannationalcorpus.org/

antonyms Pair of opposite words which refer to two extreme points on a scale (e.g. *good* and *bad*).
approximant Manner of articulation of consonants produced without audible friction. In lateral approximants, the air escapes along the sides of the tongue, in central approximants down the centre of the mouth.
articulator Part of the vocal tract which is involved in speech production. We distinguish active articulators (like the lips), which can be moved, and passive articulators (like the palate), which cannot change their position.
aspirated stop Stop (or plosive) in which the release burst is accompanied by an extra puff of air. In narrow transcription, aspirated stops are marked by [ʰ], following the relevant stop symbol: e.g. [pʰ], [tʰ], [kʰ].
aspiration Phonetic process by which stops become aspirated.
assertive See the synonymous term 'representative'.
augmentative prefix Prefix that expresses the meaning of 'large' (e.g. *mega-*).
background knowledge Cover term for world knowledge and interpersonal knowledge.
base That part of a word to which affixes can be attached.
bilabial Place of articulation of sounds that are produced with both lips.
blend Word that is created by combining material from two words into one new word (e.g. *smog* < *smoke* and *fog*).
bound morpheme Morpheme that cannot occur on its own and that appears only in combination with other, usually free, morphemes.
British National Corpus (BNC) Text collection of some 100 million words from both written and spoken British English. Website: http://www.natcorp.ox.ac.uk/.
case Inflectional category which marks the grammatical function of noun phrases in a sentence or phrase (e.g. nominative for subjects).
categorisation The classification of entities into mental categories.
clear l Label for the non-velarised realisation of the English phoneme /l/ in words like *live* and *willow*. The antonym of 'clear l' is 'dark l', or 'velarised l'.
clipping A word-formation process used to create lexemes by means of deleting a part of the base word (e.g. *lab* < *laboratory*).
coda Syllable constituent which comprises all consonants after the nucleus (e.g. [ŋk] in the word *blink*).
cognates Words from different languages that have a common ancestral form.
co-hyponym A word that shares a common hyperonym with another word.
commissive Type of speech act by which a speaker commits herself to some future action.

communicative intention   Goal a speaker wants to accomplish with an utterance.

comparative reconstruction   A method in historical linguistics, according to which word forms and grammatical constructions from different languages are compared. Based on these comparisons, systematic changes can be discovered and the genetic relationships of languages can be reconstructed.

complementaries   Pair of opposite words which refer to a dichotomous distinction where there is no in-between (e.g. *dead* and *alive*).

complementary distribution   1. The distribution of variants in environments that exclude each other. 2. In phonology, a distribution of sounds in which one sound cannot occur where the other sound occurs, and vice versa. For example, dark and clear l are in complementary distribution in British English.

complex word   Word consisting of two or more morphemes.

compositional meaning   The meaning of a linguistic expression that is derived from the meanings of the parts of that expression.

compounding   Word-formation process used to create words by combining two or more bases (e.g. *textbook*).

concatenative process   Morphological process in which a complex word is created by sequentially adding forms to each other (as in compounding and affixation).

concept   Mental category used to classify objects.

connotation   Personal affective or emotive associations connected with a particular word (in contrast to the conceptual meaning of that word). For example, 'swimming pool' or 'beach parties' may be connotations evoked by *summer*.

consonant   Type of speech sound in which the airstream is severely obstructed.

constituent   Structural unit in linguistic analyses.

conversational implicature   Pragmatic inference drawn by the speaker in a particular conversation by taking into account the Cooperative Principle and the different types of linguistic and non-linguistic knowledge.

converse relation   Sense relation between converses.

converses   Pair of words that refer to a relational state of affairs from opposite viewpoints (e.g. *buy/sell*, *parent/child*).

conversion   Word-formation process used to create lexemes without any change in form (e.g. *(the) water* > *(to) water*).

Cooperative Principle   Pragmatic principle used to account for patterns of human interaction. According to this principle, communication is viewed as a rational activity during which interlocutors cooperate with each other and follow certain maxims, such as being clear and orderly.

coordination test Syntactic test used to determine the constituent status of a syntactic string by combining the string with another string and linking both strings with a conjunction (e.g. *and*).

corpus Compilation of texts, written or spoken, from a language, usually in a machine-readable format.

Corpus of Contemporary American English (COCA) Text collection of some 385 million words from both written and spoken American English. Website: http://www.americancorpus.org/

dark l Label for the velarised realisation of the English phoneme /l/ in words like *hall* and *bulb*.

declaration Type of speech act whose purpose it is to change a given state of affairs (e.g. baptising).

definite expression Linguistic expression (for example a noun phrase) that is marked by a linguistic device (e.g. the definite article) to mark the referent of the expression as identifiable by the reader/hearer.

deictic expression Linguistic expression which refers directly to the personal, temporal, or locational characteristics of the situation it occurs in, in order to identify a referent.

denotation The set of potential referents of a word.

dental Place of articulation of sounds produced with the tongue immediately behind the upper front teeth or protruding between the upper and lower front teeth. The latter place of articulation is sometimes referred to as interdental.

derivation 1. Morphological process by which lexemes are created by adding derivational affixes. 2. Any morphological process except compounding by which lexemes are created.

derivational affix Affix that is used for the formation of complex lexemes.

derivative Word formed from a root or a base by the process of derivation.

determiner A word-class of English. Determiners typically occur in the first slot of a noun phrase and encode grammatical properties such as definiteness (*a/the*) or number (*this/these*).

diminutive suffix Suffix that expresses intimacy or smallness (e.g. *-y* in *Suzy*).

diphthong Vowel sound with a change in auditory quality within a single syllable (e.g. [aʊ] in *cow*).

direct object One of the two objects of a ditransitive verb. The direct object denotes the entity that is affected by the action denoted by the verb.

direct speech act Speech act in which the relation between the linguistic form and the linguistic function is straightforward.

directive Type of speech act used to make the hearer do something.

distribution The positions in which a linguistic item can occur.
ditransitive verb Verb that takes two objects (e.g. *give*).
expressive Type of speech act used to express the speaker's feelings and inner states.
face In Brown and Levinson's (1987) theory of politeness: the speaker's social self-image.
face-threatening act Speech act by which the hearer's face is endangered.
felicity conditions Conditions that need to be met for an utterance to be a successful speech act.
final obstruent devoicing Phonological rule by which voiced stops, fricatives, and affricates become voiceless in syllable-final position.
First Germanic Sound Shift A systematic consonantal sound change which happened around 1000 BC and separated the Germanic languages from the other Indo-European languages and language families. The sound shift is also known as 'Grimm's Law'.
flapping See 't/d-flapping'.
free morpheme Morpheme that can occur on its own without any other morphemes attached to it.
free variation Type of distribution in which different realisations of a linguistic category can occur in the same position. For example, in English the allophones [p] and [pʰ] are in free variation in word-final position.
frequency In phonetics, the rate of air vibration in a sound wave, measured in cycles per second (Hz).
fricative Manner of articulation of consonants produced with audible friction.
gapping test Syntactic test used to determine the constituent status of a syntactic string. In tag questions, for example, the VP is gapped.
gender A grammatical category of the noun. English has three genders, masculine, feminine and neuter. The three genders are only distinguishable in the pronominal system. Semantically, masculine and feminine gender are mostly reserved for animate entities, while nouns denoting inanimate entities are usually neuter.
gender-marking suffix Suffix used to create words denoting female or male versions of the base word.
General American The term used to refer to all those accents of American English which are (relatively) neutral with regard to the speaker's regional background. Being the majority accent of American English, General American is also commonly used in radio and television broadcasting.
glide Subclass of approximants, including [j] and [w]. An alternative term for 'glide' is 'semi-vowel'.

glottal Place of articulation of sounds produced with a constriction at the glottis.
glottis The opening between the vocal cords.
grammar 1. The system of phonological, morphological, syntactic and semantic information and rules that (native) speakers of a given language possess. 2. A book containing the description of the grammar (in sense 1.) of a particular language (or language variety). Such descriptions are traditionally restricted to morphological and syntactic aspects of the language.
grammatical word Grammatically fully specified form of a lexeme (e.g. *bakes*: third person singular present tense form of BAKE).
Grimm's Law Synonym of 'First Germanic Sound Shift'. Named after the German philologist Jakob Grimm, who — together with his brother Wilhelm — is also famous as a collector of fairy tales (*Grimms' Fairy Tales*).
head The most important element of a linguistic constituent, especially in syntax.
historical linguistics Sub-discipline of linguistics which is concerned with the historical relationship between languages, the histories of individual languages and the mechanisms of language change.
homonyms Set of words with the same (phonological or orthographic) form, but with different, unrelated meanings.
homonymy (adjective: homonymous) Relation that holds between homonyms.
hyperonym Word that has a meaning which is superordinate to that of other words (i.e. its hyponyms).
hyponym Word that has a meaning which is subordinate to that of another word (i.e. its hyperonym).
hyponymy Sense relation that holds between a hyponym and its hyperonym.
illocution The component of a speech act that renders a speaker's communicative intention.
indefinite expression Expression whose referent cannot be identified by the reader/hearer.
indirect object One of the two objects in a ditransitive construction. The indirect object denotes the recipient, goal or benificiary of the entity denoted by the direct object.
indirect speech act Speech act in which the relation between the linguistic form and the linguistic function is not explicit. In such cases the speaker's intention cannot be read off the semantic meaning of the utterance, but must be detected by inferencing.
inference Result of the process of decoding the pragmatic meaning of an utterance.

inferencing Cognitive procedure that makes use of situational, cotextual, or world knowledge to identify the pragmatic meaning of an utterance.
infix Affix which is inserted into a base.
inflection Morphological process by which grammatical information (e.g. on number, person, or tense) is encoded.
inflectional affixes Affixes that convey grammatical information (e.g. third person singular present tense -*s*).
initialism Word created by abbreviation and pronounced by naming each individual letter (e.g. *USA*, *UK*).
instrumental suffix Suffix used to create words denoting instruments.
inter-dental See the synonymous term 'dental'.
International Phonetic Alphabet (IPA) Commonly used system for the representation of speech sounds in writing phonetic transcription. Each symbol in the phonetic alphabet corresponds to exactly one sound.
interpersonal knowledge The interlocutors' knowledge about each other, which can be used to arrive at the pragmatic meaning of an utterance.
intransitive verb Verb that does not take an object.
labio-dental Place of articulation of sounds produced with the lower lip and the upper front teeth.
language family Group of languages that have developed from a common ancestral language.
lexeme Abstract lexical unit underlying the different grammatical realisations of a word in the mental lexicon.
lexical category See the synonymous term 'word-class'.
lexical conditioning Mechanism for the selection of allomorphs by which the shape of an allomorph depends on an individual word in which it surfaces.
lexical field Set of words with related meanings.
linguistic context What is said before and after a given utterance, i.e. its linguistic surroundings. Synonymous to 'co-text'.
liquid Subclass of approximants, including [l] and [ɹ].
locution The linguistic form of a speech act.
manner of articulation Criterion for the classification of consonants. The way in which the airstream is obstructed.
Maximal Onset Principle Rule of syllabification according to which (as many) consonants (as possible) are syllabified as onsets.
maxim of the Cooperative Principle Sub-principle that specifies the Cooperative Principle.
meaning Relation between a linguistic form and a concept. See also 'pragmatic meaning', 'semantic meaning'.
mental lexicon Facility in the human mind in which words are stored.

minimal pair Two words that share the same sound sequence apart from one sound, and differ in meaning (e.g. English *night* and *kite*). Minimal pairs are used in phonology to diagnose phoneme status.
modifier That element of a linguistic structure (e.g. of a compound or of a phrase) that describes and specifies the head.
monomorphemic word See the synonymous term 'simplex word'.
monophthong Vowel sound without a change in quality; a simple vowel, e.g. [uː].
morph The concrete physical realisation of a morpheme, e.g. an acoustic speech signal or orthographic symbols on a sheet of paper.
morpheme The smallest meaningful unit of language, traditionally viewed as a unit of form and meaning.
morphological conditioning Mechanism for the selection of allomorphs by which a neighbouring morpheme determines which allomorph has to be used in a certain linguistic environment.
morphology 1. The internal structure of words, with regard to its meaningful elements. 2. The study thereof.
movement test Syntactic test used to determine the constituent status of a given syntactic string by moving the string to a different syntactic position.
narrow transcription Method of transcription that gives more phonetic detail than standard transcription, which is essentially phonemic. For example, a narrow transcription of the word *trap* is [tɹ̥æpʰ] (standard transcription: [tɹæp]).
nasal Manner of articulation of sounds which involves the complete closure of the oral cavity and the lowering of the velum, so that the air escapes through the nose instead of the mouth.
negative affix Affix used to create words with a negative, opposite or reverse meaning.
negative face In Brown and Levinson's (1987) theory of politeness: the speaker's desire not to be imposed on by the others.
negative politeness In Brown and Levinson's (1987) theory of politeness: the speaker's linguistic strategy to minimise the threat to the hearer's negative face.
neutralisation (of phonemic contrast) Phonological phenomenon where two different phonemes have the same realisation in a particular context. For example, in German the phonemes /d/ and /t/ both have an allophone [t], which surfaces in word-final position. The contrast between /d/ and /t/ is thus neutralised in this position.
nominal compounds Compounds that have a noun in the head position.

non-concatenative process^1 Word-formation process which does not make use of adding linguistic material, but of some other means, such as deleting linguistic material or changing the word-class without any overt change in form. These include conversion and different shortening processes (e.g. *(the) water > (to) water*, *Trish < Patricia*).
non-linguistic context   The physical and social setting of an utterance.
non-rhotic   Any variety of English in which postvocalic /ɹ/ (if in the same syllable as the preceding vowel) is not realised as a consonant.
noun   A word-class of English. Nouns head noun phrases and typically take plural and genitive suffixes.
noun phrase   Syntactic phrase that is headed by a noun.
nucleus   Constituent of the syllable which contains the sonority peak of the syllable. The sounds that occur in the nucleus are typically vowels, but may also be syllabic consonants (as, for example, [n̩] in *button* or [l̩] in *tickle*).
number   A grammatical category of the noun and the verb. English distinguishes two numbers, singular and plural.
object   A type of sentence function. In English, objects can be characterised by at least four properties: case, position, obligatoriness and passivisation.
onset   Constituent of the syllable which comprises all consonants before the nucleus.
opposites   Pair of words in which the meaning of one word stands in some kind of oppositional relationship to the meaning of the other word.
palatal   Place of articulation of sounds produced with a constriction at the hard palate.
palato-alveolar   Place of articulation of sounds produced with a constriction in the region between the alveolar ridge and the hard palate.
part-of-speech   See the synonymous term 'word-class'.
performative verb   Type of verb that explicitly names the action performed by the speaker, such as *promise, advise, apologise, state*.
perlocution   The effect of a speech act on the hearer.
person   A grammatical category of the verb. We distinguish three persons in English, the first (i.e. the speaker), the second (i.e. the hearer), and the third (i.e. the entity talked about).
phone   Realisation of a speech sound. Phones which function as the realisation of the same phoneme are called allophones of that phoneme.
phoneme   Abstract phonological category which constitutes the minimal distinctive unit in the phonology of a language.
phonetics   Sub-discipline of linguistics which deals with the following sound-related aspects of language: the production of speech sounds (articulatory phonetics), their physical properties (acoustic phonetics), and the per-

ception and processing of the speech signals by the listener (auditory phonetics).

phonological conditioning Mechanism for the selection of allomorphs by which the sound structure determines which allomorph has to occur in a certain linguistic environment.

phonology 1. The sound system of (a) language. 2. The linguistic discipline concerned with the sound system of language(s).

phrase Syntactic unit that is not a clause and that is headed by a word of some syntactic category (e.g. noun, verb, adjective, preposition and adverb).

phrase structure rule Grammatical rule that formally rewrites larger constituents as strings of smaller constituents (e.g. VP → V NP PP).

place of articulation Criterion for the classification of consonants. The point of closest constriction in the vocal tract.

plosive Alternative term for oral stops.

politeness Pragmatic principle used to account for certain patterns of human interaction. In Brown and Levinson's (1987) theory of politeness: linguistic strategy used by speakers to minimise threats to the hearer's face.

polymorphemic word See the synonymous term 'complex word'.

polysemy (adjective: polysemous) Property of lexemes. Polysemous lexemes are lexemes that have more than one meaning, with the different meanings being related to each other.

positive face In Brown and Levinson's (1987) theory of politeness: the speaker's desire to be well-thought of and admired by others.

positive politeness In Brown and Levinson's (1987) theory of politeness: the speaker's linguistic strategy to minimise the threat to the hearer's positive face.

pragmatic meaning Type of meaning that conveys a speaker's communicative intention, and which can be determined with the help of situational and world knowledge in a given context.

pragmatics Sub-discipline of linguistics that deals with how speakers use language to accomplish certain communicative intentions.

predicate A type of syntactic function. That part of a sentence that says something about the subject, i.e. everything in the sentence apart from the subject. In school grammar books, the term often refers to the verb and its auxiliaries (if any).

prefix Bound morpheme that precedes a root or a base.

prefixation Word-formation process used to create lexemes by adding prefixes to bases.

preposition A word-class of English. Prepositions head prepositional phrases, typically precede noun phrases (hence the name) and do not take inflections (e.g. *to, in, about*).

prepositional phrase Syntactic phrase that has a preposition as its head (e.g. *into the mountains*).
productivity Ability of affixes to be used to create new words.
pro-form Cover term for all kinds of pronominal expressions.
projection The process by which the head of a phrase transmits (i.e. 'projects') its grammatical properties onto higher-level constituents. Also: the result of this process, i.e. a higher-level constituent.
pronominalisation The substitution of a syntactic string by a pronoun. Also used as a test for constituency.
proto-language A (usually unattested) language from which other, attested, languages developed. Proto-languages are reconstructed on the basis of comparative reconstruction.
psycholinguistics Sub-discipline of linguistics which is concerned with the representation and processing of language in the brain, and with the acquisition of language.
Received Pronunciation (RP) The standard accent of British English, which is regionally neutral, and which originated from the prestigious speech used in public schools and in Court. RP spread among the better-educated parts of society due to its association with prestige. It used to be the norm in BBC speech and is still the most common reference accent of British English in foreign language teaching.
reference Relation between a linguistic expression and its referent (i.e. an object or situation we want to talk about).
referent Entity a speaker refers to in a given situation.
register Variety of a language whose use is determined by extralinguistic parameters such as the level of formality (formal vs. informal, colloquial language), the medium (spoken vs. written language), and the social or personal relationship between interlocutors (e.g. talk among close friends vs. talk between teachers and their young students).
released Property of a plosive sound. Released plosives are plosives where the air pressure that has been built up in the oral cavity during closure is released with a sudden burst.
representative Type of speech act used to represent or assert a state of affairs as it is viewed by the speaker.
rhotic Any variety of English in which /ɹ/ is realised as a consonant in all syllabic positions, i.e. also post-vocalically.
rounded Criterion for the classification of vowels. Vowels produced with lip rounding are called 'rounded'.
root That part of a word which cannot be analysed further into morphemes.
Second Germanic Sound Shift A consonantal sound change that affected

Old High German and separated this language from other branches of Germanic. The change happened roughly between the fourth and the ninth century AD.
semantic scope The extension of the meaning of a morpheme to one or more elements in the wider linguistic context (e.g. the sentence).
semantics 1. The meaning of linguistic expressions 2. The study thereof.
semantic meaning Relation between a linguistic expression (e.g. a word, sentence, or phrase) and a concept (in the case of non-compositional meaning), or between a linguistic expression and a combination of concepts (in the case of compositional meaning).
semi-vowel Alternative term for 'glide'.
sense relation Relation between words that share crucial aspects of their meanings (e.g. synonymy, hyponymy, antonymy, complementarity, converseness).
sentence function The syntactic role of a syntactic constituent with regard to the verb. Sentence functions are subject, object, adverbial and predicate.
sentence-fragment test Syntactic test used to determine the constituent status of a syntactic string. Only constituents can be used as sentence fragments.
sibilant Member of a class of alveolar fricatives and affricates whose articulation is characterised by a hissing noise (e.g. [s, ʃ, z, ʒ]).
simplex word Word consisting of only one morpheme.
situational context The physical setting of a given utterance, including gestures, mime, posture of the participants, etc.
situational knowledge The interlocutors' knowledge about the situational context of an utterance, which can be used to arrive at the pragmatic meaning of an utterance.
social class A grouping of people in a society who are similar to each other along certain dimensions. Social classes are most commonly distinguished by education, occupation and income.
sociolinguistic variable Linguistic entity (e.g. a phoneme, a morpheme) whose realisation depends on social factors (such as social class or style).
sociolinguistics Sub-discipline of linguistics which is concerned with the social significance of language. Sociolinguists study the correlation between linguistic variables and non-linguistic variables (such as age, gender, sex, social class), or the relations between language and power, or language and ideology.
sonority Relative measure for the audibility of speech sounds. Differences in sonority play an important role in syllabification.
Sonority Sequencing Principle Principle underlying syllable structure:

onsets must rise in sonority, codas must fall in sonority, and nuclei contain the sonority peak of the syllable.

sound inventory Pool of sounds which speakers of a given language use to construct words of their language. Languages differ in their respective sound inventories.

spectrogram Graphic representation of the sound waves that create the auditory impression of speech sounds.

speech act Utterance performed by a speaker in a certain context with a certain communicative intention.

Speech Act Theory Theory developed by J. Austin (1962) that deals with how humans use language to perform different actions, such as promising, apologising, etc.

stem That part of a word which remains after the removal of all inflectional affixes. The term is often used interchangeably with the term 'base'.

stop Manner of articulation which involves a complete closure in the oral cavity, followed by a release. The term is mostly used to refer to oral stops, but may also occur in reference to nasal stops, in which the air escapes through the nose. Oral stops are alternatively termed 'plosives'.

structural ambiguity An ambiguity that arises through the possibility of assigning different structural analyses to a given string of words.

subject A type of sentence function. In English, subjects can be characterised by at least four properties: case, subject-verb agreement, position, obligatoriness.

subject-verb agreement A syntactic rule of English according to which subject and verb need to share the same person and number features.

suffix Bound morpheme that follows a root or a base.

suffixation Word-formation process used to create lexemes by adding suffixes to existing bases.

syllabic consonant Consonant that occupies the nucleus of a syllable.

syllabification Process of assigning the chain of speech sounds to syllables and syllabic constituents.

syllable Unit of phonological organisation. Based on general and language-specific principles of syllabification, sequences of sounds are grouped into syllables.

synonyms Set of words with the same meaning.

synonymy (adjective: synonymous) Sense relation between words with the same meaning.

syntactic category See the synonymous term 'word-class'.

syntax 1. The structure of sentences, or more generally, of linguistic constructions. 2. The study thereof.

t/d-flapping A phonological rule commonly associated with North American varieties of English by which /t/ and /d/ are realised as [ɾ] in particular phonetic contexts.
transitive verb A verb that takes an object.
truncation See the synonymous term 'clipping'.
unique morpheme Bound morpheme that occurs in only one word of a language.
unreleased Property of a plosive. In unreleased plosives the air pressure that has been built up in the oral cavity is not released.
utterance Unit of analysis in pragmatics that refers to what the speaker says at a given point in time at a given location with a given intention.
velar Place of articulation of sounds produced with a constriction at the velum.
velarised l Synonym of 'dark l'. The articulation of dark l involves the raising of the tongue body towards the velum (in addition to the standard articulatory characteristics of [l]).
verb A word-class of English. Verbs head verb phrases and take person, number and tense inflections.
verb phrase Syntactic phrase that has a verb as its head.
verbal compound Compound that has a verb in its head position.
vocal cords Also called 'vocal folds'. Two small muscular folds which are located at the lower end of the larynx. The position of the vocal cords is flexible: they can be close together or apart. If the vocal cords are close together, the passing air from the lungs causes them to vibrate. Sounds produced with the vocal cords vibrating are said to be 'voiced', those produced with the vocal cords apart and not vibrating are called 'voiceless'.
vocal tract The organs above the larynx (including nasal and oral cavities) that participate in the production of sounds.
voiced Property of sounds that are produced with vibration of the vocal cords.
voiceless Property of sounds that are produced without vibration of the vocal cords.
vowel Type of speech sound in which the airstream is modulated, and not obstructed.
vowel alternation The systematic variant realisation of a vowel depending on phonological or morphological factors.
vowel change 1. In morphology: the expression of an inflectional or a derivational category through the change of the root vowel (as in *keep* vs. past tense *kept*). 2. In historical linguistics: the change of the length or quality of a vowel over time.

vowel epenthesis   Insertion of a vowel into a string of sounds.
vowel frontness   Criterion for the classification of vowels. Vowels are placed on a front-back continuum according to their auditory quality. This corresponds roughly to the position of the tongue during production. Three levels are usually distinguished: front, central, and back.
vowel height   Criterion for the classification of vowels. Vowels are placed on a high-low continuum roughly according to the height of the tongue during production. Three levels of vowel height are commonly distinguished: high, mid, and low. Sometimes a further distinction is made between mid-high and mid-low vowels.
wh-pronoun   A pronoun that is used to introduce a question (e.g. *who, why, where*). In English most of these pronouns (but not all of them, cf. *how*) are written with initial <wh>, hence the name for this class of pronouns.
word-class   A category according to which words can be grouped syntactically. Criteria for classification involve chiefly syntactic distribution and morphological make-up.
word-form   See the synonymous term 'grammatical word'.
word-formation   Sub-discipline of morphology that deals with the ways of creating words on the basis of other words.
world knowledge   The interlocutors' knowledge about the world and the socio-cultural aspects of the society they belong to, which can be used to arrive at the pragmatic meaning of an utterance.
zero form   A linguistic form whose realisation is zero.
zero morph   Morph that has no (acoustic or orthographic) manifestation.
zero-affixation   See the synonymous term 'conversion'.
zero-derivation   See the synonymous term 'conversion'.

References

Aarts, Bas
    2008   *English Syntax and Argumentation.* 3nd ed. Basingstoke/New York: Palgrave.

Adams, Valerie
    2001   *Complex Words in English.* Harlow: Longman.

Aitchison, Jean
    2003   *Words in the Mind — An Introduction to the Mental Lexicon.* 3rd ed. Malden: Blackwell.

Aronoff, Mark and Kirsten Fudeman
    2005   *What is Morphology?* Malden: Blackwell.

Ash, Sharon and John Myhill
    1986   Linguistic correlates of inter-ethnic contact. In: David Sankoff (ed.), *Diversity and Diachrony,* 33–44. Amsterdam/Philadelphia: John Benjamins.

Austin, John L.
    1962   *How to Do Things with Words.* Oxford: Claredon Press.

Bauer, Laurie
    1983   *English Word-Formation.* Cambridge: CUP.

Bauer, Laurie
    2003   *Introducing Linguistic Morphology.* 2nd ed. Edinburgh: Edinburgh University Press.

Bogart, Leo
    1950–1   The spread of news on a local event. A case study. *Public Opinion Quarterly* (Winter), 769–772.

British National Corpus (British National Corpus World)
    2001   Distributed by Oxford University Computing Services on behalf of the British National Corpus Consortium.

Brown, Penelope and Stephen Levinson
    1987   *Politeness: Some Universals of Language Use.* Cambridge: Cambridge University Press.

Campbell, Lyle
    1998   *Historical Linguistics: An Introduction.* Edinburgh: Edinburgh University Press.

Chambers, Jack K. (ed.)
    2002   *The Handbook of Language Variation and Change.* Malden: Blackwell.

Chambers, Jack K.
    2003   *Sociolinguistic Theory. Linguistic Variation and Its Social Significance.* 2nd ed. Oxford: Blackwell.

Clark, Eve
   1993   *The Lexicon in Acquisition*. Cambridge: Cambridge University Press.

Collins, Beverly and Inger M. Mees
   2008   *Practical Phonetics and Phonology. A Resource Book for Students*. 2nd ed. Oxon: Routledge.

Cutting, Joan
   2008   *Pragmatics and Discourse. A Resource Book for Students*. 2nd ed. London/New York: Routledge.

Davis, John F.
   2004   *Phonetics and Phonology*. Stuttgart: Klett.

Downing, Angela and Philip Locke
   2006   *English grammar. A university course*. 2nd edition. London/New York: Routledge.

Field, John
   2003   *Psycholinguistics: A Resource Book for Students*. London: Routledge.

Gelderen, Elly van
   2006   *A History of the English Language*. Amsterdam: Benjamins.

Giegerich, Heinz J.
   1992   *English Phonology*. Cambridge: Cambridge University Press.

Goffman, Erving
   1967   *Interaction Ritual: Essays on Face to Face Behaviour*. New York: Garden City.

Greenbaum, Sidney and Randolph Quirk
   1990   *A Student's Grammar of the English Language*. London: Longman.

Grice, Herbert Paul
   1975   Logic and Conversation. In: Cole, Peter and Jerry Morgan *Syntax and Semantics*, vol. 3: Speech Acts, 41—58. New York: Academic Press.

Grundy, Peter
   2008   *Doing Pragmatics*. 3rd ed. London: Arnold.

Haspelmath, Martin
   2002   *Understanding Morphology*. London: Arnold.

Hawkins, John A.
   1999   The relative order of prepositional phrases in English: Going beyond Manner-Place-Time. *Language Variation and Change* 11, 231—266.

Hogg, Richard and David Denison (eds.)
   2006   *A History of the English Language*. Cambridge: Cambridge University Press.

Holmes, Janet
   2001   *An Introduction to Sociolinguistics*. 2nd ed. London: Longman.

Huddleston, Rodney and Geoffrey Pullum
   2002   *The Cambridge Grammar of the English Language*. Cambridge: Cambridge University Press.

Huddleston, Rodney and Geoffrey Pullum
　2005　*A Student's Introduction to English Grammar.* Cambridge: Cambridge University Press.
International Phonetic Association
　2006　IPA Fonts. http://www.arts.gla.ac.uk/IPA/ipafonts.html. Retrieved October 21, 2008.
Jenkins, James J.
　1970　The 1952 Minnesota Word Association Norms. In: Postman, Leo and Geoffrey Keppel (eds.), *Norms of Word Association*, 1—38. New York: Academic Press.
Johnson, Keith
　2003　*Acoustic and Auditory Phonetics.* 2nd ed. Malden/Oxford/Carlton: Blackwell.
Jones, Daniel
　2006 English Pronouncing Dictionary. 17th edition. Cambridge: Cambridge University Press.
Jones, William
　1786　Third anniversary discourse, 1786. In: *Asiatick Researches; or, Transactions of the Society Instituted in Bengal, For Inquiring into the History and Antiquities, the Arts, Sciences, and Literature, of Asia.* Volume I, 1: 415—431.
Katamba, Francis and John Stonham
　2006　*Morphology.* Basingstoke: Macmillan.
Kenstowicz, Michael
　1994　*Phonology in Generative Grammar.* Cambridge, M.A.: Blackwell.
Kortmann, Bernd and Edgar W. Schneider (eds.)
　2004　*A Handbook of Varieties of English*, Volume 1: Phonology. Berlin: Mouton de Gruyter.
Kreidler, Charles
　1998　*Introducing English Semantics.* London/New York: Routledge.
Kreidler, Charles
　2003　*The Pronunciation of English: A Course Book.* Malden: Blackwell.
Labov, William
　1972　The social motivation of a sound change. In: Labov, William (ed.), *Sociolinguistic Patterns*, 1—42. Oxford: Blackwell.
Ladefoged, Peter and Ian Maddieson
　1996　*The Sounds of the World's Languages.* Oxford: Blackwell.
Ladefoged, Peter
　2003　*Phonetic Data Analysis. An Introduction to Fieldwork and Instrumental Techniques.* Malden/Oxford/Carlton: Blackwell Publishing.
Ladefoged, Peter
　2006　*A Course in Phonetics.* 5th edition. Boston: Thomson Wadsworth.

Laver, John
    1994   *Principles of Phonetics*. Cambridge: Cambridge University Press.

Leech, Geoffrey and Jan Svartvik
    2002   *A Communicative Grammar of English*. 3rd ed. London/New York: Longman.

Levinson, Stephen C.
    1983   *Pragmatics*. Cambridge: Cambridge University Press.

Lipka, Leonhard
    2002   *English Lexicology: Lexical Structure, Word Semantics and Word-Formation*. Tübingen: Narr.

Löbner, Sebastian
    2002   *Understanding Semantics*. London: Arnold.

LoCastro, Virginia
    2003   *An Introduction to Pragmatics. Social Action for Language Teachers*. Ann Arbor: University of Michigan Press.

Longman Dictionary of Contemporary English
    2003   Harlow: Longman Pearson Ltd. and Langenscheidt.

Marchand, Hans
    1969   *The Categories and Types of Present-day English Word-formation*. 2nd ed. München: Beck.

McCarthy, John and Alan Prince
    1993   *Prosodic Morphology I: Constraint Interaction and Satisfaction*. Ms. University of Massachusetts, Amherst/Rutgers University, New Brunswick.

Mey, Jacob L.
    2001   *Pragmatics. An Introduction*. 2nd ed. Oxford/Malden: Blackwell.

Meyerhoff, Miriam
    2006   *Introducing Sociolinguistics*. Oxon: Routledge.

Oxford English Dictionary (2nd ed) on CD-ROM 1997
    Oxford: Oxford University Press.

Peccei, Jean Stilwell
    1999   Pragmatics. London/New York: Routledge.

Plag, Ingo
    2003   *Word-formation in English*. Cambridge: Cambridge University Press.

Portner, Paul H.
    2005   *What is Meaning? Fundamentals of Formal Semantics*. Malden, MA: Blackwell.

Pyles, Thomas and John Algeo
    1993   *The Origins and Development of the English Language*. 4th ed. Fort Worth: Harcourt Brace Jovanovich.

Quirk, Randolph, Sidney Greenbaum, Geoffrey Leech and Jan Svartvik
    1985   *A Comprehensive Grammar of the English Language*. London/New York: Longman.

Radford, Andrew
    1988   *Transformational Grammar: A First Course.* Cambridge: Cambridge University Press.

Radford, Andrew
    2004   *English Syntax. An Introduction.* Cambridge: Cambridge University Press.

Roca, Iggy and Wyn Johnson
    1999   *A Course in Phonology.* Oxford: Blackwell.

Saeed, John Ibrahim
    2000   *Semantics.* Oxford: Blackwell.

Schreuder, Robert and Harald Baayen
    1997   How complex simplex words can be. *Journal of Memory and Language* 37: 118—139.

Searle, John
    1969   *Speech Acts. An Essay in the Philosophy of Language.* Cambridge: Cambridge University Press.

Spencer, Andrew
    1996   *Phonology.* Oxford: Blackwell.

SIL (Summer Institute of Linguistics)
    2006   Speech Analyzer. Version 3.0.1. http://www.sil.org/computing/sa/sa_download.htm#download. Retrieved October 26, 2008.

Trask, Robert Lawrence 1996
    A Dictionary of Phonetics and Phonology. London: Routledge.

Trask, Robert Lawrence
    1997   *Historical Linguistics.* London: Arnold.

Trudgill, Peter
    1974   *The Social Differentiation of English in Norwich.* Cambridge: Cambridge University Press.

Webster's New Encyclopedic Dictionary
    1996   Revised Edition. New York: Black Dog and Leventhal.

Subject index

abbreviation 107–108
acronym 107–108
adjectival compounds 103
adjective 122–126, 160
adjective phrase 122, 126, 128
adjunct 133
adverbial 128–131
affix 77–78
affricate 12, 15, 62, 212–214
agentive suffix 96
allomorphs 83–88
allophones 33–53, 63–65, 83
alveolar 10, 15
ambiguous 154, *see also* structural ambiguity
antonyms 160–161
approximant 12, 15
articulators 9, 10–12
aspirated stop 46–48, 214, 217
aspiration 46–47
assertive *see* representatives
augmentative prefix 97
background knowledge 193–194
base 76–82
bilabial 10–15
blend 107
bound morpheme 76–77

British National Corpus (BNC) 105, 110, 167–169

case 122, 130–133
categorisation 143–144
clear l 43–45, 63
clipping 106
coda 57–64

cognates 58, 215
co-hyponym 157–159, 173–174
commissives 185
communicative intention 176–189
complementaries 160–161
complementary distribution 34–37, 42, 44–45, 47, 49, 63
complex word 72, 78–82
compositional meaning 149–154
compounding 99–104
concatenative processes 104–105
concept 94, 141–147, 213
connotation 159
consonant 10, 15
conversational implicature 199–200
converse relation 161–162
converses 161–162
conversion 104–105
Cooperative Principle 195–201
corpus 166–167

dark l 43–45, 63–65
declaration 183–184
definite expression 124–125, 146–147
deictic expression 147–148, 193
denotation 146
dental 10, 15
derivation 90
derivational affixes 89–93
derivational morphology 89–93
derivative 76
determiner 125–126, 147
diminutive suffix 96
diphthong 21–23, 52, 223–224

direct object 133
direct speech act 187–189
directives 184–185
distribution 34–39, 42–49, 51, 63–65, 83, 85–86, 122–125, 132, 220–222

expressives 184

face 203–205
face-threatening act 203–205
felicity conditions 189–192
final (obstruent) devoicing 41
First Germanic Sound Shift 217
free morpheme 76
free variation 37, 44–45, 47–49, 50–51
frequency 7–8
fricative 12–16, 213–217

gapping test 117
gender 96, 123, 131
gender-marking suffix 96
General American 5–6, 20, 23, 48–57
glide 12
glottal 11, 15
glottis 11, 14
grammar 35, 112–113, 128–129
grammatical word *see* word-form
Grimm's Law *see* First Germanic Sound Shift

head 103, 121
historical linguistics 210–217
homonyms 164, 169
homonymy 164, 169
hyperonym 156–158
hyponym 156–158
hyponymy 156–158, 162

illocution 179–180, 182
indefinite expression 82–85, 125, 146–147
indirect object 133
indirect speech act 187–189
inference 151, 193–199
inferencing 151, 193–199
infix 77–78
inflection 90
inflectional affixes 89–93
inflectional morphology 89–93
initialism 107–108
instrumental suffix 96
interdental 11
International Phonetic Alphabet (IPA) 3–5
interpersonal knowledge 192–195

labio-dental 10,15
language family 215–216
lexeme 90–91
lexical category *see* word-class
lexical conditioning 87–88
lexical field 156
linguistic context 186
liquid 12
locution 179

manner of articulation 11–16
Maximal Onset Principle 59–60
maxims of the Cooperative Principles 197–202
meaning 35–37, 39, 45, 47, 51, 71–77, 80–83, 89–93, 95, 97, 101–102, 123–124, 140–170, 179–180, 187–189, 192–195, 211–212, 218–219
mental lexicon 155–162, 224–227
minimal pair 36–37, 42, 45
modifier 103

monomorphemic word *see* simplex word
monophthong 22
morph 74, 83
morpheme 71–77
morphological conditioning 88
morphology 70–110
movement test 116

narrow transcription 33
nasal 14, 15
negative affix 97
negative face 204
negative politeness 205
neutralisation (of phonemic contrast) 41
nominal compounds 103
non-concatenative processes 104
non-linguistic context 186, 195
noun 121–125
noun phrase 121–123, 125, 131, 146
nucleus 57, 59–61
number 102, 129, 131

object 128–136
onset 57–65, 226
opposites 159–162

palatal 11, 15
palato-alveolar 11, 15
part-of-speech *see* word-class
performative verb 187
perlocution 179
person 89–90, 92, 124, 129–131
phone 33, 35–36
phoneme 29–37, 40–42, 44–45, 47–48, 49–50, 51–52, 83
phonetics 1–28
phonological conditioning 83

phonology 29–65, 71
phrase 114–128, 131
phrase structure rule 128
place of articulation 10–11
plosive 12, 15, 37–42, 45–46, 212–214, 217
politeness 202–206
polymorphemic word *see* complex word
polysemy, polysemous 163, 168, 169–170
positive face 203
positive politeness 203
pragmatic meaning 152, 180, 192–195
pragmatics 176–209
predicate 128–129
prefix 77, 79–82, 96–97
prefixation 94
preposition 122–123, 161–162
prepositional phrase 122, 126
productivity 97–99
pro-form 115–116, 125
projection 123
pronominalisation 115–121, 123, 131
proto-language 215–216
psycholinguistics, psycholinguistic 155–156, 224–227

Received Pronunciation 4–6, 15, 18, 20, 22–23, 26–27, 42, 49–54, 67–68
reference 146–148, 195
referent, referential 146–148
register 169
released, release 11–12, 37–40, 45, 50
representatives 184
rhotic 51–54, 57

root 77–79
rounded 20

Second Germanic Sound Shift 211–217
semantic meaning 152, 171, 179
semantic scope 154
semantics 140–171
semi-vowel 12–13
sense relations 157–162
sentence function 128–136
sentence-fragment test 111–112, 117
sibilants 85
simplex word 72
situational context 193–195
situational knowledge 193–195
social class 221–223
sociolinguistic variable 220–224
sociolinguistics 219–224
sonority 60–62
Sonority Sequencing Principle 61–62
sound inventory 1
sound system 29–65
spectrogram 29–32, 37–38
speech act 177–187
Speech Act Theory 178
stem 76
stop 12, 13, 37–42, 45–50, 212–214, 217
structural ambiguity 119–120
subject 128–137
subject-verb agreement 129
suffix 77, 79–82, 94–96
suffixation 94
syllabic consonant 57
syllabification 59–63

syllable 54–65
synonym, synonymy, synonymous 164–170
syntax 111–139
syntactic category *see* word-class

truncation 106

unique morpheme 73
unreleased 11–12, 37–39, 45, 50
utterance 180, 192–193

velar 11, 15
velarised l *see* dark l
verbal compounds 103
vocal cords 8, 14–15
vocal tract 8–9
voiced 15, 48, *see also* voiceless
voiceless 14–15, 33–34, 42–43, 48
vowel 9, 16
vowel alternation *see* vowel change
vowel change 75, 86–88
vowel epenthesis 58
vowel frontness 17–19
vowel height 17–19

word-class 81, 92–93, 102–104, 123–128
word-form 90
word-formation 93–94
world knowledge 151, 159, 194–195

zero form 75, 86
zero morph *see* zero form
zero-affixation *see* conversion
zero-derivation *see* conversion